TRILLION DOLLAR TRIAGE

TRILLION DOLLAR TRIAGE

How Jay Powell and the Fed Battled
a President and a Pandemic—
and Prevented Economic Disaster

NICK TIMIRAOS

Little, Brown & Company
New York Boston London

Little, Brown and Company
Hachette Book Group
1290 Avenue of the Americas, New York, NY 10104
littlebrown.com

First Edition: March 2022

Little, Brown and Company is a division of Hachette Book Group, Inc. The Little, Brown name and logo are trademarks of Hachette Book Group, Inc.

The publisher is not responsible for websites (or their content) that are not owned by the publisher.

The Hachette Speakers Bureau provides a wide range of authors for speaking events. To find out more, go to hachettespeakersbureau.com or call (866) 376-6591.

ISBN 9780316272810
Library of Congress Control Number: 2021950353

Printing 1, 2021

LSC-C

Printed in the United States of America

*To my parents, Carol and Vicente, for encouraging
me to follow my dreams*

And to Mallie, whose support makes everything possible

CONTENTS

Contents

TRILLION DOLLAR TRIAGE

INTRODUCTION

O ver the weekend of February 22, 2020, Saudi Crown Prince Mohammed bin Salman hosted the finance ministers and central-bank governors from the Group of Twenty nations, a forum for the leaders of the world's largest economies. The prince was eager to use the event in Riyadh to showcase his country's modernization, although the progress was relative; one of his most radical steps was allowing women to drive.

The summit featured icons of Saudi culture — which explains how Federal Reserve Chair Jerome Powell and Treasury Secretary Steven Mnuchin each ended up donning a leather glove and posing with a gray feathered falcon, Saudi Arabia's national bird. The most powerful players in the global economy also held up their iPhones to video a white camel parading through a palace courtyard. The animal, named Most Beautiful Camel at the annual King Abdulaziz Camel Festival, had won hundreds of thousands of dollars based on criteria such as hair color and lip plumpness. Powell's colleague at the Fed, governor Randal Quarles, and François Villeroy de Galhau, governor of the Banque de France, snapped a photo together in front of the mammal.

The trim, silver-haired Powell, who had spent his career at top-flight law firms, investment companies, and as a White House appointee, moved comfortably in these rarefied settings. He had survived a tumultuous first two years at the top of the Fed, earning the respect of Democrats and Republicans for his levelheaded leadership in the face of constant attacks from President Donald Trump. By most metrics, the US economy he was responsible for monitoring was in very good shape after the central bank had shifted from raising rates in 2018 to cutting them in 2019, a humbling U-turn. But the conference's luxuries and cultural trappings offered just a temporary distraction from unsettling news about a virus that had recently emerged in the Hubei province of China.

That weekend, the novel coronavirus had gone viral, with outbreaks now multiplying in Iran, South Korea, and Italy. In Riyadh, there was little opportunity for Powell or other global economic leaders to officially discuss global responses to the virus — the summit had been planned down to the minute many weeks earlier. Talk on the sidelines of the conference, however, quickly turned to how northern Italy was sealing off eleven towns inside a quarantined *zona rossa*, or red zone, enforced by military police. Major events such as the Venice Carnival were being canceled. Guests didn't know what to think — it all sounded like something out of *The Andromeda Strain*, the 1969 Michael Crichton techno-thriller about a deadly rogue pathogen from outer space. Would it be a worse repeat of the 2003 SARS outbreak, which killed hundreds, primarily in East Asia? Or something more serious? Over 2,300 people had already died, almost all of them in China.

Powell — who was not trained as an economist — had spent hours poring over economic papers and textbooks when he first joined the central bank in 2012 so he could take part in monetary debates. In recent weeks, he had added the latest epidemiological research to his evening reading diet. There were still more questions than answers — the virus appeared to be less lethal than Ebola or SARS, but it was extremely contagious.

In Riyadh that weekend, Powell walked away from a private meeting with Lee Ju-yeol, the head of South Korea's central bank, struck by Lee's firsthand report over the stringent public-health measures already being deployed in South Korea to prevent outbreaks. *Not good*, thought Powell. Until then, Powell shared the consensus view that the virus might sap Chinese demand and roil supply chains for a couple of quarters, denting growth in Asia, but it would not be memorable for the United States. The previous week, for example, Apple had announced it would miss its quarterly sales goal because of chaos caused by the coronavirus in China.

Unfazed investors sent the tech-heavy Nasdaq stock index to a record high the following day.

When it was his turn to address the international delegations, Powell slapped a huge disclaimer on his cautiously positive outlook. "I hold these views with very, very low confidence," he said, "and I'm really wondering whether they're right at this point." His private remarks would have been especially notable if they became public because the Fed leader's words can cause huge, nearly instantaneous drops in investor confidence and stock markets.

Officials from Hong Kong and Singapore — areas that had been heavily affected by similar earlier viruses — skipped straight past standard monetary-policy measures and discussed extensive, much more radical, fiscal measures, such as income-replacement programs, that were being rolled out to defend against the virus's disruptions. It was a wake-up call for Western financial officials.

On his last day in Riyadh, Powell began to think it was only a matter of time before virus clusters would multiply through US cities. He called his colleagues at the Fed. "What capabilities are available to the Treasury to do anything specific about this?" he asked. "And by the way, what authorities do we actually have?" During the previous year's trade war, Trump had come up with a farmer-bailout program that ultimately directed nearly $25 billion to offset losses in exports. Was there a similar way for the Treasury Department to quickly make government payments available if American cities had to start shutting down commerce to stop the spread of the virus?

During a television interview from Riyadh on Sunday, February 23, Mnuchin, a former partner at Goldman Sachs with jet-black hair and black-framed eyeglasses, said there was "no question" that the US government had a backup plan to deal with a contagious virus, but he also said it was too soon to say what that would entail. "In another three or four weeks, we'll have much better data," he said. "I don't think people should be at the point where they're panicked. On the other hand, it is concerning."[1]

On Monday, February 24, Powell climbed on a jet for the flight back to Washington, DC. In 2018, he'd been asked at a forum if he slept well at night. "No one wants a central banker who sleeps well," he joked. "What good is that?" But there wasn't much he could do for the moment. He switched off his phone and settled in for the fourteen-hour flight.

When the plane touched down at Dulles International Airport outside Washington, Powell switched on his phone. The news was all bad. Italy and South Korea had announced more deaths. Additional countries were imposing travel restrictions. The Dow Jones Industrial Average had tanked, falling 1,000 points. The Centers for Disease Control wasn't calling it a *pandemic* yet, but the markets were treating it like one.

There are two sides to Powell's job. One could fairly be described as boring — regulating banks and the supply of credit to keep the economy growing steadily. These decisions on dry monetary policy, however, can have tremendous influence over people's lives. Setting the price of money influences the prices Americans pay on their credit-card balances, their car loans, their mortgages. Changes in the prices of stocks and bonds can influence how much large and small companies are willing to hire, invest, and save.

The other side of his job is harder to quantify: maintaining confidence in the financial system. In a few hours on that Monday, investors had erased the Dow's gains for the year to date. The Fed's job, of course, isn't to respond to normal ups and downs in markets. But when investors and corporate finance chiefs are forced to make very sudden changes in their investment plans, the risk of a market crack-up or panic soars. In late February, those risks accelerated. The Federal Reserve had been created 107 years earlier to prevent a rerun of debilitating banking panics by serving as a lender of last resort — a role that it had embraced during the Great Recession of 2008.

Even with interest rates at historically low levels, that episode illustrated how Powell had plenty of tools at his disposal. He led an institution with almost magical powers — lending money that it creates out of thin air. American presidents can order troops to war and a midnight air strike, but they can't spend $1 trillion unilaterally. The Fed can.

At the same time, politics, monetary theory, and decades of Fed history meant that Powell's job wasn't as simple as pointing a money hose at a problem. The central bank can help boost demand when the economy slumps; there was no precedent for what policymakers would soon face — the equivalent of an economy placed into a medically induced coma. And rash action risked panicking the markets further. As he disembarked from the plane, Powell already knew one thing: doing nothing was not an option.

———

The next day, Dr. Nancy Messonnier, director of the CDC's National Center for Immunization and Respiratory Diseases, offered an austere assessment of the public-health situation. "It's not so much of a question of if this will happen anymore, but rather more of a question of exactly when this will happen and how many people in this country will have severe illness," she said at a press briefing.[2]

Messonnier described how she had told her children that morning about the potential for severe disruptions to everyday life, including school closures and telework, and she calmly advised Americans to begin preparing for similar "significant disruption of our lives." Unnerved by the candor, the Dow dropped another 879 points on Tuesday.

The White House continued to deny that the virus would have much impact. That same Tuesday, February 25, after two straight days of a plunging Dow average, Larry Kudlow, Trump's director of the National Economic Council, appeared on CNBC. Fed governor Lael Brainard, at a conference in Amsterdam, caught part of the interview. Kudlow had just walked out of a meeting with senior health advisers and thought he was simply reiterating the points they had covered. "We have contained this," Kudlow said from the briefing room. "We have contained this — I won't say airtight, but pretty close to airtight...I don't think it's going to be an economic tragedy at all."[3]

Brainard couldn't believe what she was hearing. *Oh my God,* she thought. *These guys think this is all about the stock market. They just don't get it.*

The next morning, President Trump fired off a tweet blaming cable news for overhyping the "Caronavirus" and panicking markets. Then he called Powell to tell him how big a loser he was. The dollar had strengthened over the prior week — as it usually does when investors get nervous about financial volatility. The strong dollar was killing the United States, Trump said.

The president envied negative interest rates in Germany and incorrectly believed that if the US had negative rates, he could call due existing Treasury debt, like the mortgage on a hotel, and replace it with new, negative-yield debt. After decades in real estate and three years as president, Trump still didn't understand the difference between public and private debt. Trump told Powell the Germans were laughing their heads off at the Fed chief. "They think it's so funny that you don't understand any of this, how they're picking our pockets because of you, and they tell me this personally," Trump said to the man he had put in charge of the central bank two years earlier.

On this and other occasional calls, Trump would also refer to the CEO of Caterpillar, the giant maker of construction equipment and engines, who, the president alleged, had said the Fed was the reason the economy was not growing faster. After Trump first brought up the company, Powell read Caterpillar's earnings reports and found no such mention of the Fed or a strong dollar. But with Trump, reality didn't matter.

Powell summoned the discipline that had served him well over the past year of similar outbursts. *The only promise I can make you,* Powell would offer politely, *is to do my absolute best for the people that we both serve.* He pledged that the Fed was devoting lots of thought and analysis to what was happening, and that it would use whatever tools would be needed. Trump's public threats and needling would soon be the least of Powell's worries.

At 10 a.m. Wednesday morning, Powell and a dozen Fed officials convened their first Covid-19 crisis-planning meeting in a wood-paneled conference room on the fourth floor of the Marriner S. Eccles Federal Reserve Board Building overlooking the National Mall. The Fed had already put in place certain safeguards, such as quarantining paper money returning from Asia just in case it might spread the virus. The discussion turned to what might happen to the US economy if and when the virus arrived.

At the time, the Fed was preparing for a one-quarter slowdown. Officials could see anecdotal reports that foot traffic at shopping malls was declining. It seemed likely that air travel and hotel bookings would soon follow. But they believed the economy — then in the middle of the longest continuous expansion since the Civil War — could still avoid a recession. It was a classic case of the human tendency to absorb big news slowly. What's more, none of the experts around the table had any historical context for what happens when a $20 trillion economy shuts down, either voluntarily or by government decree.

Powell, who sat at the head of the conference room, had encouraged his board members to ignore received wisdom and economic orthodoxies. He turned to Vice Chair Richard Clarida and pressed him for his worst-case scenario. "Don't tell me what's plausible," said Powell. "What's the real worst case?"

"Well, Jay, if we become Italy, and we shut down the entire economy, then this will be a bigger hit than the Great Depression," Clarida said.

———

The names of Fed chairs are often well known — Paul Volcker, Alan Greenspan, Ben Bernanke, Janet Yellen — but the central bank's leaders operate mostly in the background, giving bland speeches in drab hotel ballrooms to chambers of commerce and economics clubs, away from the harsh political glare bathing other institutions such as Congress and the Supreme Court.

There are certain moments, however, when the Fed sheds those reservations and becomes what is tantamount to a fourth branch of government. In crisis, the Fed chair's words are more closely watched by global money managers and CEOs than anyone else's in the world, including those of the US president. On the precipice of catastrophic financial meltdowns, the normally staid and predictable Fed can move faster and more powerfully than any other arm of the government.

The Pandemic Crisis would be one of those moments.

Chapter One

HAWKS, DOVES, AND JAYBIRD

Jerome "Jay" Powell grew up the second of six children in Chevy Chase, Maryland, a Washington DC suburb with picturesque Cape Cod–style homes that sits about seven miles from the Fed headquarters.

His upper-middle-class family were among the first Catholics to join the prestigious Chevy Chase Club, where his father, also named Jerome, would serve as president. The elder Powell saw combat as an Army infantryman in Europe during World War II before a career as an accomplished lawyer who represented companies in labor disputes. Powell learned from his father how to measure his words carefully. Patricia Hayden, Powell's mother, graduated valedictorian from Trinity College in Washington before going to work as a statistician for the Army Map Service. After marrying the elder Powell, she volunteered widely and worked part-time for the Republican National Committee.

Powell, whose family called him "Jaybird," followed his father to Georgetown Prep, a strict all-male Jesuit high school in nearby Bethesda. Students wore jackets and ties, attended Mass every day, and were assigned to detention called *JUG*, short for *Justice Under God*, for minor violations — such as arriving late to class. Georgetown Prep graduated future diplomats, congressmen, senators — and the first two justices Donald Trump would seat on the Supreme Court, Neil Gorsuch and Brett Kavanaugh. Powell was popular, played center for Prep's "Little

Hoyas" football team, and was a good student. His classmate Francis Rooney, later a two-term Republican congressman from Florida, recalls Powell as "killer smart."

Despite a first-rate education — he graduated from Princeton University, where he majored in government, in 1975 — Powell considered himself a bit of a late bloomer. That summer, he traveled through Europe with his guitar, entertaining a crowd at a Paris café with "I'm So Lonesome I Could Cry" and other Hank Williams ballads. Back in Washington, he took a job working for a friend's father at an office-supply company, then became an assistant to a senator on Capitol Hill. After watching former classmates take high-paying and prestigious jobs, he rediscovered his drive at Georgetown University's law school.

After graduating from Georgetown, Powell went on to a clerkship and a few years at prestigious Manhattan law firms before switching to investment banking in 1983, joining Dillon, Read & Company, led by a low-key but well-connected New England blueblood named Nicholas Brady.

Two years later, in 1985, Powell married Elissa Leonard, a Harvard-educated producer and writer of science television shows who was friends with Powell's younger sister. Leonard kept her last name and would eventually put her career on hold after their first two of three children were born.

At Dillon Read, Powell snagged a meeting with Brady and introduced himself as a Washington native who was interested in public service and ready to make himself helpful however he could. His colleagues at Dillon Read rolled their eyes: Time spent in Washington was time wasted; it didn't generate new banking business. Powell didn't care, and his connection to Brady paid off.

A few months later, Dillon Read found itself defending the petroleum exporter Unocal Corporation in a takeover bid from T. Boone Pickens, the corporate raider. Brady called Powell down to Washington to accompany him on meetings with top officials at the Treasury, White House, and Congress.

President Ronald Reagan tapped Brady to chair a task force that reviewed the Black Monday stock market crash of 1987, then named him Treasury secretary a few months before Brady's friend, George H. W. Bush, became president. It seemed like a plum opportunity for Powell, but to his disappointment, Brady had agreed not to bring anyone from his firm down to DC.

Two years later, a partner at Dillon Read leaned into Powell's office to tell him Brady was looking for a new assistant secretary:

"Nick wants someone who's like a carbon copy of Jay Powell."

Powell offered a few names before adding, "But why settle for a cheap imitation?"

He got the job. A few months later, Powell called up his old Wall Street law firm, Davis Polk & Wardwell, and said he needed a hardworking assistant. They recommended a thirty-three-year-old, Ivy League–educated lawyer, Randal Quarles. Powell hired him, launching the public-policy career of another future Fed colleague.

Financial crisis 101

1990 wasn't the easiest year to start work at the Treasury. Over the previous few years, the country had been rocked by financial collapses and corruption. A rolling savings-and-loans crisis had resulted in the collapse of over 1,000 banks and depositories and still wasn't fully contained. The bank-deposit insurance fund — which guarantees that bank customers will be able to withdraw their money even in a crisis — was depleted. The economy entered a recession.

It was, however, the perfect time to learn firsthand how to deal with unpredictable crises. In early 1991, Powell found himself at the center of a disaster involving the Bank of New England, a large regional bank on the brink of failure as a result of the recent collapse of the commercial and residential real-estate markets. Powell and other regulators wrestled with the potential consequences of a bailout. The immediate stakes were not catastrophic — the Bank of New England was only the 33rd largest bank in the country — but the basic questions were the same as when a Citigroup or Lehman Brothers was courting insolvency. A fraction of the

$19 billion in deposits at the bank and two of its sisters were in accounts that exceeded the amounts guaranteed by the Federal Deposit Insurance Corporation. Should the government let market forces wash away poorly managed institutions? Or did it have a responsibility to prevent shocks to the bigger economy?

Robert Glauber, a Harvard academic whom Powell reported to, came down firmly on one side: he hated bailouts. Powell huddled with Fed governor John LaWare at a Treasury Department conference room where Glauber pounded the table and insisted the depositors take a haircut and pay for the sins of the bank. *If we always run to the rescue,* he said, *it creates a "moral hazard"* — a term the insurance industry uses to refer to people who take risks knowing they're protected against larger losses.

After Glauber got off his soapbox, LaWare calmly laid out the Fed's line: "You're the government, and you can do whatever you want, but here's what we think will happen if we haircut uninsured depositors. There will be a run on every American bank when they open Monday, and all these money-center banks will be at our door. Do you really want to run that test, Bob?"

The fear of a bigger crisis trumped the concern about bailouts.

"We chose the first option, without dissent," Powell said.[1]

Upping the ante

A few months later, Powell again wrestled with the problem of what to do with a financial institution on the verge of insolvency — this time, with greater stakes. Salomon Brothers had dominated 1980s Wall Street, both financially — the investment bank was consistently one of the most profitable firms — and culturally. It was the fictional backdrop for *The Bonfire of the Vanities*, Tom Wolfe's 1987 satire of an ambitious bond salesman, as well as the actual setting for Michael Lewis's 1989 *Liar's Poker*, a searing critique of testosterone-driven trading culture. But by 1991, as the Wall Street party was quickly turning into a hangover, the all-powerful Salomon Brothers had hit a wall.

The trouble for the bond-trading giant began in late May, when federal regulators started investigating how Salomon and a few of its customers had ended up controlling 94 percent of the market for two-year Treasury notes. By cornering the market, Salomon could force dealers who had been shut out of the auction — together with arbitrageurs who had bet prices would fall and had sold such securities "short" — to buy the notes back from Salomon at higher prices.

Salomon was one of an elite group of thirty-nine "primary dealers" authorized to trade directly with the New York Fed, which transacts in markets on behalf of the US Treasury. Primary dealers buy Treasury securities directly from the government and resell them to other investors. The total purchases of any one buyer are limited, but Salomon had gotten around that rule by buying securities in its clients' names — without their knowledge — and then using the combined purchases from multiple clients to corner the market.

As the regulators kept digging around, Salomon executives hoped to put the scandal behind them when they disclosed how a senior trader had flouted government rules and rigged the bidding. The revelations sent ripples through the $2.2 trillion market for Treasury securities. Had other dealers joined Salomon in manipulating pricing? Why had Salomon executives not come clean earlier? Was the US government paying more to finance the federal debt as a result of the rigging? And why hadn't regulators noticed sooner?

In the messy aftermath, the New York Fed forced out Salomon's legendary CEO and chairman, John Gutfreund.[2] The government was also contemplating a harsher penalty: suspending the firm's privileged status as a primary dealer in Treasury securities. Even though government bond trading didn't account for much of the firm's total revenues, the move could still be tantamount to a death sentence for the firm in the eyes of its creditors. Salomon depended heavily on short-term borrowing to finance its trading operations. If the Fed cut off Salomon, its lenders could refuse to extend new loans, forcing a fire sale of its assets that would almost surely dissolve the storied firm into bankruptcy.

Revered investor Warren Buffett, the firm's biggest shareholder, had agreed to help clean up the mess and soothe markets by stepping in to serve as chairman. But he threatened to back out if the Treasury decided not to allow Salomon to keep its privileged relationship with the Fed. A game of high-stakes brinksmanship ensued.

On Sunday, August 18, 1991, Powell found himself in the middle of a series of urgent calls among some of the most powerful people in finance — Brady, Greenspan, New York Fed president Gerald Corrigan, and Buffett — about the fate of one of the most powerful firms on Wall Street.

The clock was ticking. Salomon's board was set to meet that afternoon to elect Buffett — known as the "Oracle of Omaha" — as chairman. The board had already called a 2:30 p.m. press conference to make the announcement. But Buffett balked when, that same morning, Treasury announced that it would follow through with the sanctions that would revoke Salomon's status as a primary dealer.

Buffett wanted to shore up confidence in the existing firm, not mop up a total mess. "I am not going to spend the rest of my life shepherding the greatest financial disaster in history," he said.[3]

Corrigan thought Buffett was bluffing. He figured there was no way Salomon's biggest shareholder would flush his stock down the drain. He also thought Buffett was exaggerating the consequences of revoking Salomon's status.

Buffett countered with an ugly picture of handing off a bankrupt Salomon: "We were going to find a judge someplace in Manhattan, walk in on him while he's watching baseball probably and eating popcorn at two in the afternoon, and tell him, we're handing you the keys, you're running the place now. By the way, what do you know about Japanese law, because we owe ten or twelve billion dollars in Japan?"[4]

Powell himself had doubts about taking a hard line on Salomon. He knew Treasury had no plan for handling the failure of a firm that big. And what if Buffett was right? If Salomon's board met and then didn't announce a new chairman, would traders in Tokyo set off a chain reaction when trading opened that evening by refusing to roll over the bank's loans?

Buffett made a final emotional appeal to Brady that Sunday.

"Well, I don't think you're right, but I believe that *you* believe that you are right," Brady said. Buffett would later call it "among the most important sentences I've ever heard."[5]

Brady, Powell, and the other regulators agreed among themselves to a compromise: if Buffett would stay, they would partially reverse the penalties. Salomon could bid in Treasury auctions for its own accounts, but not for other customers.

Powell was nominated to deal directly with Buffett, but Corrigan wanted him to update the rest of the team before agreeing to any final deal. Brady shot Corrigan down. He was the type of boss who, once he trusted someone, would throw them into the deepest part of the ocean.

"I trust him. Just go do it, Jay," Brady said.

So Powell called Buffett and explained the new offer. "Will that do?" Powell asked.

"I think it will," Buffett said.[6]

Powell was finally able to exhale. "The firm's failure," he said years later, "would almost certainly have caused massive disruption in the markets."[7]

After persuading Buffett to stay on, Powell had another, more-public role in the Salomon mess: a Senate hearing. Lawmakers want to appear firm when dealing publicly with the bosses of big financial institutions — it showcases their independence from moneyed elites.

Wednesday, September 4, 1991 was Salomon Brothers' turn in the hot seat. In this case, though, it was a chair behind a large wooden table in a cavernous hearing room on Capitol Hill. Dark red curtains covered the floor-to-ceiling windows. And the first person to occupy the seat had been an executive at Salomon for less than a month.

Cameramen crowded around Buffett in the standing-room-only hearing chamber. He used his homespun Nebraska charm to placate angry lawmakers, beginning with this apology that vowed changes in the bank's culture: "Lose money for the firm, and I will be understanding; lose a shred of reputation for the firm, and I will be ruthless."

Later, lawmakers hauled up the Treasury regulators to find out what had gone wrong on their end. Had the government been asleep at the wheel?

The thirty-eight-year-old Powell, with a shock of silver in the middle of his dark hair, had been at Treasury for only about a year, but he wielded a notable ability to dial down the pressure in a room. He assured law-makers the government would treat the scandal that was roiling the market for US debt with the utmost seriousness.

The Treasury market "is the bedrock of the world financial system," said Powell.

When a skeptical congressman from Kansas asked him why Treasury hadn't detected Salomon's false bids earlier, Powell raised his eyebrows and lifted his hand.

"The fact is, we did catch it, and that's why we're sitting here," said Powell.

Another representative from Ohio piled on: Hadn't the Treasury simply gotten lucky because Salomon's behavior grew so sloppy?

"They fumbled the ball," the congressman said. "You recovered the fumble."

Powell held his ground. "But why did they fumble? They were hit. They didn't just fumble in open field."

His retort drew laughs from the chamber, and even Powell's interlocutor cocked his head and grinned.[8]

Brady had given Powell a chance to cut his teeth in public service, and Powell seized it. When Glauber returned to Harvard in 1992, Brady promoted Powell to be the undersecretary for domestic finance.

Finding fortune

After Bush left office in 1993, Powell returned to the private sector, primarily in mergers and acquisitions. Over the next decade and a half he made a ton of money, although he didn't always jibe with the culture on Wall Street. Not long after he joined Bankers Trust, traders of novel securities called derivatives were caught on tape bragging about how they had screwed over the bank's unsophisticated customers. Lawsuits followed. Powell wanted no part of it and left.

He rejoined Dillon Read as head of mergers in 1995 for a couple of years before moving back down to Washington to join the Carlyle Group, a growing private-equity firm. Powell started and led the industrial group within the firm's buyout fund. His biggest hit was the acquisition of Rexnord Corp., a Milwaukee-based maker of auto parts, which Carlyle sold a few years later to another private-equity firm for more than double what it initially paid. But by 2005, the corporate-buyout market looked more and more like a bubble. Powell, a conservative, cash flow–oriented investor, didn't like being part of the perilous game of hot potato. He also didn't mesh with Dan Akerson, a former naval officer and technology executive who had been brought in to run industrial buyouts for Carlyle. Powell confided in one of Carlyle's partners that he was unhappy in his work.

"You were great," the partner told Powell, "but other people are making a shitload of money doing deals at ten times earnings, and that's just not going to be you." Powell decided to leave.

"Jay was not as driven by making large sums of money as people often can be in this business," said Carlyle's founder, David Rubenstein. "You get on what I call a money merry-go-round, and when you get on it, you can't get off it. Jay was not seduced by that — and he had already made a fair amount of money by any normal human standards."[9]

Powell, at fifty-two, was indeed financially secure — his financial disclosures years later would report assets worth between $19.7 million and $55 million[10] — but he wasn't ready to retire. One venture with another Carlyle alumnus never advanced beyond a business card. After a few more years in the wilderness — Powell did a stint at an asset manager run by his late brother-in-law called the Global Environmental Fund — he pursued a dream his father had deferred: As a college student in 1973, Powell had seen his father turn down a chance to accept a posting in Richard Nixon's Labor Department. Government work simply wouldn't pay college tuition for six kids. But the wealthy, younger Powell didn't have to worry about that.

There was one problem. By the time Powell decided to return to government work in 2010, there was no obvious place for him. Powell, a registered Republican, was unlikely to find work in the Democratic administration of Barack Obama. So he did what people in Washington do when their party is out of power: he joined a think tank. Powell signed on at the centrist Bipartisan Policy Center as an unpaid adviser.

Hitting the ceiling, opening a door

Republicans scored huge wins in the November 2010 midterm elections, retaking control of the House of Representatives with a commanding majority. The influence of the Tea Party movement within the GOP surge ratcheted up the partisanship, quickly choking legislative action.

The success of the insurgents also emboldened conservative lawmakers to take a hard line: they refused to raise the federal borrowing limit. Their strategy was to use the threat of a default on US government debt to bring the White House to the bargaining table, where they could demand steep cuts in spending.

One critical issue in the debate was when the government would run out of money. If the Treasury invokes "extraordinary measures," it's able to operate for a few weeks or months past the date when it is unable to increase borrowing by employing emergency cash-management measures. Powell, who had the luxury of being in an academic position, decided to pinpoint when, exactly, the government could no longer keep the lights on.

That spring, Powell compiled a spreadsheet that modeled daily cash flows — estimating future payments owed and incoming revenues — to approximate what he termed the "X Date," or the specific day on which the US would no longer be able to make required payments to veterans, retirees, or bondholders.

A couple of weeks after he published the analysis online, his blog post went viral. As the standoff heated up, Powell began getting calls from newspapers and radio stations across the country.

The loudest conservative commentators held seemingly contradictory positions. Some accused the Obama administration and business leaders of exaggerating the consequences of default when talking about the necessity of coming to an agreement. But at the same time, they argued that the crisis they were inviting would be so serious as to force their longstanding goal of cutting government retirement and health-care spending programs.

In a May 14, 2011 *Wall Street Journal* interview, billionaire investor Stanley Druckenmiller encouraged conservative lawmakers to hold firm.[11] He claimed the US was heading toward a "Greek situation" of unsustainable borrowing "in six or seven years." Druckenmiller encouraged delaying debt payments for "six, eight or 10 days" to force a grand bargain to entitlement-spending programs.

Powell agreed that government spending was on an unsustainable path. His experience supervising debt-management policy at the Treasury in the early 1990s, however, led him to a different conclusion about the budget standoff. Powell believed Republicans were being led down a dead end by partisans. They were playing politics without really understanding the consequences of taking hostage the nation's sterling credit. He also thought the arguments advanced by people like Druckenmiller were crap.

Powell wrote in a letter to the *Journal*, "Any credible threat of a default would run unacceptable risks for the markets, the economy and our standing in the world.... We must fix our entitlements. It won't happen in 'six, eight or 10 days.' Threats of default will not help to build the broad public support and bipartisan agreement that will be necessary."[12]

While Powell was pushing pragmatism, White House officials were pulling out their hair trying to convince rank-and-file Republicans of what boiled down to the same arguments. This partisan logjam opened Powell's unlikely path back into government.

In the spring of 2011, Powell visited the Treasury to make sure his cash-flow estimates weren't way off base. *If I'm wrong here,* he told Treasury Secretary Tim Geithner's staff, *I'll throw this in the trash. If I'm right, I'll be a big advocate for raising the debt ceiling and explaining it.*

The GOP had stopped listening to Obama or Geithner. Maybe

intransigent conservatives would listen to the silver-haired Powell? The former finance executive was a Republican with solid markets cred.

Soon Geithner was back-channeling regularly with Powell. Treasury officials — who don't publicly release their own estimates — began to refer journalists to Powell. He also began meeting with lawmakers and their staffs.

On Capitol Hill, Powell stuck with his "Just the facts, ma'am" approach. He wasn't lobbying. His presentation simply spelled out what would happen when the government ran out of money. The facts spoke for themselves.

Powell estimated the Treasury would be unable to pay its bills after August 2. On Wednesday, July 13 — twenty days before "X Date" — he briefed Republican congressional leaders. Impressed, they brought him back to brief the entire House GOP conference at a raucous 8 a.m. meeting that Friday. The leadership said Powell was simply there to provide information, not persuade. The response to his take-your-medicine message was mixed. Some conservatives and Tea Party members were elaborately rude, but his analysis clicked with establishment Republicans who needed to hear an outsider say, "There is no other credible choice."

Powell's visit to the lion's den burnished his appeal as a non-ideologue who wasn't going to sugarcoat things. Afterward, House Speaker John Boehner explained to Obama that Boehner still lacked the votes to raise the debt limit, despite bringing in "this Powell guy" to explain everything.

After Congress and the White House reached an intricately crafted compromise to raise the debt limit on August 2, a grateful Geithner asked Powell if he would accept a government appointment. Powell was, of course, enthusiastic.

The debt limit showdown was resolved, but partisanship was creating another headache for Geithner: Obama had nominated a professor at the Massachusetts Institute of Technology named Peter Diamond for one of two seats on the Fed's Board of Governors. Diamond had recently won the Nobel Prize in economics. Republicans said he was unqualified.

Looking for a way to assuage the GOP, Geithner suggested pairing

Powell, a Republican, with the other nominee, Harvard professor Jeremy Stein, a Democrat, to break the impasse.

Just before Labor Day, Geithner's chief of staff asked Powell if he wanted to join the Federal Reserve's Board of Governors. Powell took the night to think it over, then called back.

"Yeah, I do," he said.

At the end of 2011, Obama formally nominated Powell to fill the final two years of a vacant term. The Senate confirmed him the following spring. He was joining an institution with loads of experience navigating messy political battles.

Chapter Two

"THIS FEDERAL RESERVE PLACE"

In October 1907, a group of investors attempted to corner the market on shares of the United Copper Company. They failed spectacularly, causing a run on the lenders that had financed the scheme, which in turn instigated a more generalized panic. Over the next few weeks, New York City's third-largest trust and numerous regional banks failed. The crisis subsided only after the financier J. P. Morgan put up a large sum of his own money to stabilize banks.

Relying on the country's wealthiest citizens to manage future crises was clearly no way to run a national financial system. Lawmakers began a series of negotiations, encouraged by Wall Street financiers, which in 1913 led to the creation of America's own central bank: the Federal Reserve.

From its beginning, the Fed was criticized by populists as too close to wealthy banking interests, but the institution was also relatively weak. In a compromise with agrarian interests who were suspicious of a national bank controlled by East Coast bankers, the Fed had been created as a decentralized network of private banks based in different major cities across the country. On the eve of the Great Depression and the 1929 crash, the Fed had little power — and failed to use what it did have — to stem what is still considered the worst economic crisis in the nation's history. Officials made a series of policy errors, standing by while hundreds of banks failed.

The autonomy that the Fed would later carve out for itself took decades to build and featured high-stakes battles and some painful mistakes. A brief history of the Fed demonstrates why the modern central bank and Jay Powell never took this hard-won independence for granted.

A centralized central bank

The failures of the Fed in the first years of the Great Depression led to the most significant overhaul in its history. Franklin D. Roosevelt's Fed chair, Marriner Eccles, was in many ways the embodiment of the American dream. His Scottish-born Mormon parents immigrated to Utah when the state was still a territory and, through hard work, built up extensive business interests. Only twenty-two years old when his father died, Eccles capably guided the businesses, which had expanded into banking, through the early years of the Great Depression.[1]

Despite never graduating from high school, Eccles came to the kind of radical ideas on government spending that made him an American version of John Maynard Keynes — before the celebrated British economist had published his most important works. Among these ideas was that the way out of the Great Depression was a fiscal policy that increased government spending to fill the gap left by anemic private demand.

Eccles accepted Roosevelt's offer to lead the Fed in 1934 only after the president agreed to back a series of changes to centralize the Fed's authority in Washington. The extreme economic crisis — unemployment stayed above 20 percent for all of 1934 — was the perfect environment for a fundamental redesign of the Fed. The regional Fed banks, which were jointly owned by private local banks, would stay in places like St. Louis and Dallas. But on the "really important questions of policy, authority and responsibility," Eccles wrote, authority would now be "concentrated in the board."[2]

To address concerns from Congress about the increased potential for political meddling in monetary policy, the seven presidentially appointed governors on the Washington-based board would enjoy fourteen-year terms to insulate the central bank system from radical shifts in direction or political pressures. No longer would the Treasury secretary or Comptroller of the Currency serve as *ex officio* members of the board. And to further limit the chances of a single president dominating the makeup of the Fed, the governors' terms would be staggered; a new term begins every two years.

The Eccles reforms put decisions about expanding or contracting the money supply in the hands of a twelve-member group called the Federal Open Market Committee, or FOMC. The seven presidential appointees on the Washington-based board would become permanent members, along with the president of the New York Fed. The other four would rotate among the presidents of the other eleven Fed banks. The reserve-bank presidents underscore the private-public hybrid of the Fed system. Nationally chartered banks are required to own stock in their regional Fed, each of which is a private institution with a board that names its president, subject to the approval of the board of governors in Washington.

In 1937, the Fed consolidated its growing staff in a downtown DC building across from the National Mall. With an exterior of imposing Georgia marble, the four-story structure is known, appropriately, as the Marriner S. Eccles Building.

Eccles didn't rush to use the Fed's considerable new power. He believed the Fed's tools were better suited for slowing down an overheating economy than for jump-starting a contracting one. "One cannot push on a string," he told lawmakers at hearings in 1935.[3] In the years after Roosevelt's initial reforms, "the Treasury usually led and the Federal Reserve usually followed," historian Allan Meltzer wrote.[4]

After the attack on Pearl Harbor drew the United States into the Second World War, long-term Treasury yields jumped. Higher yields send borrowing costs up and can curb investment, spending, and economic growth. To free up resources for the war effort, the Fed agreed to cap certain Treasury yields by purchasing securities as needed to hold rates down. On March 20, 1942, the Fed and Treasury agreed that the Fed would cap long-term Treasury yields at 2½ percent, although the policy was never formally announced — "perhaps to avoid embarrassment in case the policy proved unsuccessful," Fed economists later concluded.[5]

The Missouri populists

Following World War II, US officials relaxed wartime wage and price controls. Combined with demand for American goods from war-torn Europe, consumer prices rose an enormous 17.6 percent between June 1946 and June 1947, and another 9.5 percent over the following 12 months. As prices exploded upward, Eccles decided to end the wartime policy of capping government borrowing costs. Easy money wasn't needed in a rapidly expanding peacetime economy, and it was stoking inflation (a preview of the post-pandemic debates of 2021).

Eccles's move was fiercely resisted by the President Truman's Treasury Secretary, John W. Snyder, who didn't want the government to pay more on its war debts. Snyder, an old army buddy of Truman's, had the president's full support. He and Eccles eventually came to a compromise in which the government's borrowing costs were allowed to rise subject to Treasury approval.[6]

The president's confused understanding of finance further drew the Fed into conflict with the White House — something that Powell would encounter with a different president shortly after he became Fed chair. Truman was a populist who never attended college, worked his family's farm, and was left in debt for years after his haberdashery business went bust. By pushing back on raising interest rates, the president felt that he was resisting a "non-productive tax burden on the public." Years later, Truman would describe rising interest rates as a "hardship on the consuming public" that "only benefits the privileged few."[7]

Truman especially hated the idea that long-term rates might rise because, decades earlier, he had lost money when he sold his World War I Liberty savings bonds early. Truman erroneously feared that those who had invested their savings in wartime bonds would suffer similar losses if the Fed prevailed now. Truman didn't realize — and couldn't be convinced by Snyder — that bondholders could suffer losses only if they sold their bonds before they matured, as he had.[8]

Truman replaced Eccles when his term as Fed chair expired though Eccles, whose term as governor ran for another ten years beyond the chairmanship, chose to stay on the Fed board, where he wielded an unusual amount of influence.[9] Secretary Snyder recommended a friend of his, business executive Thomas McCabe, for the Fed job, claiming he'd stand down on any fight over interest rates.[10] But the administration quickly learned they had misjudged their choice for Fed chair, which became a common theme for future presidents.

A 1949 recession helped cool inflation, but the next year, the prospect of a wider war in Korea drove new fears of inflation. The FOMC voted in June to increase the one-year rate, but the Treasury refused. The Fed's purchases of securities soared.[11] Eccles and New York Fed president Allan Sproul encouraged McCabe to dig in and defend the bank's autonomy. If the central bank "expected to survive as an agency with any independence whatsoever, [it] should exercise some independence," Eccles said.[12] When the FOMC voted to raise rates in June 1950 to tamp down inflation, Snyder and Truman were completely opposed.[13] Ralph Leach, who joined the Fed board as the head of the government finance section in 1950, later wrote about the confrontation: "The chasm that existed was unbridgeable. Truman and Snyder were populists who believed that banks, not the market forces of supply and demand, set interest rates."[14]

When communist China entered the Korean war and repelled US forces at the end of 1950, consumer spending surged in anticipation of new shortages, and prices soared.[15] Truman framed his desired Fed policy in stark terms of national security in a letter to McCabe: "I hope the Board will...not allow the bottom to drop from under our securities," he said. "If that happens that is exactly what Mr. Stalin wants."[16]

The dispute boiled down to which entity should have control over interest-rate decisions — and the Fed's independence from Treasury. More debt issued by the Treasury to finance war spending risked sending up yields unless the Fed purchased the securities, something economists refer to as "monetizing" the debt. When the Fed buys debt from the government, it adds reserves to the banking system, which can boost lending and spur inflationary pressures. Eccles explained to lawmakers how the Fed's policies made the banking system, through the actions of the Fed, "an engine of inflation."[17]

The Treasury-Fed accord

On January 31, 1951, Truman summoned the entire FOMC to the White House, the first and only time any such meeting has been called. The "present emergency is the greatest this country has ever faced, including the two World Wars and all the preceding wars," Truman told the FOMC, somewhat hyperbolically.[18]

The next morning, the White House press secretary blindsided the Fed by declaring that the central bank had "pledged its support to President Truman to maintain the stability as long as the emergency lasts."[19] When newspaper reporters called Eccles, he said Truman had utterly misconstrued the Fed's position. Eccles regarded Truman's treachery as "the final move in a Treasury attempt to impose its will on the Federal Reserve," he wrote. "If swift action was not taken...the Federal Reserve would...be reduced to the level of a Treasury bureau."[20]

Eccles decided to leak a confidential FOMC memorandum summarizing who had said what during the White House meeting, exposing the administration's perfidy. "The fat was in the fire," Eccles wrote in his memoirs.[21]

The opening for a resolution between the Fed and White House emerged after Snyder, the Treasury secretary, checked into the hospital on Sunday, February 11, for a previously scheduled cataract operation. One of Snyder's lieutenants, William McChesney Martin Jr., began secret discussions with Fed staffers at his house in Washington.[22]

Martin's conversations with the Fed ultimately produced a formal agreement that Snyder and Truman reluctantly supported. The central bank announced the Treasury-Fed accord on March 4, 1951, in an unexceptional, two-paragraph bulletin. Its significance would grow over time because it marked the beginning of what many commentators refer to as Fed independence. Going forward, the Fed would set interest-rate policy to ensure the economy functioned well rather than to support cheaper financing for the government, as the Fed had done since 1942 to support the war effort. Those boundaries have largely remained to the present day. The Treasury manages all of the money the government receives and pays out, while the Fed manages the supply of money in circulation to keep the economy stable.

The Fed had two things in its favor in 1951: support from key members of Congress and the president's weakening political standing. The month in which the Treasury-Fed accord was reached coincided with Truman's discovery that General MacArthur had discussed defying direct orders, which ignited one of the worst storms of his presidency when he fired MacArthur on April 11.[23]

"Traitor"

The end of Treasury-Fed hostilities did nothing to reduce personal hostilities. Snyder, still furious with the Fed's McCabe for pushing ahead with plans to sever the rate peg while he was in the hospital, secured Truman's agreement to accept the resignation that McCabe had angrily offered.[24] To find Truman his second new Fed chair, Snyder recommended Bill Martin, thinking the fellow Missourian who had so ably negotiated the accord might be more tractable.

At a White House meeting, Truman asked Martin if he would commit to keeping rates stable. The president patiently explained how his Liberty bonds had gone down in value after World War I. "You wouldn't ever let that happen again, would you?"

Martin's reply was blunt. Without responsible fiscal and monetary policies, a rate increase "will probably happen again. Markets will not wait on kings, prime ministers, presidents, secretaries of the Treasury, or chairmen of the Federal Reserve."[25] Even if it wasn't the answer Truman wanted, the politically weakened president gave him the job.

The initial reaction on Wall Street and at the Fed was that with Martin's appointment, the Fed had "won the battle but lost the war," recalled Leach, the Fed staffer. "That is, the Fed had broken free from the Treasury, but then the Treasury had recaptured it by installing its own man."[26]

The conventional wisdom was wrong. Under Martin, the Fed forced Treasury to issue short- and medium-term debt that was higher than Snyder wanted. This show of independence from his new chair incensed

Truman. In late 1952, while leaving the Waldorf Astoria Hotel in midtown Manhattan, Martin ran into the president on the sidewalk.

"I said, *Good afternoon, Mr. President*," Martin recalled later. "The president looked me right in the eye and said only one word in reply: *Traitor!*"[27]

Getting pushed around

President Dwight Eisenhower reappointed Martin twice, a precedent that helped validate the Fed's independence. Despite disagreements between Martin and President Kennedy's more liberal advisers, they recognized that Martin enjoyed the confidence of the broader financial community and recommended his reappointment in 1963. Kennedy didn't bully Martin, but he did become the first president to seek out candidates for Fed governorships with the academic or technical heft to push or pull a consensus toward the administration's policies. "About the only power I have over the Federal Reserve is the power of appointment, and I plan to use it," he said.[28]

Whatever peace Martin forged with Kennedy unraveled under President Lyndon B. Johnson. Early on, Johnson told Martin that he came from "a part of the country that liked interest rates to be low — all the time."[29] In contrast, Martin worried credit conditions were too easy and that, by 1965, inflation could become a more difficult problem. Martin, who had once quipped that it was the Fed's job to take away the punch bowl before the party got out of hand, later learned that spending on the Vietnam War was growing faster than Johnson's advisers would publicly admit. The higher deficits might also fuel more inflation.

Martin believed he needed to act soon by raising the discount rate, which the Fed charges banks for short-term loans and which is controlled by the seven-member board of governors, as opposed to the larger FOMC. One of Martin's allies on the board was set to retire in January 1966, potentially depriving Martin of a majority of support for an increase in the discount rate. The economy was looking strong. An expansion that had started in early 1961 was more than four and a half years old, the longest since World War II. The discount rate had been raised only twice in two years. The unemployment rate, which peaked at 7 percent in 1961, was nearing a low level of 4 percent. Taking away the punch bowl could stop the possibility of inflation taking off.

But such a policy went against Johnson's low-rate mantra. At an October 6, 1965, meeting at the White House, Martin suggested the president think of it as a way to extend the economic expansion and aid small banks, which were disadvantaged by statutory ceilings on interest rates for savings certificates.[30]

Johnson didn't bite. "'It would,' he said with an arm outstretched and fingers clenched, 'amount to squeezing blood from the American working man in the interest of Wall Street,'" recalled Paul Volcker, then a thirty-eight-year-old assistant secretary of the Treasury.[31]

On Friday, December 3, 1965, Martin called a meeting of the board to make his move. After sleepless nights, he cast the deciding vote in favor of raising the discount rate by half a percentage point, to 4.5 percent. Martin also warned his colleagues about the potential ferocity of Johnson's ire. "We should be under no illusions," said Martin. Their decision could lead to a wholesale "revamping of the Federal Reserve System, including its structure and operating methods."[32]

The president summoned Martin, along with other top economic advisers, to his Texas ranch on December 6, 1965. Johnson saw the battle in historic terms. Before Martin's rate increase that week, in a phone call with Treasury Secretary Henry Fowler, Johnson had alluded to the fight over the Second Bank of the United States, a Philadelphia-based and federally authorized national bank that had operated from 1816 until 1836. In 1832, President Andrew Jackson had vetoed the renewal of that bank's charter in an epic clash with bank president Nicholas Biddle.

"I would hope that he wouldn't call his board together and have a Biddle-Jackson fight," Johnson told his Treasury secretary. "I'm prepared to be Jackson if he wants to be Biddle — have a fight like that. Right now, I don't want that in public."[33] He also told Fowler, who had earlier recommended that Volcker take Martin's job, to find a new chair — "a real articulate, able, tough guy that can take this Federal Reserve place."[34]

It would be a showdown. Johnson had already asked his attorney general whether language in the Federal Reserve Act that allowed the president to fire a governor "for cause" gave him grounds to dismiss Martin. The answer was no.[35]

Alone in the president's living room, Johnson let Martin have it: "You took advantage of me, and I just want you to know that's a despicable thing to do."[36] Johnson advanced on Martin, pushed him around the room and shouted in his face, "Boys are dying in Vietnam, and Bill Martin doesn't care!"[37]

Martin allowed he might have made the wrong decision, "but I do have a very strong conviction that the Federal Reserve Act placed responsibility for interest rates with the Federal Reserve Board. This is one of those few occasions where the Federal Reserve Board decision has to be final."[38]

After the lashing, Martin and his economic advisers sat with Johnson on the porch of the ranch house in a line of folding aluminum chairs for a press conference. All sides played down any conflict.

"Your job [in the press] is to provoke a fight. Mine is to prevent one," Johnson said diplomatically.[39]

Lawmakers pilloried Martin. He took solace from a surprise note he received from Eisenhower, who wrote of "the intense pride I have in seeing you stand 4-square for what you know to be right."[40] Eisenhower told Martin history would regard his path-setting tenure at the Fed the way it did for John Marshall, the first chief justice of the Supreme Court.[41]

For all the drama, it turned out that the 1965 rate increase ultimately did little to slow the growth of inflation. The Fed would reverse course in 1967, after the economy appeared to be entering a downturn, and Martin held off on raising rates after that because he wanted to support a White House proposal to raise taxes.

"You've got a problem"

For all the fireworks of the Johnson presidency, the wheels really came off the bus under Richard Nixon. The new president wanted to turn the Fed over to Arthur Burns, his longtime economic adviser. In 1960, Burns had warned the then–vice president that Martin's monetary policy would cause a slowdown, derailing Nixon's campaign for the presidency. "Unfortunately, Arthur Burns turned out to be a good prophet," Nixon later wrote.[42] Martin wanted to take care of the growing inflation problem before leaving and rejected an offer Nixon made to install him as Treasury secretary. By the time Nixon took office, the rate of annual price growth had reached an unsettling 4.7 percent.

Shortly after Nixon became president, Paul Volcker, now an undersecretary at Treasury, went to the White House to deliver some straight talk. "You're in here. The inflation rate is up. You've got a problem. Deal with it now. If you have to have a recession, take it early," Volcker told Nixon. "Don't sit around because it will be worse for you later." Volcker laughed as he later recalled the new president's reaction: "He didn't believe a word."[43]

Meanwhile, Martin's Fed again raised rates. Nixon was furious, recalling the Republican Party's wipeout during the 1958 congressional elections. "We cooled off the economy and cooled off 15 senators and 60 congressmen at the same time," he said.[44]

The economy fell into recession in 1970, ending the longest US expansion since the Civil War, but inflation didn't entirely subside. Martin was ashamed of the situation he was leaving behind and feared that he had deferred too much to Johnson. At a Saturday black-tie sendoff at the White House, Martin lamented how the central bank had allowed inflation to fester: "I wish I could turn the bank over to Arthur Burns as I would have liked," he said. "But we are in very deep trouble."[45]

At Martin's final luncheon at the Fed board, "He said simply, 'I've failed,'" recalled FOMC secretary Bob Holland. "He felt that inflation had crept into the American economy on his watch, and he saw it as his failure."[46]

When Martin met with Richard T. McCormack, a Nixon adviser who was overseeing a council studying how to better organize the executive branch, Martin told him the story about what had happened at Johnson's ranch in 1965, implying that he should have raised rates sooner — or higher — than he actually did. "To my everlasting shame," Martin said, "I finally gave in to him."[47]

"We got his attention"

Nixon didn't care much for the idea of Fed autonomy either. The president figured he was going to get the credit or blame for the economy's performance, so he should be able to decide on the money supply.[48] He announced Arthur Burns's nomination on October 17, 1969, and from the start, made clear to Burns that he had little regard for "the myth of the autonomous Fed."[49]

Like many economists who came of age during the Great Depression, Burns believed government policy had an obligation to prevent a recurrence of the unacceptably high levels of unemployment that followed and should focus on that task above all else.

By the time Burns was nominated, however, inflation was on a sharp upward turn. He began advocating for an unorthodox "incomes policy" that would use wage and price controls, not interest-rate increases, to hold down inflation. Nixon was furious when he read press reports about the proposal, which he didn't support. After White House adviser John Ehrlichman delivered a stern admonition from the president, Burns's reply revealed his sense of devotion to Nixon: "The idea that I would ever let a conflict arise between what I think is right and my loyalty to Dick Nixon is outrageous."[50]

By the summer of 1971, the economy was six months into a recovery, and inflation held at a still-high 4.4 percent. On July 16, the Fed raised the discount rate for the first time under Burns, to 5 percent from 4.75 percent. A week later, at a July 23 congressional hearing, Burns again strayed from Nixon's political goals. Instead of offering the optimistic spin the president desperately wanted, he publicly puzzled over the phenomenon that had begun in the late 1960s. "The rules of economics are not working in quite the way they used to. Despite extensive unemployment in our country, wage-rate increases have not moderated. Despite much idle industrial capacity, commodity prices continue to rise rapidly."[51]

Nixon had heard enough. That evening, during a Friday-night cruise on the Potomac River aboard the presidential yacht *Sequoia*, Nixon and a few advisers hatched a plot to manipulate Burns.[52] With Burns pushing for wage controls, they leaked a story saying the chair was simultaneously seeking to increase his own $42,500 annual salary by $20,000.[53] White House press secretary Ron Ziegler carefully refused to deny the story.

In case Burns hadn't gotten the message, Nixon adviser Charles Colson enlisted Alan Greenspan — a Burns protégé and an economic consultant for the Nixon campaign — to telephone the Fed chair. Colson had helped hatch the pay-raise-smear pressure tactic on the *Sequoia*, and he would later go to jail for his role in other White House dirty tricks. According to Sebastian Mallaby's 2016 biography of Greenspan, notes from Colson suggest Greenspan spoke at length to Burns about his policy dilemma and loyalties to Nixon.[54] According to those notes, Greenspan reported Burns as being "very disturbed" and "pissed off."[55]

H. R. Haldeman, Nixon's chief of staff, relayed Colson's account to the president. "The Arthur Burns ploy worked with a bang," he reported to Nixon. "Greenspan says Arthur's ego is so great that honestly he thinks he is doing the right thing, and he doesn't think until now Arthur really realized he was doing political harm."[56]

Nixon was delighted. "We got his attention," the president said of Burns in a phone call with Treasury Secretary John Connally.[57]

Confident that Burns had gotten the message, Nixon turned from foe to friend. At an August 4 news conference, he said his budget office had proposed the idea of a pay raise for the Fed chair and that Burns had rejected it.

"He has taken a very unfair shot," Nixon told reporters.[58]

A copy of Nixon's remarks was later sent to Burns. "It warmed my heart," Burns said. "I haven't been so deeply moved in years."[59]

The anguish of central banking

Nixon faced a bigger problem in August 1971: the postwar international monetary system was breaking down. The system relied on the convertibility of gold to a fixed-exchange rate of $35 per ounce, redeemable by the

US government. Other currencies, in turn, pegged to the dollar. In essence, the United States found itself in the position of supplying the rest of the world with reserve assets — dollars backed by gold. For it all to work, the US had to maintain the purchasing power of the dollar by avoiding inflation. But there weren't enough dollars in a growing global economy with increasing demand for reserves. Now, with inflation rising, the dollar link to gold was unraveling.

On Friday, August 13, 1971, Nixon gathered his economic team at Camp David in the Catoctin Mountains of western Maryland, where they decided in favor of abandoning the gold link. Nixon also relented on the incomes policy and announced a ninety-day freeze of all prices and wages, which was to be followed by some form of price and wage controls. For Volcker, the end of the fixed exchange-rate system gave more responsibility to the Fed by indicating "widespread understanding that the dollar's value now depended on the Fed's ability to control the money supply and end the inflationary process."[60]

Meanwhile, the pressure on Burns appeared to pay off. The FOMC cut rates twice before the end of 1971. Despite Nixon's continued paranoia about the Fed, the economy accelerated at a breakneck pace. In a clear surrender to Nixon's political schedule, the Fed held rates at 4.5 percent through the November 1972 election, then raised them aggressively over the next year, to 7.5 percent by September 1973. Fed governor Dewey Daane later contrasted Burns unfavorably with his predecessor. Martin "was always seeking to strengthen the system to make it work. Burns was always trying to get invited to the White House."[61]

Burns's second term proved as challenging as his first. A bad harvest in 1972 and the oil shock of 1973 drove prices up rapidly, leading to a recession at the end of 1973. As would be expected in a contracting economy, unemployment shot up over the course of 1974. But so did inflation, reaching levels not seen since the immediate postwar era.

Normally, central bankers look past one-time price increases from such transitory shocks. But the rising inflation of the late 1960s and early 1970s meant consumers were getting accustomed to paying higher prices, leading to self-fulfilling expectations of still-higher prices. Consumer prices rose nearly 9 percent in 1973 — more than double the rate when price controls took effect two years earlier — and 12 percent in 1974. Burns feared raising interest rates too high would lead to levels of unemployment not seen since the Great Depression. When he retired in the spring of 1978, unemployment was at 6 percent and inflation hit 9 percent — and both were still rising.

In the ongoing crisis, Congress passed Democratic legislation in 1977 and 1978 that set forth a so-called *dual mandate* for the Fed. The legislation directed the Fed to maintain stable prices and low unemployment. Until then, Congress hadn't been so specific about the Fed's goals. The legislation creating the Fed in 1913 focused not on defined economic objectives but on supervising banks and furnishing an "elastic currency." The Employment Act of 1946, passed as millions of American soldiers returned home and with memories still fresh of the Great Depression, declared it the responsibility of the federal government, but not specifically the Fed, to "promote maximum employment, production and purchasing power." Now, Congress had given the Fed two very specific goals.

At a speech in Belgrade in September 1979 entitled "The Anguish of Central Banking," Burns offered a litany of excuses for the decade of economic-policy failures. "It is illusory to expect central banks to put an end to the inflation that now afflicts the industrial democracies," he said.[62] Whether he had been a victim of bad luck, misreading the economy, or political pressure — or a combination of all three — economic historians would later judge Burns harshly for not even trying to use monetary policy to constrain inflation once the genie was out of the bottle. The lesson to future Fed chairs was clear: Don't be like Burns.

Tall Paul

In 1978, President Jimmy Carter named corporate executive G. William Miller to succeed Burns. Miller used an egg timer at committee meetings to keep his colleagues from droning on and posted a sign that said THANK YOU FOR NOT SMOKING. Both proved as ineffective as his monetary policy.[63] Inflation was soaring, but rising unemployment made the Fed reluctant to raise rates. Miller's job grew harder after the second oil shock of the decade, again driven by events in the Middle East.

On July 19, 1979, after Carter outlined his measures for dealing with twin energy and economic crises, he sacked his Treasury secretary. Miller would take his place. He called Volcker, who was then president of the New York Fed, and asked him to fly down to see Carter.

Volcker stood a looming six feet seven and had a gruff and rumpled disposition. A former colleague described him as badly dressed and often in need of a haircut. Though he had served in the Treasury under three presidents, he had never met Carter. At their Oval Office meeting, Volcker slumped on a couch, cigar in hand, and told Carter, "You have to understand, if you appoint me, I favor a tighter policy than that fellow," pointing a friendly finger at Miller.[64]

Carter telephoned him the next morning at 7:30 to offer him the job. Volcker hadn't even gotten out of bed yet.[65]

Volcker's appointment signaled the beginning of a new era in central banking. Ten days into Volcker's term, the Fed raised the discount rate to 10½ percent — its highest level ever. The board voted again on September 18 to raise rates, but this had been a closer 4-3 decision. The split vote stoked concern in markets that the Fed and its new chair might lose their nerve. An unnamed Treasury official told *The Wall Street Journal* that the Fed would soon be forced to cut rates because unemployment would hit 7 percent "and Congress isn't willing to bear that burden."[66]

Volcker decided new tactics were needed. One week after returning from international financial meetings in Belgrade, where he had attended Burns's defeatist jeremiad, he called a rare Saturday meeting of the FOMC. Over six hours on October 6, 1979, he secured agreement to a drastic change in how the Fed would conduct monetary policy.

No longer would the Fed manage the daily level of the federal-funds rate — the price of money — to achieve desired credit conditions. Instead, it would focus on the overall supply of money to achieve its goals. The price of money — short-term interest rates — would fluctuate dramatically, if needed, to hit the money-supply targets. The old, established pattern of making small, steady changes to the short-term rates "tended to be too little, too late to influence expectations," Volcker concluded.[67]

When Volcker's press aide, Joe Coyne, phoned news outlets to tell them about an unusual 6 p.m. news conference, an assignment editor at the CBS bureau protested he didn't have a camera to spare. Pope John Paul II happened to be in Washington that Saturday. Without hesitating, Coyne told the editor to send a crew:[68] "Long after the pope is gone, you'll remember this one."[69]

Just how high rates would rise under Volcker's new strategy was anyone's guess. Eventually, rates on three-month Treasury bills exceeded 17 percent and the commercial bank prime-lending rate peaked at 21.5 percent. Mortgage rates neared 18 percent. All were unheard of, and it was terrible timing for Carter's reelection. A recession began in January 1980.

Carter mostly kept any frustrations to himself, but the public pressure on the Fed was intense. Angry farmers drove their tractors around the Fed's headquarters. Home builders mailed two-by-fours bearing the message LOWER INTEREST RATES, and realtors and car dealers sent in keys to represent unsold homes and autos. After an armed man broke into the Fed's headquarters in December 1980 and threatened to take hostages, Volcker was forced to accept a personal security detail.[70]

Economic misery was again poison for the incumbent; Carter lost the 1980 election in a landslide to Ronald Reagan. Following Reagan's inauguration in January 1981, someone from the White House asked Volcker if he'd like to host the president at the Fed. Volcker was concerned about the optics. "I'm glad to meet with the president and I'm at his beck and call, but if he comes to the Federal Reserve, a lot of questions will be raised about why the hell you have this new president meeting at the Federal Reserve," Volcker said.[71]

Volcker didn't know what to expect when they agreed to meet for lunch at the Treasury Department on January 23, 1981. Volcker had been told that some "gold bugs" had enlisted Reagan's support in returning to the gold standard. The new president disarmed him immediately when the meeting began by poking fun at that crowd: "What about all this crazy gold-standard stuff?" the president said, laughing.[72] He applauded the drop in gold prices as a sign that Volcker's inflation fight was succeeding.

"I don't kiss men," Volcker said, "but I was tempted."[73]

Even though Reagan declined to attack the Fed, his senior officials occasionally fired off criticisms of Volcker, and congressional Democrats were unsparing. They wanted to hold Volcker to the Fed's new dual mandate. Yet in the early 1980s, the dual mandate wasn't just hard to achieve, it was contradictory. With the unemployment rate rising to 10.8 percent in November 1982 from 7.2 percent in early 1981, Volcker appeared to be disregarding the jobs half to achieve the stability half. Texas Democrat Henry Gonzalez said he intended to file impeachment proceedings against Volcker. Massachusetts Senator Edward Kennedy said he supported legislation to put the Fed in the Treasury Department, "where it belongs."[74]

Volcker's comments at FOMC meetings during a crucial period in 1981, when the economy was in a painful double-dip recession, underscored his concern that they had one shot to defeat inflation. He acknowledged "great restiveness and anger" that could be "relieved, obviously, by some decline in interest rates," at a meeting on October 6. But giving temporary comfort by lowering rates, only to have to raise them later because inflation hadn't been reined in, would be the worst outcome. "The public patience for climbing up the hill very rapidly again may be extremely limited," he said.[75]

By July 1982, economic activity appeared to hit a trough, and Volcker began easing up. A few months later, inflation had fallen below 5 percent for the first time in a decade. Volcker conceded the Fed had reached the limits of what the public would accept. "If we get this wrong, we are going to have legislation next year without a doubt. We may get it anyway," he told the FOMC on October 5, 1982.[76]

Things quieted down after that as the economy revved up, with one exception. Reagan's advisers had packed the board with governors who favored looser monetary policy. In February 1986, four of them — a majority — proposed a cut in the discount rate that Volcker opposed.

The chair saw it as a coup and told James Baker he would submit his resignation to the president that day. To defuse the situation, one of the governors agreed to reverse his vote and wait to cut rates, as Volcker had proposed. But for Volcker, life at the Fed "was never quite the same."[77]

The lessons of Fed history were becoming clear: Autonomy from day-to-day political pressure served the central bank well in any effort to hold inflation down, but there was no such thing as true independence. Congress could revamp the Fed at any time, as it did after the Great Depression and again when lawmakers spelled out the dual mandate in the late 1970s. George Shultz, who served as Reagan's secretary of state and Nixon's Treasury secretary, stated the case well years later: "To do something difficult, even if you are the independent Federal Reserve, it makes a huge difference if the president is on your side and is strong and understands the problem, and when things get tough, he doesn't go the other way and denounce you."[78]

The Rubin Rule

The boom years that followed the defeat of high inflation strengthened the argument for the Fed's political autonomy. It would be up to Alan Greenspan — appointed by Reagan and confirmed in August of 1987 — to consolidate those gains by holding inflation low.

The Greenspan era was marked by economic expansion and generally low unemployment and inflation. Greenspan caught some flak during the first Bush administration for not reducing rates more after the 1990–91 recession. Treasury Secretary Nick Brady — Jay Powell's boss — canceled their weekly breakfasts, and the president later blamed Greenspan for his 1992 election loss. Still, it was nothing compared with Johnson's hectoring or Nixon's dirty tricks.[79]

Even this mild reproach would fade away under President Bill Clinton. Robert Rubin, the co-chairman of Goldman Sachs, disapprovingly watched the entire Greenspan-Bush fracas play out. When he was appointed to run Clinton's National Economic Council, Rubin advised Clinton to make it a policy of his administration that neither the president nor anyone else would ever weigh in publicly on monetary policy. Demanding something the president couldn't attain made Bush look weak, Rubin concluded. And it could be counterproductive. Some Fed officials might feel obligated to stiffen their backs against presidential pressure, lest markets question the central bank's inflation-fighting credibility.

"It was clear what we should do," Rubin said. "If you looked at the Paul Volcker experience, for example, having an independent Fed in terms of its decisions and credibility was critically important."[80] Thus was born the "Rubin Rule." A few advisers wavered at first in following it, but the booming economy of the late 1990s made it a moot point.

The hands-off policy carried through into the next administration, led by Bush's son. At a breakfast meeting in Washington shortly before his inauguration, George W. Bush assured Greenspan he would not comment on Fed policy during his time in office. "And he never did," said Greenspan, continuing Rubin's practice.[81]

Declining inflation, rising incomes, a booming stock market, and low unemployment allowed Greenspan — dubbed "the Maestro" — to cultivate an aura of technocratic omniscience and gave the Fed license to be mostly left alone by politicians. Term limits forced Greenspan to retire in 2006, and George W. Bush nominated Ben Bernanke — a distinguished economist with experience in academia and government — to serve as the 14th chair of the Federal Reserve. The next year, a nationwide housing bubble collapsed, triggering the worst financial crisis since the Great Depression. The messy aftermath plunged the Fed into grueling policy and political battles. Jay Powell watched closely, and he would later borrow extensively from Bernanke's playbook.

Chapter Three

"WE WOULD TREAT HIM PRETTY UGLY"

The problems boiled over in 2007, when Ben Bernanke had been slow to recognize how the subprime mortgage crisis had stretched its tentacles through the entire economy. But after the collapse of Lehman Brothers in September 2008 plunged the financial system into its worst crisis since the Great Depression, Bernanke moved quickly and creatively to prevent a rerun of 1929.

The Fed deployed scarcely used emergency-lending authorities — first to rescue the investment bank Bear Stearns, and later the insurance giant American International Group — to stem a financial panic. But these tools weren't enough. Congress was pressured in October 2008 to approve what became a $700 billion bill to recapitalize the nation's banking sector.

Bernanke's initial response to the economic turmoil was a standard monetary tool: reducing the federal-funds rate. The Fed moved interest rates down by purchasing short-term Treasury bills with money it created out of thin air to expand the money supply.

This standard monetary response would not be enough. The financial panic that followed the collapse of Lehman Brothers in September 2008 ultimately prompted Bernanke to slash the rate to effectively zero by the end of the year — the first time it had ever been so low. With the interest-rate tool maxed out (officials weren't willing to push the fed-funds rate below zero) but the economy still hobbled by the wreckage from the housing bust, Bernanke moved to deliver more stimulus with a tool dubbed *quantitative easing,* or *QE.*

Buying and selling short-term Treasury bills was a well-tested practice for expanding or shrinking the money supply to set interest rates. Quantitative easing went a step further: instead of just buying ultra-safe Treasury bills, the Fed bought riskier assets such as longer-dated Treasury bonds and government-guaranteed mortgage-backed securities. QE fueled lots of scaremongering in the financial press, but it was just another way to increase the money supply and encourage lending and investment.

Although Washington had moved quickly to rescue the financial system, these salvage jobs carried a steep political cost. The Fed—and Congress—hadn't expended nearly as much effort or money to stem the millions of foreclosures across the country. Following the rescue of the overleveraged and poorly managed insurance company AIG, the Fed found itself defending the company's payout of huge bonuses to executives. The sense that the Fed would do anything to prop up Wall Street while average Americans saw their dreams repossessed by banks stirred an intense populist backlash—one that was seized upon by the emerging Tea Party.

The humbling of the technocrats

Depending on who you asked, the Fed had kept rates too low in the early 2000s and inflated the housing bubble; failed to regulate the banks; didn't cut rates soon enough in 2007; made irresponsible bailouts in 2008; embarked on risky and unproven stimulus campaigns between 2009 and 2011; grew too involved with Congress and the White House in drawing up new regulations; and invited runaway inflation and new bubbles by keeping easy-money policies in place for too long once the crisis passed. Some criticisms were valid. Some weren't. But the range of criticism was intense, and it made the Fed's desire to remain aloof from politics increasingly difficult to achieve.

Democrats proposed stripping the Fed of its regulatory powers. When the Fed fended off those efforts and dived into negotiations over the regulatory overhaul that became the Dodd-Frank Act, Republicans saw a central bank too eager to collaborate with Democrats. Wasn't the Fed supposed to be independent?

But the fiercest political battles cropped up around quantitative easing. The tool was controversial because it wasn't well understood, and it stepped outside the parameters of traditional monetary policy. To some, QE seemed to encroach on the fiscal policy — changes to spending and taxes — that is traditionally the domain of Congress, by making it cheaper to run bigger deficits. Critics of QE claimed that all the "made-up money" purchasing assets could also lead to runaway inflation in the future.

Bernanke was unconvinced of either argument. A bald and bearded Princeton economist — brilliant, if sometimes socially awkward — Bernanke had spent his academic career focused on policymakers' failures during the Great Depression. Bernanke was determined not to repeat their mistakes, and to avoid a similar spell of deflation that had struck Japan in the 1990s, causing wages and prices to fall. Bernanke kept the Fed rate near zero for the rest of his tenure. QE also remained the Fed's go-to tool whenever economic growth threatened to peter out.

Bernanke's innovations

The bond-buying stimulus programs that Ben Bernanke pioneered after the 2008 financial crisis were not his only innovations. The first was designing a more robust apparatus for communicating, a step that would have been anathema to an earlier generation of central bankers.

Montagu Norman, the famously secretive governor of the Bank of England from 1920 to 1944, took as his personal creed, "Never explain, never excuse." Alan Greenspan had started largely in the Norman mold. "Since I've become a central banker, I've learned to mumble with great incoherence. If I seem unduly clear to you, you must have misunderstood what I said," Greenspan quipped shortly after becoming Fed chair.[1] He was only half-joking. Greenspan frequently testified in Congress but gave just one television interview; it occurred at the start of his 18½-year tenure, and he never gave a second.

The Fed had opened up more to the public during the Greenspan years, but it could go further still. Until 1994, the Fed didn't officially announce changes in the federal-funds rate. Instead, investors and reporters who covered the central bank figured it out from changes in short-term money markets after policy meetings.

Communications took another leap forward in 2003, when the Fed offered more explicit guidance in what had become a regular, post-meeting statement about the future path for interest rates. The US no longer faced the threat of inflation staying too high, the big risk since the Volcker years. Instead, officials contemplated a grim scenario of interest rates hovering close to zero and inflation drifting lower.

In the event of economic contraction or deflation, the Fed would have very little conventional firepower to stimulate growth while the fed-funds rate sat at an all-time low of 1.25 percent. Bernanke, then a Fed governor, suggested that communicating with the market was not just desirable, but perhaps the central bank's best option: "When we get close to the zero bound, we run out of traditional tools, and the only way we can influence interest rates is by manipulating expectations."[2]

Bernanke figured that if officials gave specific projections about Fed policy, they could influence the expectations that shaped credit decisions. "Ambiguity has its uses, but mostly in noncooperative games like poker," Bernanke told his colleagues in 2003. "Monetary policy is a cooperative game. The whole point is to get financial markets to do some of our work for us."[3]

Bernanke expanded his practice of "information as monetary tool" by becoming more specific about the Fed's intentions for achieving its goal of price stability. Before becoming chair, Bernanke had urged the Fed to consider setting an explicit target, but he didn't get far with Greenspan. He made that his goal after becoming chair, and arrived there in several steps over the course of five years.

By 2009, once the fed-funds rate had been lowered below even 2003 levels, Bernanke believed even more strongly that setting an official target would be desirable to assure the public that the Fed was committed to making sure inflation wouldn't be too high or *too low* — again, to avoid the paralyzing problem of deflation. The Fed finally adopted a formal 2 percent target in 2012.

Another Bernanke change in communications — quarterly news conferences after every other FOMC meeting — made the Fed chair's job more important. Now, Bernanke would summarize the committee's different viewpoints and explain the policy decision four times a year. Some analysts referred to his charm offensive as *Open Mouth Operations*, a play on *open market operations*.

QE3

In May 2012, Jay Powell walked past the twin staircases with intricate wrought-iron railings and through the arresting two-story atrium of the Eccles Building, his footsteps echoing off the polished stone floors and cream-colored, travertine-marble walls. From the ground level, the stairs lead up to a mezzanine flanked by Greek columns under a large skylight decorated with the outline of an eagle. On each side of the atrium's second floor are six bays with office doorways; the city of each of the twelve districts of the Federal Reserve system is carved into the marble above one of the doors. Powell continued past the boardroom and down the yellow-carpeted hallway to his office. He recognized the enormity of his opportunity and was thankful for the public-service comeback that his father had felt constrained not to accept. But once he settled inside the grand Beaux Arts hall, he found Bernanke's Fed was still licking its wounds from 2008.

The biggest issue facing the Fed that spring was how to shore up a still-lackluster economy. By 2010, the Fed's asset portfolio had ballooned — from $900 billion before the crisis to $2.3 trillion in March 2010, at the end of the first round of quantitative easing. A hoped-for "V-shaped" economic recovery never materialized; the economy was limping toward restored health. On November 3, 2010, with unemployment still well above 9 percent, Bernanke had led his colleagues in launching a second round of bond buying, or "QE2."

Easy money, Republicans howled, would obscure the cost of exploding federal deficits and ease any impetus for spending cuts. The day before, the Tea Party movement had propelled Republicans to a commanding majority in the House of Representatives. Within days, conservatives were taking aim at Bernanke's policies. On November 15, 2010, several prominent conservative economists and investors published an open letter in national newspapers asking Bernanke to abort QE2.[4] They warned that the Fed's money printing would lead to runaway inflation or currency debasement.[5]

A few days later, the four most-senior Republicans from the Senate and House sent Bernanke a letter expressing their "deep concerns" over QE2. "Printing money is no substitute for pro-growth fiscal policy," said Mike Pence, then an Indiana congressman.[6] Others reasonably grumbled that these policies were unfair to retirees and other savers who had sheltered their money in low-risk accounts away from the stock market.

On August 15, 2011, Texas Governor Rick Perry, then seeking the GOP nomination for president, turned up the volume at a candidate debate in Cedar Rapids, Iowa. It would be "almost...treasonous" for Bernanke to play politics by expanding the money supply, he said. "If this guy prints more money between now and the election, I don't know what y'all would do to him in Iowa, but we would treat him pretty ugly down in Texas."[7] The Fed had faced intense political pressure before, but usually because presidents and politicians demanded easier money. Now Bernanke was running arguably the easiest money policy ever — and getting hammered for it.

By September 2012 — long after Perry's presidential aspirations had flamed out — Bernanke still wasn't happy with the state of the economy. Economists and pundits were talking about two economies: the stock market, which had almost bounced back to its pre-crisis records, and the still-high unemployment numbers. The chair leaned on his go-to tool again, launching an even more aggressive bond-buying program: Dubbed "QE3," this initiatve was the most controversial of all; unlike the first two, the Fed hadn't set a limit on its purchases. Instead, the Fed announced that it would continue to buy Treasury and mortgage securities until certain goals had been met.

The FOMC met on September 12 to review Bernanke's proposal, one of its eight annual meetings scheduled roughly six weeks apart. The meeting consisted of the twelve reserve-bank presidents from across the country, joining the Fed chair and six other Washington-based governors in a massive boardroom in the Eccles Building. The men and women would crowd around a huge table of polished Honduran mahogany and granite. Overhead hung a half-ton chandelier of brass and glass. Rows of chairs at one end of the silk-walled boardroom would fill with several dozen economists, market specialists, and other senior staffers. Over two days of detailed presentations, they would engage in seminar-like debates on whether to move rates slightly up, slightly down, or to signal a more subtle change in their growth outlook.

A few months into his term as governor, Powell supported the program with reservations. His concern was that the Fed was headed far beyond emergency monetary policy. Whereas the earlier asset-purchase programs were designed to improve dysfunctional markets and bring down long-term interest rates, he worried the Fed now appeared to be embarking on QE as a "straightforward jobs program."[8] Powell thought the central bank could manage the risks frequently cited by the Fed's Wall Street critics, including fueling undesirable levels of inflation. But he raised other concerns, including the prospect that the Fed's holdings might one day lead the Fed to lose money — a political problem that central banks strive to avoid.

Janet Yellen, who was now the Fed's vice chairwoman, argued that those risks paled next to the "human and economic costs of failing to reduce the unemployment rate as aggressively as we can."[9] Raised in a Brooklyn brownstone where her physician father maintained a basement office, Yellen credited her mother — an elementary-school teacher who had quit her job to raise the family — with stoking her interest in economics. The older woman managed the family's finances and was an avid reader of the business press, and mother and daughter would debate the pros and cons of selling a stock. "My view, which I argued vigorously with her, was that history and what you paid were fundamentally irrelevant," Yellen recalled.[10]

Yellen graduated at the top of her class from Fort Hamilton High School and planned to study math at Brown University. But then she met visiting Yale economist James Tobin, an adviser to Kennedy and Johnson, and was taken by Tobin's Keynesian belief that the government had an obligation to combat the human suffering caused by unemployment. Yellen went on to earn her PhD at Yale, with Tobin as her mentor. Her notes of his lectures were so meticulous that he asked her to turn them into a textbook.[11] After a teaching stint at Harvard, Yellen joined the Fed's staff in the fall of 1977. She met her future husband, economist George Akerlof, at lunch in the cafeteria.[12] They collaborated often on provocative research topics, including why workers were more likely to quit their jobs when the economy was strong, what caused out-of-wedlock births, and how community norms could deter gang crime.

At the Fed's meeting in December 2012, Yellen warned against repeating the mistakes of the Bank of Japan, which in its long-running battle with declining prices had conveyed skepticism about the benefits of QE. She believed this had undermined their policy and required ever-larger purchases. "Every time there is even a whiff of recovery, the BOJ makes clear that it is ready, willing, and able to end quantitative easing and is prepared to reduce its balance sheet back to normal in a heartbeat," she said. Then Yellen turned to address the arguments that Powell and others had made. Capital losses "can raise questions among politicians and the public about a central bank's performance. But prolonged failure to meet the central bank's mandate can be just as damaging to its reputation and independence."[13]

The "Three Amigos"

Powell didn't arrive at the Fed with the same sterling academic credentials as many of his peers, but he did develop a reputation for studying the nuts and bolts of the place. He tackled unheralded operational tasks and technical matters, including an overhaul of interest-rate benchmarks and the management of payment-processing systems. The job could be intimidating with hundreds of PhD economists around, and Powell groused in a good-natured way to a colleague after he had joined the board about how the staff patronized someone who wasn't a trained economist.

"They talk to me like I'm a golden retriever," Powell said.

But he also used that as fuel to devour briefing books and show up well-prepared for meetings. To tap into an alternate stream of information from the heavily manicured and formal Fed staff presentations, Powell sought outside voices who could help him sharpen critical counterarguments. He rounded out a heavy diet of technical papers by following economic debates on blogs and Twitter (though he didn't tweet).

Powell was regarded by colleagues as an exceptionally good listener. He had developed a quirk in high school: repeating sentences backward. As that "talent" suggests, Powell also had a killer memory. In the fall of 1971, Powell and Alan Tonelson had been playing cards inside a freshman dorm at Princeton. Powell suggested they listen to an album by the band Dan Hicks and His Hot Licks.

Tonelson, not into the folk-rock scene, dismissively responded, "Dan Hicks sucks."

The two didn't keep in touch during college or immediately afterward. Once Powell became a Fed governor, however, Tonelson — a frequent commentator on trade policy — reconnected with his former classmate at a chance meeting of Princeton alums in Washington.

"So 'Dan Hicks sucks,' huh?" Powell deadpanned.

"I was floored," Tonelson later told the Associated Press.[14]

Jeremy Stein, the Harvard economist who was confirmed to the Fed board at the same time, found Powell to be "deeply curious, in the best possible way. He threw himself into it with the best possible attitude."[15]

Soon after joining the Fed, Powell and Stein struck up a friendship — as well as some shared policy goals. The two would often visit Bernanke together before FOMC meetings, where they voiced concerns about the open-ended nature of the new bond-buying campaign. Bernanke sought to reassure them by estimating it would probably result in $500 billion to

$750 billion in new purchases—about the size of the $600 billion in Treasury purchases during QE2.

By the spring of 2013, it became clear the program would likely run for longer. A third governor, Elizabeth "Betsy" Duke—a bank executive appointed by George W. Bush—joined Powell and Stein in expressing reservations. All three were troubled by Wall Street investors' complacency that the programs might last indefinitely. Analysts were throwing around terms like *QE-finity*.

The three governors became a driving force in encouraging Bernanke to find an off-ramp for the program. Michelle Smith, Bernanke's communications consigliere, dubbed them the "Three Amigos."[16] The trio occupied an important middle ground on the FOMC because they sat in between the hawkish and outspoken presidents of Fed banks in Dallas, Philadelphia, Kansas City, and Richmond, who vocally opposed the program, and the dovish leadership of the Fed in Washington and New York, which strongly supported continued bond buying. (In Fedspeak, *hawks* tend to favor higher rates to ward off any risk of inflation, while *doves* favor lower rates to push unemployment lower.)

Broker-dealers were now projecting the Fed's balance sheet would swell to $4 trillion, from $2.8 trillion before the program began. Powell openly wondered when—if ever—the program would end. "Why stop at $4 trillion? The market in most cases will cheer us for doing more," said Powell at an FOMC meeting in October 2012.[17] "Our models will always tell us that we are helping the economy, and I will probably always feel that those benefits are overestimated."

Powell also thought his colleagues were "way too confident" they could smoothly slow down or reverse the purchases once they finally agreed that time had arrived. The purchases were already fueling "bubble-like terms" in corporate borrowing. "There is every reason to expect a sharp and painful correction," he said in January 2013.[18]

By May of that year—with unemployment at 7.5 percent and falling—the Three Amigos thought Bernanke should signal the program might end sooner than some on Wall Street expected. At a May 1 policy meeting, Powell conceded the program was providing more support than the Fed's critics allowed but said he wanted to slow the pace of purchases, or "taper," as soon as possible. "This is not an unmanageable thing," Powell said. "This is not going to be done in a way that provokes a massive reaction of shock from the market."[19]

He was wrong.

Bernanke made an initial effort to build the off-ramp at a congressional hearing three weeks later. His attempt to smoothly introduce the possibility of reducing bond purchases confused the markets. Some investors thought — erroneously — that by suggesting a slowdown in purchases, the Fed might likewise be rethinking its other commitment to hold rates near zero for longer. In response, yields on ten-year Treasury notes began to accelerate sharply. On May 21, the day before Bernanke's hearing, yields sat below 2 percent. By the end of the summer, they were nearing 3 percent.

Higher long-term rates, dubbed the "taper tantrum," rippled through the economy, threatening the nascent recovery underway in the housing market. It also spurred a violent rush of cash out of emerging market economies. The ordeal undermined the original point of the purchases — exactly the scenario Yellen had cautioned against months earlier. Partly due to the way the rate rise slowed the economy's progress, the central bank delayed its plans to slow the asset purchases until December 2013. As a result, the Fed's securities holdings swelled to $4.5 trillion.

In 2014, Powell was confirmed to a full fourteen-year term, and Janet Yellen took over from Bernanke as chair. Yellen's appointment did not signal a change in the direction of Bernanke's Fed, and throughout the ups and downs of a Fed policy that Powell had at times privately expressed concerns about, he never went public with them. In 2015, he praised the decisions Yellen and Bernanke had made in navigating the post-crisis tumult. The Fed's actions "are a major reason why the US economy is now outperforming those of other advanced nations," he said. He pointed to the fact that other central bankers were now following "some of the same bold steps undertaken much earlier by the Fed."

The more conservative and populist Republicans in Congress, together with left-wing detractors such as Bernie Sanders, didn't share Powell's positive appraisal. They pushed proposals to give a government-oversight authority the power to review the Fed's monetary-policy decisions — something the Fed feared would simply give its critics another way to drum up opposition to its policies. As the lone Republican on the board, Powell became a forceful defender of the Fed's approach — a reprise of his role in the debt-ceiling crisis of 2011. Powell slammed these "Audit the Fed" proposals as "misguided" and "troubling," the equivalent of fighting words for the normally subdued central bank.[20]

Removing the punch bowl

It was in the 1950s that Chair Bill Martin had described the Fed's job as that of the chaperone who removes the punch bowl just as the party is getting rowdy. But how exactly does it know when the guests are enjoying themselves? This was precisely the dilemma that Janet Yellen faced during her first two years. The growing economy had largely recovered from the financial crisis. Inflation was very low. Unemployment was back to precrisis levels. But how much was the economy being propped up by Fed purchasing programs and ultralow interest rates?

Since the 1960s, academics had adhered to prescriptions originating from the work of John Maynard Keynes, who in 1936 argued that increased deficits could boost growth. Economists had been guided by a concept referred to as the Phillips curve, named for New Zealand economist A. W. Phillips, who first advanced it in 1958 by studying British labor markets at the turn of the 19th century. The framework holds that inflation rates go up as unemployment moves down, and vice versa. The economists who populated Kennedy's White House pushed for lower levels of unemployment because they mistakenly believed there was more slack in the labor market. Some also thought a little more inflation was worth the tradeoff.

Most economists, including Yellen and others at the Fed, were guided by basic beliefs: first, that there is a direct inverse relationship between inflation and unemployment — if one goes down, the other must go up — and second, that there is a "natural rate of unemployment," a level that evenly balances the supply and demand for labor. When unemployment falls below it, companies must compete for workers by driving up wages at a rate that can feed into higher prices. In order to tamp down an overheating economy, the Fed had traditionally raised interest rates.

The natural rate isn't easily observable. It is an invisible target. So economists had been coming up with their own best estimates and setting interest rates accordingly. (Think of an archer shooting an imaginary arrow at this invisible target.) Monetary policy works over a year or two, not right away. If inflation went up one year, consumers expected it to rise the next year. Left unchecked, inflation could accelerate sharply. As a result, the Fed saw its job as slowing job growth so that unemployment would hold near the natural rate.

In September 1996, then-governor Yellen had been at the center of a big debate over the inflation-and-unemployment tradeoff — the so-called Phillips curve. The unemployment rate had just fallen to 5.1 percent — close to twenty-year lows, and many economists' estimates of the natural rate of unemployment. Yellen was so concerned that she and another governor, Laurence Meyer, visited Greenspan in his office the week before. Mindful that governors rarely dissented on policy decisions, they made their case for Greenspan to resume raising rates. "We just think the time has come. It's utterly essential to raise rates, and we're not sure we're going to be able to support you if you don't agree to do that," Yellen said.[21] She wasn't normally considered someone with a bias toward higher rates — a hawk — but the experience of the 1970s was weighing on her then.

Greenspan listened but said little. At the September 24, 1996 meeting he finally shared his thinking. Greenspan had been curious why the proliferation of computing hadn't boosted worker productivity, or output per hour of work, and he suspected that higher profits at companies investing in new technologies meant the US was on the cusp of a productivity boom that government statistics had failed to capture. If he was right, the economy could grow faster without generating inflation.[22]

History proved him right. Productivity growth was on an upswing after a two-decade lull, allowing the Fed to hold off on raising interest rates even as the unemployment rate fell to lower levels. Nonetheless, the idea of the natural rate lived on.

More than a decade later, Yellen showed no fears about keeping interest rates low. She was a fierce advocate for Bernanke's easy-money, low-interest-rate policies. In late 2012, when Powell grew nervous that the risks of continued stimulus were outweighing the benefits, Yellen reminded her colleagues of the promises they had made to support a stronger jobs recovery: "We communicated that we will at least keep refilling the punch bowl until the guests have all arrived and will not remove it prematurely before the party is well underway."[23]

As vice-chair and then chair, Yellen had borne the brunt of years of unhappiness with the Fed's post-crisis policies, including at a testy three-hour congressional hearing in February 2015. Republicans criticized Yellen for her speech on rising economic inequality, which they said was too political. "You're sticking your nose in places that you have no business to be," said Mick Mulvaney, a South Carolina Republican.[24]

Yellen was already preparing for the Fed to increase the fed-funds rate for the first time since it had been lowered to near zero in 2008. Her decision was — again — guided by the Phillips curve and the natural rate of employment, as well as by a growing group of colleagues who were pushing the Fed to get on with "normalizing" rates. Unemployment was at 5.5 percent and moving closer to officials' comfort level of 5 percent. Inflation readings were held down by a drop in energy prices, but staff economists expected those effects to fade over time. According to the Phillips curve, a drop in labor-market slack, reflected in the dropping unemployment rate, should push up wages, which would in turn drive inflation upward.

"This seems like a simple matter of demand and supply," Yellen told her colleagues at the FOMC meeting on March 17, 2015. The speed at which unemployment was falling made it "imprudent to wait until inflation is much closer to 2 percent to begin to normalize policy. I consider this a strong argument for an initial tightening with inflation at low levels, and it's one that I plan to make."[25]

By December 2015, the unemployment rate had reached 5 percent.

Even though inflation was still running below 2 percent, Yellen and her colleagues expected inflation would pick up when they voted to raise interest rates away from near zero for the first time in seven years. Nonetheless, she allowed for the possibility that inflation dynamics weren't operating as they had in past periods. "A more radical rethinking... would surely be in order," she said, if inflation remained "persistently subdued...despite further improvements in the labor market."[26]

The Fed raised interest rates just once in 2016 amid a slowdown in manufacturing. If all went well in 2017, the Fed would be able to show that it could keeping moving farther away from the emergency policies it had deployed after the 2008 financial crisis. But whether Yellen would get a new four-year term remained an open question. Given what would transpire, it wasn't clear why anyone would want the job.

Chapter Four

THE KING OF DEBT

G OP presidential candidate Donald Trump called in to CNBC on September 12, 2016 to unleash a tirade at Fed Chair Janet Yellen. "She's keeping [rates] artificially low to get Obama retired. Watch what is going to happen afterwards. It is a very serious problem, and I think it is very political. I think she is very political and to a certain extent, I think she should be ashamed of herself because it is not supposed to be that way." The celebrity developer, who had long supported low rates, had opportunistically turbocharged Tea Party–style conservatives' critique of the central bank.[1]

Yellen needn't have taken the attacks personally. Trump's insurgent bid was many things, including an apotheosis of anti-establishment anger — and what could be more establishment than the Fed? Trump's rants were also transparently self-interested and fickle. Trump knew from his real estate career that low rates could goose growth, and in 2016 he figured a weaker economy would help his election chances. What's more, he knew that any flavor of Obama bashing would play to his base. In the closing days of his presidential run, a Trump campaign spot alleged a global plot to take wealth from workers. The ad, which flashed images of Goldman Sachs CEO Lloyd Blankfein, financier George Soros, and Yellen, tapped into centuries-old anti-Semitic conspiracy theories.

Trump's surprise victory didn't bode well for Yellen's reappointment as Fed chair. But neither did it suggest Powell had much of a shot at winning her seat. To populist conservatives like Trump's supporters, the

Fed's technocrats personified the Beltway bourgeoisie. Its culture prized fidelity to the institution's nonpartisan, analytical, and consensus-oriented process. Jay Powell embodied those very traits. So how did Trump end up choosing him to lead the Fed in 2018, when Yellen's term came to an end?

For starters, Trump actually preferred the low-rate policy he had savaged. As the self-proclaimed "King of Debt," Trump knew better than any other presidential aspirant what a quarter-point increase in interest rates could do to heavily leveraged businesses. Once he was president, Trump had no desire to see interest rates rise or the Fed's asset holdings shrink. Anticipating big tax cuts, less regulation, and a burst of spending on roads and bridges, Wall Street celebrated Trump's election. Stocks jumped, long-term interest rates rose, and the dollar strengthened.

"My geniuses"

When Trump was elected, Gary Cohn had been the No. 2 at Goldman Sachs for a decade; realizing that Blankfein, the chief executive, wasn't going anywhere, however, he decided it was time to move on. Cohn knew Trump's son-in-law, Jared Kushner, who invited him to meet with the president-elect. At a Trump Tower meeting on November 29, 2016, Cohn dazzled Trump with a discussion of interest rates and deficits. Trump was so enamored with the Goldman president that he half-jokingly suggested Cohn be named Treasury secretary, creating an awkward moment for Steven Mnuchin, the odds-on favorite for the job, who was sitting in on the meeting.[2] As a candidate, Trump had spoken about installing a hard-charging dealmaker — a "killer" — at the Treasury. The astute but awkward Mnuchin didn't exactly fit the bill, and Cohn did. After the Cohn meeting, the Trump team put out word that Mnuchin would be named Treasury secretary, lest the famously fickle Trump change his mind.

Instead of Treasury secretary, Cohn became director of the White House National Economic Council. Its first director, Robert Rubin, had also spent a career at Goldman Sachs, rising to become the investment bank's co-chairman.

Trump went through a honeymoon phase with Cohn. He referred to the bald-pated, linebacker-built Cohn as one of "my geniuses" and tasked him with running the process to determine who would lead the Fed when Yellen's term expired. Trump even toyed with the idea of making Cohn the Fed chair. But Cohn's relationship with Trump broke down in August 2017. On August 15, days after violent clashes spurred by neo-Nazi white nationalists in Charlottesville, Virginia, Cohn stood behind Trump at an impromptu news conference in which the president said there had been "very fine people, on both sides." Cohn, as one of the most prominent Jews in the administration, faced intense pressure to resign. He broke his silence in an August 25 interview with the *Financial Times* where he rebuked Trump for failing to provide moral leadership.[3]

It left Cohn on the outs with the president during the weeks in which Trump would decide what to do about the Fed. To the extent that Trump listened to any of his advisers, Mnuchin — who is also Jewish — replaced Cohn as the most senior voice on the economy.

Mnuchin (pronounced Meh-NOO-shin) had become Treasury secretary without the political pedigree of such recent predecessors as Rubin or Hank Paulson, who had both run Goldman, cultivating contacts in Washington and foreign capitals that proved invaluable once they became Treasury secretary. While Mnuchin enjoyed a closer relationship with the president than other advisers, that didn't confer the kind of outsize influence that previous Treasury secretaries — from Roosevelt's Henry Morgenthau to Reagan's James Baker — enjoyed. That wasn't Trump's way.

After graduating from Yale in 1985, Mnuchin worked in the mortgage-investments department at Goldman Sachs (where his father had spent his career as a star trader), rising to partner. He left the firm in 2002 after Blankfein won a promotion that put him in line to lead Goldman. Mnuchin ran various hedge-fund firms and led a group of investors in buying the defunct California-based mortgage lender IndyMac. After being appointed chief executive of the rebranded OneWest Bank, Mnuchin moved with his wife and three children from their Manhattan apartment in 740 Park Avenue, one of the city's most exclusive addresses, to a 20,000-square-foot mansion in Los Angeles. In 2015, Mnuchin made a tidy profit selling OneWest to a financial-services company. Mnuchin also dabbled in film investments and considered investing in the firm that owned Trump's hit reality-TV show, *The Apprentice*.

On April 19, 2016, Mnuchin stopped by Trump's New York primary-election victory party. Trump spotted him while stepping off the elevator and invited him up onto the stage. "The next thing I know, I'm standing right behind him, and I'm on national TV, on four different monitors, my phone is, like, going crazy buzzing," said Mnuchin.[4]

Trump called Mnuchin the next morning and asked him to manage the campaign's finances. Before 2016, Mnuchin's political involvement extended only to donating money to campaigns, primarily those of Democrats. His decision to join the Trump campaign shocked some of his business partners, but he knew a good trade when he saw one. Other Wall Street moneymen spent years positioning themselves for a plum White House job. If Trump's long-shot bid for the presidency worked out, the payoff for Mnuchin would be enormous.

"Nobody's going to be like, 'Well, why did he do this?' if I end up in the administration," Mnuchin told Bloomberg Businessweek.[5]

Two weeks before he became Treasury secretary, Mnuchin dropped $12.6 million on a nine-bedroom Washington home with an indoor pool off Rock Creek Park. But he struggled to master the new world of DC politics. For one, Mnuchin — who often wore large, distracting, self-darkening transition glasses — projected an uncomfortable disposition in almost any setting. His share of awkward moments included an instantaneously viral photograph with his new wife, an aspiring actress named Louise Linton, who wore black gloves and gazed into the camera while the couple displayed a sheet of new one-dollar bills bearing Mnuchin's signature during a tour of the Bureau of Engraving and Printing.

Faced with Republicans' suspicion that he was a Wall Street Democrat, GOP leaders sent word to political advisers in the West Wing to keep Mnuchin away from high-stakes negotiations over tax reform on Capitol Hill.

But Mnuchin, a sharp financier, excelled at keeping his head down in the daily Trump-show drama. In the summer of 2017 the president attended Mnuchin's wedding to Linton — which Vice President Mike

Pence officiated. Mnuchin never missed a chance to prove his unflinching loyalty to the president, and his fealty was on full display after Charlottesville. Under the same pressures as Cohn to break with Trump, Mnuchin instead defended the president's comments, putting Cohn's rebuke in even starker relief. Cohn's subsequent falling-out with Trump presented the kind of opportunity for Mnuchin to position himself as the economic adviser whose counsel Trump was least likely to ignore.

The Apprentice: Fed edition

After savaging her during his campaign, Trump initially played up Yellen's prospects for reappointment. Privately, however, his advisers never considered her reappointment a serious possibility. Trump's inner circle thought Yellen opposed the administration's signature tax cut. As the selection process heated up, Yellen's public defense of the post-crisis financial regulatory architecture, which the president had campaigned on rolling back, may have sealed her fate. Trump's advisers invited her for a courtesy meeting with Trump, but only several weeks after his advisers had presented him with three other contenders: Powell, Stanford professor John Taylor, and former Fed governor Kevin Warsh.

Conservatives and other GOP establishment figures favored Taylor and Warsh, who had served in Republican administrations. Taylor was a trained economist who had been among the most vocal critics of Fed policy under Bernanke and Yellen, arguing their unconventional tools were stunting growth by making lenders less willing to extend credit. In 1993, he had advanced an especially influential mathematical formula for setting interest rates, the "Taylor rule," which called for considerably higher rates.

Warsh had become the youngest governor in Fed history, at age thirty-five. His ambition alienated him from some graybeards of GOP economic policymaking circles. As a White House aide in the year before securing his appointment to the Fed, he had campaigned so hard for a top Treasury Department posting that President George W. Bush was forced to weigh in. Bush deferred to his Treasury secretary, who picked Randal Quarles, a more experienced Treasury official.

Warsh, who was not an economist, had extolled his background in finance when he joined the Fed, but like the rest of the central bank, he had severely misjudged markets in the run-up to the 2008 crisis. In June 2007, as the seeds of the mortgage bust were sprouting, Warsh gave a speech hailing the Wall Street trading desks that had churned out increasingly esoteric derivatives and securities. Warsh liked giving speeches with affected, smart-sounding turns of phrase, and this one touted how "financial innovation" had "made markets substantially more 'complete.'"[6]

As the crisis accelerated, though, Warsh found his groove. He used his extensive Rolodex to serve as Fed chair Ben Bernanke's bridge to Wall Street executives. And he proved a loyal guardian of Bernanke in GOP circles.

In November 2010, however, Warsh publicly broke with Bernanke's policy, echoing critiques made in GOP policy circles; for example, that the bond purchases were enabling the White House to hide the cost of a bulge in federal borrowing. He then left the Fed for Stanford's Hoover Institution, where he established himself as a conservative proponent of tighter monetary policy and a vociferous critic of the Fed. By 2016, Warsh was perfectly positioned to serve as Fed chair under a traditional Republican president — including the campaign version of Trump. As it became clear that the new president actually favored an easy-money policy, though, Warsh rebranded once again — this time as a reformer offering a grab bag of platitudes with little substance.

Warsh also had a potentially helpful connection to Trump. He was married to the daughter of the billionaire art collector Ronald Lauder, who had been a classmate of Donald Trump's at the University of Pennsylvania. Lauder donated more than $1 million to pro-Trump political advocacy groups.

Looking the part

Ironically, Powell — who hadn't done as much political maneuvering as Warsh — ended up in a better position. Warsh's record proved the perfect foil for Powell, who for years had strongly defended the Fed's policies against Republican critiques.

In contrast to Warsh, Powell hadn't set his eye on becoming Fed chair. After quietly and dutifully handling thankless tasks for several years at the board, Powell thought maybe he could become Janet Yellen's vice chair during her second term or maybe the next president of the New York Fed, whose leader would hit a mandatory retirement in less than two years.

In December 2016, a few weeks before Trump took office, Powell met with Marc Sumerlin, an economic adviser to President George W. Bush. Sumerlin offered Powell some advice: *Why couldn't you be Fed chair? You're the only person with a Republican background who didn't fall for the inflation fearmongering after 2010,* he said. Powell hadn't signed on to GOP proposals to link interest-rate policy more tightly to the Taylor rule — which by 2017 proposed interest rates well above where the Fed had been setting them — and Trump didn't favor hawkish policy or seem likely to keep Yellen.

"Your odds might be better than you think," Sumerlin told him. He forwarded Mnuchin's contact information after the meeting.

After Trump took office, Powell signaled his interest in a different vacancy — the vice chair for bank supervision. But Cohn made clear that the White House wasn't interested in him for the job. Due to his seniority at the Fed, Powell took the position on an interim basis, which gave him a chance to build a relationship with Mnuchin. Powell recommended that Mnuchin consider Quarles, his former assistant, for the appointment, which Trump ultimately did.

Powell and Mnuchin had gotten along well as the administration put together its deregulation blueprint, and Powell's solid, pragmatic track record made him appear the safest choice in Mnuchin's eyes. Both men also shared an interest in cycling: As Treasury secretary, Mnuchin stayed in shape by taking his Secret Service detail on thirty-five-mile bike rides to Mount Vernon and back.

Powell had told the administration it would be a mistake not to reappoint Yellen but realized they weren't seriously considering her when he was invited to a preliminary interview with Mnuchin and other White House advisers that August. The meeting went well enough that on

September 27, 2017, Powell found himself sitting across the Resolute Desk from Trump in the Oval Office, the first candidate invited to do so. Mnuchin attended along with two aides who were running the process. Chief of Staff John Kelly listened in but sat against a wall off to one side. Powell's case was straightforward: He offered continuity with the policies of Yellen, which Trump clearly preferred; he was a Republican; and he would be a moderate on regulation. The bottom line: if Trump wanted a Republican version of Yellen, he didn't have to look any further.

Trump had been coached before the meeting to give a nod to the Fed's quasi-autonomy, but he didn't seem especially well-briefed on what the central bank was doing with interest rates. Trump had essentially ignored the central bank's two rate increases that year, as well as the fact it was projecting several more. "I understand you're independent. I understand you're gonna do what you think is the right thing," Trump said to Powell.

Powell had no idea what to expect going into the meeting, but he figured he had connected with Trump in a way that was unexpectedly good when Kelly flashed Powell a wide smile on his way out. No one asked Powell how he had voted in the election.

Warsh interviewed with Trump the next day. Viewing Yellen as his stiffest challenger, he spent part of his interview making his case by arguing against her reappointment. While Warsh had lots of friends in Washington, his years-long yearning for the job had made him his share of enemies, too. And that summer, many of them lined up to trash him as a flip-flopping empty suit — messages that were conveyed both to Mnuchin and to the president. Mnuchin made it clear to Trump that he considered Powell the better pick.

It didn't hurt that Powell — a trim, distinguished-looking man with neatly parted silver hair and the occasional eyeglasses — was straight out of central casting for the role. For the image-conscious Trump, appearances mattered. When Randal Quarles had walked into the Oval Office to interview with the president earlier that year, Trump took one glance at the patrician, sandy-haired investment executive and exclaimed, "Well, he certainly looks the part!" Quarles did, in fact, get the job.

At the start of a different Oval Office meeting that summer, Trump had left another adviser speechless with an unusual opening question: "Is Janet Yellen tall enough to be Fed chair?" Never mind that Yellen, around five feet tall, was *already* the Fed chair at that point.[7]

Likewise, at the meeting with the forty-seven-year-old Warsh, Trump expressed surprise at the former banker's youthful looks. "Your son-in-law's great, but he's a little bit too young," Trump later volunteered to Warsh's father-in-law, Ronald Lauder.

Trump interviewed Taylor a few days after meeting with Powell and Warsh. A short time later Taylor gave a pair of speeches that sought to cast his advocacy for a rules-based policy in a less-inflexible light, but they failed to mollify Trump or Mnuchin.

On October 19, Trump finally met for thirty minutes with Yellen, who may have made the strongest impression on him. During their meeting, Trump relayed to Yellen his fascination with emerging-market economies, where growth rates could exceed 6 percent annually. Afterward, Trump struck some of his advisers as thoroughly intrigued with the notion of reappointing Yellen. The president sometimes wondered out loud whether he could pick Yellen: *I know I can't, but could I?* But none of his advisers supported the move, in part because it might spark an uproar among the Senate Republicans who were shepherding his tax-cut bill.

The president who had created a smash-hit TV show about hiring an apprentice reveled in the high-stakes drama surrounding his selection of the next Fed chair. At a luncheon on Capitol Hill with GOP senators on October 24, Trump took an informal poll by asking for a show of hands: Powell or Taylor? Most of the room went for Taylor. Trump called Quarles, who had worked directly for both Powell and Taylor at the Treasury, and asked him to recommend one man over the other. "People are anxiously awaiting my decision as to who the next head of the Fed will be," Trump teased in an Instagram video. "I think everybody will be very impressed."[8]

Trump called Powell to tell him his decision on Tuesday, October 31, 2017. At 3 p.m. on November 2 — a sunny, 70-degree day — Powell and Trump walked out of the White House to the Rose Garden for the formal announcement.

Years earlier, Powell had dispensed the following counsel when a business-school student sought out Powell for career advice: *Keep your head down and work hard. You'd be surprised by how many otherwise competent people self-sabotage with poor behavior.*[9] As he had in 1990 and again in 2012, Powell found himself in the right place at the right time.

"There are few more important positions than this, believe me, in our government," Trump said in his introduction of Powell. Yellen didn't attend because she hadn't been invited. Powell's wife, Elissa, who had donated money to Democratic politicians before her husband joined the Fed, might have volunteered to give up her seat. She had asked her husband beforehand if she *had* to join him at the White House ceremony.

After the ceremony, Trump gave Powell a few words of encouragement. "You're gonna be great," the president told him. "And I know you're independent. You're going to do what you think is right, so I think it's gonna be great."

Like presidents before, Trump would soon come to regret his choice.

Jam sessions

By the time Powell assumed his role as Fed chair in February 2018, President Trump, after just one year in office, had replaced his national security adviser, FBI director, press secretary, communications director, and chief of staff. It didn't take much political savvy to realize that political volatility in the West Wing was perhaps the only permanent feature of this new administration. Powell knew he needed to use his honeymoon period to ensure that the most important positions at the Fed were filled with people he could trust.

Ever since Marriner Eccles's reforms in 1935, Fed policy had officially been decided by the sometimes-unwieldy Federal Open Market Committee. But policy gets shaped before the FOMC meetings by just three people, informally known as the Fed Troika: the Fed chair, the vice chair, and the president of the New York Fed, who also serves as vice chair of the FOMC. The Troika sets the agenda for each FOMC meeting. They refine the policy options and decide which papers or briefing memos should go out to committee members before each meeting. They steer the FOMC toward consensus. This was the power center of the Fed, and Powell had a historic opportunity to influence the selection of the Troika's other two members.

The vice chair of the Fed, Stanley Fischer, had resigned in October 2017. The next month, a few days after Trump announced Powell's selection as Fed chair, New York Fed President William Dudley announced his plans to retire the following summer. There was no precedent for having an entirely new Fed Troika—chair, vice chair, and New York Fed president—taking office within just a few months.

Powell's first choice to replace the retiring vice chair was San Francisco Fed President John Williams. But by late January 2018, his effort to groom Williams for vice chair had faltered because the monetary-policy specialist failed to impress the White House.

With the Williams nomination looking unlikely, Powell backed Richard Clarida, a sixty-year-old Columbia University professor of economics who had served as chief economist in George W. Bush's Treasury Department. Obama had considered Clarida for a position at the Fed—the one that ended up going to Powell. But Clarida, who had taken a lucrative job advising the bond giant Pimco a few years earlier, took himself out of the running.

When the Trump White House called, this time Clarida said he was interested. Clarida began seven rounds of interviews, including with Cohn, Mnuchin, and Kevin Hassett, a White House economic adviser who knew Clarida from their time on the Columbia faculty together in the 1990s.

Powell also invited Clarida to the Fed for a chat. Even though the two men didn't know each other, they had a number of friends in common. Their first meeting was in the Fed's "special library"—an ornate, wood-paneled room containing the boardroom table used by the original governors in 1914. The get-together, scheduled for thirty minutes, ran for over an hour.

Before he studied economics, Clarida's biggest interest had been music. His father had directed the school band; Clarida learned to play clarinet, saxophone, guitar, and piano, performing in jazz and rock bands in high school.

In 1975 Clarida enrolled at the University of Illinois in Champaign-Urbana, planning to major in accounting. It was a very practical strategy for a kid from the small southern-Illinois town of Herrin: seek a marketable degree, go to work for a Chicago accounting firm, and get a nice home in the suburbs. But after taking a required introductory course, Clarida decided he was more interested in teaching economics.

His academic turn proved to be a good decision. Clarida earned his PhD in 1983 from Harvard, taught at Yale, took leave to serve as a staff economist on Reagan's Council of Economic Advisers, then joined the faculty of Columbia in 1988, where he would teach until 2018. Clarida was best known for his research on models that predict how the economy reacts when buffeted by shocks. Those models are at the center of the tools used by the Fed and other major central banks to analyze how various monetary policies influence the economy and how central banks might react to any number of shocks.

Powell was looking for a team player who could help him lead a review of the Fed's policymaking strategy. Clarida had the academic credentials, which Powell lacked, to add heft to the task. Clarida told Powell he wanted to be involved in every debate about strategy. In exchange, he offered to advocate for whatever decisions they made. Clarida also promised Powell never to surprise him in his speeches — he would make news only when that was their express goal.

Then he added a pitch that he knew would resonate with Powell and that would prove more prescient than both men knew at the time. "I want you to understand," Clarida said, "if I come here, I'm not going to come here to be the defender of the models. I built the models. I know both their virtues and pitfalls. And I'm not going to be shy to tell you when we should just ignore the models. I'm here to tell you when we should pay attention to them and when we should not."

Clarida felt the meeting had gone well when Powell informed him he was a guitar player too. "So when you get down here, we'll take a break and play guitar together," Powell said.

When Trump called Powell to talk about the vice chairmanship, Powell made it clear he wanted Clarida. Mnuchin and Cohn had already signed off on Clarida's selection when they invited him to visit Trump in the Oval Office for a brief meeting on Feb. 14, 2018. Trump did most of the talking. When the subject of Fed independence came up, Trump preached from the same songbook that Cohn had urged. "Well, you know, the Fed is independent. I understand that," Trump said. "We've got a great economy, I hope you understand that."

Before too long, Trump offered Clarida the job. "I put Jay Powell there. Jay Powell's a good man, and Jay Powell wants you, and Steven Mnuchin wants you, so I want you to take the job," the president explained. Oddly, Trump also asked Clarida what he thought of one of the other candidates who had been under consideration for the job, Mohamed El-Erian. Clarida explained that they had worked at Pimco together for twelve years. "He used to be my boss," Clarida began.

"Some people are talking about him," Trump interjected. "But Jay and Steve really want you, so that's what we're doing." The White House formally nominated Clarida two months later, and the Senate confirmed him on August 28, 2018.

The "R-Star" aficionado

The New York Fed is far and away the most powerful of the reserve banks scattered across the country, a first among equals. Physically located just a few blocks north of Wall Street, the bank is the US government's real-time eyes and ears on trillions of dollars that move through global markets daily. Its markets desk manages the plumbing through which that money flows, and is itself a major participant — intervening to implement rate-setting decisions or to clear any blockages that emerge. During the 2008 crisis, the markets desk designed creative emergency-lending programs on the fly. It also executed the Fed's bond-buying stimulus campaigns and devised new tools to later reverse those operations.

Unlike the board of governors, the presidents of the New York Fed and the other eleven reserve banks don't need White House sign-off on their appointments. They are instead chosen by the private-sector directors of each bank — a hallmark of the federated system produced by the 1913 compromise that created the Fed. That meant Powell might have another opportunity for John Williams in his inner circle after the White House had passed on him as vice chair.

Williams grew up in Sacramento, California, the son of an attorney who worked for four consecutive governors in the state capital, including Ronald Reagan and Jerry Brown. Williams was drawn to public policy more than politics, so he studied economics at the University of California at Berkeley. He spent four years after college as the general manager of Blondie's, a popular local pizza joint, before getting a PhD at Stanford, where John Taylor was his dissertation adviser.

Unlike most previous New York Fed presidents, Williams lacked any experience in markets. But few could dismiss his knowledge of monetary policy or his understanding of the Fed system. He had spent virtually his entire career there, first as a staff economist for the board, and later as an economist at the San Francisco Fed. Yellen, then the bank's president, named him research director there in 2009, and he succeeded her as president two years later, after Obama brought her to Washington.

Like Clarida, Williams brought strong academic chops. In 1999, Williams published an important paper about how monetary policy might need to change rapidly if the nation confronted an environment where low inflation, not high inflation, became a problem. The ideas in the paper didn't seem relevant at the time, but they moved to the forefront of policy discussions after the Great Recession. Williams had coauthored seminal research on policy-setting rules and models to estimate neutral levels of interest rates, working with Thomas Laubach, a soft-spoken German economist who had been promoted to run the Fed's influential division of monetary affairs in 2015.

Powell also had a personal relationship with Williams from their tenure on the FOMC. Every year, a Fed governor takes a weeklong Asia trip with the San Francisco Fed president, and Powell and Williams had toured Beijing and other Asian capitals annually for the past three years.

The New York Fed directors running the search initially were focused on Raymond McGuire, Citigroup's co-head of investment banking. The search committee had prized the recruitment of diverse candidates, and McGuire was one of the most prominent Black executives on Wall Street. They were so impressed with McGuire that they asked Powell to meet him, even though Powell kept raising concerns about giving the job to someone whose bank had required significant government aid as part of the 2008 bailout, known as the Troubled Asset Relief Program. Officials in Washington feared a public relations disaster if they now picked such a candidate to lead the New York Fed. The connection with Citigroup doomed McGuire's candidacy.

On April 3, 2018, the New York Fed announced the selection of Williams. A well-known video-game junkie and an aficionado of punk music and classic rock, the fifty-seven-year-old Williams eschewed neckties and sprinkled his speeches with lyrical references to Led Zeppelin and The Clash. When he left San Francisco for New York in 2018, staffers presented the nerdy Williams with a T-shirt: on the front, spelled out in the gothic lettering of the AC/DC logo, was *R-Star*, the phrase economists use to refer to the neutral level of interest. On the back of the shirt were the cities in his district that had Fed branches, evoking concert-tour merchandise.

Williams's selection fell flat with some who thought the post should go to someone with more gravitas in finance. Williams could be dismissive of even the most successful Wall Street traders, who could be notoriously fickle about their economic convictions. He had pooh-poohed paying too much attention to financial-market gyrations by bragging that he didn't even have a Bloomberg terminal, the ubiquitous trading-desk tool. In his first month on the job in New York, he received an hourlong tutorial on the device.

The Jimmy Stewart of monetary policy

Getting close allies in the most senior jobs off the bat was a remarkable and underappreciated achievement. After all, Paul Volcker had been undermined at times by senior leaders who were loyal to President Reagan. With his team in place, Powell worked to establish a plainspoken approachability — demystifying the Fed even more than Bernanke had. He enjoyed public speaking and thought he was good at it. Early in Yellen's term as Fed chair, the central bank had fallen into a pattern of announcing big changes only at meetings preceded by a quarterly press conference. Powell had encouraged her to consider more frequent press conferences, but Yellen, always so meticulous about preparations, had decided it would be too time-consuming. In June 2018, Powell announced he would hold a press conference after every meeting, which he believed would give the Fed more flexibility in sequencing its policy moves. More regular public communication wouldn't stop the president from criticizing the Fed, but it wouldn't hurt.

Powell's conversational style reflected his desire to reach an audience he felt the Fed at times overlooked — average citizens who didn't work in markets and whose livelihood didn't require hanging on every word of the Fed chair. They knew the Fed was important, but they might not know much more than that. At his briefings, Powell delivered short answers, used simple language, and spoke in a breezier manner than his academic predecessors — "a Jimmy Stewart of monetary policy," as a former senior Fed economist put it.

An important part of communicating with the outside world focused on the 535 people who could make Powell's life more difficult, or easier, if the going got tough: the lawmakers on Capitol Hill. And he wasn't shy about letting people know that he thought this was one of the most important things the Fed chair could do. "I'm going to wear the carpets of Capitol Hill out by walking those halls and meeting with members," he said in a July 12, 2018 radio interview.[10]

People who knew or interacted with Powell for long enough agreed on one thing: He had excellent EQ — emotional intelligence. He wasn't necessarily an extrovert, but he was good with people. "He's not a braggart. He's not a tell-you-how-great-he-is kind of guy. If you ran into him in a restaurant and you had a conversation with him for an hour, you wouldn't know he's chairman of the Fed — he wouldn't tell you," said

David Rubenstein, the Carlyle cofounder. Few elements of the job reflected this strength as well as his interactions with lawmakers.

Powell enjoyed the informal discussions he'd had during his confirmation process and, before that, as a governor. The meetings weren't fancy — usually no more than thirty minutes spent dropping by a representative's office to talk about what the economy looked like and to hear what concerns they might have. Powell would often remind them he wasn't an economist, which played well with most members of Congress — neither were they.

Powell used the meetings to build a rapport and to see where the Fed might be able to improve its outreach. He also reminded the legislators that in the US system, the Fed's accountability ran straight through Congress — an indirect observation that the Fed was *not* accountable to the president. Lawmakers appreciated Powell's bridge-building. It helped that he had been nominated by both President Obama and President Trump.

Powell also urged humility. The Fed should "give serious consideration to the possibility that we might be getting something wrong," he said at his formal swearing-in ceremony.[11]

Powell received 84 votes in the Senate — more than either Yellen or Bernanke had received in 2010 or 2014. The vote was a hopeful sign for Powell that whatever frustration Congress had with the Fed after the financial crisis, there was now the chance of a reset. The economic expansion may have been slow, but it was starting to pay dividends. Powell saw an opening to capitalize on a moment where someone who had backed the at-times-unpopular policies of Bernanke and Yellen could win a wide majority of support. *This is a different moment*, he thought. *This is my opportunity.*

Building up the Fed's brand and making the institution a paragon of diligent, apolitical analysis struck Powell as something he might be uniquely equipped to accomplish. It might have lacked the ambition of Bernanke's *glasnost* or inflation-targeting reforms. And it might not require the courage of Bernanke's crisis-fighting innovations or Yellen's delicate work to show that their extraordinarily easy policies could be gradually reversed. But if Powell could get a hyper-partisan Congress to agree that the Fed should have some freedom, who knew what might bloom? Reflecting on his large bipartisan vote of support, he thought, *I'm determined to hold onto that if we can.*

Trade wars: "easy to win"?

Unfortunately for Powell, the White House's guardrails around economic policy were falling away. Trump's centrist aides were losing their battle to contain his impulses to unleash a pugnacious economic nationalism. Gary Cohn had played to Trump's obsession with stock markets to impress the importance of letting the Fed set interest rates as it saw fit. Recognizing that the president hated high interest rates, Cohn also warned the president he should be prepared for rates to go up — especially if their tax and regulatory policies injected the "jet fuel" into the economy that Trump boasted about.

The president's goals were captured in a framed copy of *The Wall Street Journal* that hung in Mnuchin's office. Trump had signed the edition announcing Mnuchin's appointment with a black felt marker and inscribed an audacious aim: *5% GDP.* The last time the GDP growth rate had broken 5 percent was in 1984, when Trump owned the New Jersey Generals of the United States Football League.

During Trump's first year in office, Cohn and Mnuchin had convinced him not to start a trade war when he needed pro-trade Senate Republicans to secure his push for $1.5 trillion in tax cuts. With the tax cuts procured by the end of 2017, Trump turned his attention to another favorite tool: tariffs. Cohn's professional economic-policy apparatus — created to impose a sense of order on a chaotic West Wing — began fracturing just weeks after Powell took office. Trump announced tariffs on China, claiming "trade wars are good and easy to win." Cohn quit.

His departure removed the strongest shield between the White House and the Fed. It was a sobering reminder that the staff could not ultimately shake Trump from what he believed: *Tariffs were good. Trade deficits were bad. Low interest rates were good. High interest rates were bad.* In April 2018, outgoing New York Fed President William Dudley spoke for most of the FOMC: "I don't really think a trade war is a winnable proposition."[12]

Cohn's replacement, the courtly TV host Larry Kudlow, also opposed tariffs, but he was eager to be in a White House job after being passed over for one at the start of the administration. It was a trend that would play out elsewhere across the West Wing as the first wave of advisers gave way to more ingratiating loyalists. Kudlow had begun his career as an aide to Volcker at the New York Fed before working as a Wall Street economist, punctuated by a stint as a budget aide in Reagan's first term. But Kudlow's promising career imploded during a debilitating bout with drug and alcohol addiction in the 1990s. After getting clean and sober, he launched a comeback as a conservative columnist and television pundit.

Kudlow didn't encourage attacks on the Fed, yet he regarded the "Rubin Rule" as an exaggerated custom that shielded the central bank from the accountability faced by other government agencies. He joined a faction of White House officials who thought reporters and economists fetishized Fed independence to an unhealthy degree. Kudlow, who had supported Warsh and Taylor for the top job, worried that Powell would be too deferential to the Fed's model-obsessed staff. Worse, Kudlow suspected Trump didn't understand any of this, and that the more jobs the economy created, the more the Fed's models would say *Raise rates!*

Kudlow did try to sand down the rougher edges of Trump's trade policy, but time would prove him powerless to stop Trump from being Trump. Inside the White House, Kudlow was seen as a skilled communicator rather than a hard-charging dealmaker or policy whiz.

On March 22, about a week after Kudlow accepted the job, Trump escalated his trade war with China. The Dow fell more than 1,400 points that week, the largest weekly percentage loss in more than two years. "Six months ago...you couldn't find a reason to sell stocks," one analyst told *The Wall Street Journal*. "Now you can't find a reason to hold them."[13]

———

With the stock market wobbling, Trump went looking for someone to blame. Trump's harping on the Fed started off harmlessly enough. The president, who loved to assign pejorative nicknames to his political opponents, didn't even mention Powell by name. "I put a very good man in the Fed…and I don't necessarily agree with [raising interest rates]. I must tell you, I don't," the president said during a taped interview with CNBC outside the Oval Office on Thursday, July 19. "I'm not thrilled because [the economy goes] up and every time you go up, they want to raise rates again."[14]

This initial confrontation was noteworthy not only because a president hadn't made such a blunt critique of monetary policy in a quarter-century, but also because rates were still low by historic standards. The Fed's benchmark rate, around 1.9 percent, was still slightly negative when adjusted for inflation, which was finally edging up to the Fed's 2 percent goal for the first time in years. Unemployment was near 4 percent, and the economy had posted its strongest growth rate in years. If the Fed couldn't get interest rates up in this environment, then when?

The trade war wouldn't be easy to win, but it would lead Trump, in his characteristically chaotic and roundabout fashion, to get some of what he wanted from the Fed.

Chapter Five

HOT SEAT

Every August, central bankers from around the world gather at the Jackson Lake Lodge in Wyoming's Grand Teton National Park to discuss academic papers in the morning, then hike, river-raft, or fly-fish in the afternoon. The Kansas City Fed, which organizes the affair, picked the serene spot in 1982 to lure Paul Volcker, an avid fisherman, away from the summertime humidity of Washington. In 2018, attendees were treated to a "horse whispering" exhibition at a nearby ranch that weeks earlier had hosted the listening party for the release of hip-hop super-celebrity Kanye West's album *Ye*. The hosts had threatened to kill the power on Kanye's entourage when the raucous bash continued past midnight. The central bankers required no such admonitions.

Jay Powell used his speech opening the Jackson Hole conference on the morning of Friday, August 24, to unfurl a little skepticism about rigidly following macroeconomic folk wisdom. Even though Alan Greenspan had punctured a big hole in the Phillips curve lore, worries that inflation would pick up as joblessness dropped to lower and lower levels continued to haunt economists inside and outside the Fed. It made intuitive sense: when the supply of something (workers) fell, the prices paid for that item (wages) rose. Eventually, businesses would pass those costs on to consumers, and inflation would take hold.

While everyone accepted that interest rates were the Fed's best tool to cool down the economy, there was still the question of how long the Fed should raise them. What would tell the Fed to stop?

To help answer this question, officials had come up with more fancy models over the past two decades. They estimated a "neutral" rate of interest that should prevail when the economy was at its equilibrium. A neutral rate would be the setting that depressed neither the gas pedal nor the brake. If the economy needed more gas, the Fed would cut or hold rates below "neutral." And if it needed more brake, it could raise rates above neutral. It was yet another example of an invisible arrow being shot at an invisible target.

The new Fed chair had plenty of reasons to feel exultant as he stepped to the dais that day. His colleagues had managed to finally raise interest rates up from zero, and they were slowly shrinking their $4.5 trillion asset portfolio, which had been swollen by successive rounds of quantitative easing. Unwinding Bernanke and Yellen's crisis-era policies marked an accomplishment, especially when compared with Europe and Japan, where central banks were still struggling to push up inflation or interest rates.

In his speech, Powell fired a warning shot at traditional invisible arrows and targets. He discussed the neutral rate of interest and the natural rate of unemployment with a different metaphor: celestial stars that help sailors navigate the open seas. "Navigating by the stars can sound straightforward. Guiding policy by the stars in practice, however, has been quite challenging of late because our best assessments of the location of the stars have been changing significantly," Powell said. "The stars are sometimes far from where we perceive them to be."[1] Powell lauded the "considerable fortitude" of Greenspan's approach in the mid-1990s, when the Fed had delayed rate increases once interest rates were at a supposedly neutral setting in order to await evidence that inflation was actually a threat.

A changing economy also argued against relying too much on old models. During and after the 1990s, technology and globalization allowed advanced economies to sustain lower levels of unemployment without facing the same inflationary pressures they had in the 1960s. Fewer unionized workers meant wage contracts with automatic raises were less prevalent. Still, modified versions of the Phillips curve lived on at central banks. There was nothing better to use as a replacement.

Powell's speech reflected a Fed that was reaching the brink of a paradigm shift. A couple of Powell's colleagues on the Federal Open Market Committee had grown even more skeptical of the Phillips curve and thus even more hesitant to step on the brakes. "We are too focused on the unemployment rate number," said Minneapolis Fed President Neel Kashkari, who had got his start in public service managing Hank Paulson's $700 billion bank bailout in 2008 before an ill-starred bid for governor of California as a Republican in 2014.[2] Kashkari thought economists paid too much attention to this unreliable gauge. One of its biggest flaws: many potential workers stay on the sidelines and don't get counted as unemployed because they aren't actively seeking jobs. But if the economy heats up, they could enter the fray, making the supply of workers more elastic than unemployment rates suggest.

But these voices were in the minority. Many Keynesian economists worried that Trump's big deficit-financed tax cuts might produce a "sugar high" that could lead to speculative bubbles or inflation, especially with unemployment so low. The last two recessions, in 2001 and 2007, had begun when bubbles burst — in tech stocks and housing, respectively. Most Fed officials in the summer of 2018 thought a neutral interest rate, their invisible target, might be in the neighborhood of 3 percent. With interest rates slightly below 2 percent at that time, this meant at least another year of increases before the Fed's foot could ease off the gas pedal. Several Fed policymakers thought they would need to raise rates beyond that point, including some who had most strongly resisted rate increases a few years earlier.

They had plenty of company outside the central bank in the form of economists and financial pundits. The "Fed needs to wake up and admit the economy is overheating," read the headline of a *Financial Times* column that summer by a former Fed economist who worked at a large hedge fund. He summed up the conventional wisdom: "A high-pressure economy feels great during the party. But the recessionary hangover can be brutal." Better to "recognize the economy is overheating rather than hoping that it's not, announce that policy will need to be more restrictive sooner than expected, and get on with it."[3]

In the end, Powell's speech carefully avoided coming down firmly on one side or another. Was Powell saying he thought the Fed should keep raising rates until something broke in the economy? Or did his remarks mean the Fed could stop raising interest rates, following the Greenspan example that Powell had approvingly cited? Those questions could wait as long as markets and the economy chugged along.

"A long way from neutral"

On Wednesday, October 3, Powell sat down on a white leather couch for an interview with journalist Judy Woodruff at the "Atlantic Ideas Festival." It was an unscripted format that showcased his plainspoken appeal. Most of the interview went well until Powell made a clumsy attempt to deflect speculation that the Fed would need to raise rates above the neutral rate in order to deliberately slow down the economy. "We're gradually moving to a place where [rates] will be neutral.... We may go past neutral, but we're a long way from neutral at this point, probably," he told Woodruff.

Taken at face value, Powell's unscripted remark suggested the Fed needed to raise rates a lot more. With all the guesswork involved in where this invisible "neutral" target sat, Powell's words set off feverish interpretations.

On Thursday and Friday, bond yields rose and stocks fell as investors grew more nervous about inflationary pressures. When stocks slid even more the next week and investors looked for a culprit, they began to obsess over the "long way from neutral" comment. From October 3 to 11, the Dow Jones Industrial Average fell more than 1,775 points, or 6.6 percent.

Watching the Wall Street carnage unfold, Trump fumed. "The Fed has gone crazy," he told reporters during a visit to Erie, Pennsylvania, on October 10, after stocks dropped 832 points. On Fox News that night he exclaimed, "The Fed is going loco, and there's no reason for them to do it."

Trump wasn't picking up the phone to yell at Powell, but he was effectively doing the same thing through the media — turning what Truman, Johnson, and Nixon had done privately into a public spectacle. "Every time we do something great, he raises the interest rates," Trump said of Powell in an interview with *The Wall Street Journal* on October 23.

"How the hell do you compete with that?...He was supposed to be a low-interest rate guy. It's turned out that he's not."[4] At Oval Office meetings, Trump erupted at Mnuchin for recommending Powell: "I thought you told me he was going to be good."[5] Even Trump's advisers ignored these initial verbal broadsides. Powell's first few rate increases had been widely telegraphed and were universally expected by financial markets.

At the root of Trump's frustration was the trade war with China, which wasn't going well. A weak growth spell in Germany, Japan, and China added to fears of a global slowdown, sending the stock market into a swoon at the end of November. Trump made no secret of his admiration for Beijing's tightly managed economy, where the idea of an independent central bank was as foreign as a free press. "The Fed right now is a much bigger problem than China," he told the *Journal* on November 26.[6]

Even if Powell never flinched publicly, Trump's continual attacks on the Fed put him in a bind. If he stopped raising rates because he thought economic conditions demanded the change in policy, he would appear to be capitulating to Trump. The attacks "locked in that [the Fed] can't pause," said Jeremy Stein, the governor who had joined the Fed with Powell in 2012 and returned to Harvard two years later. "At that point you're saying, 'Do I want to be Paul Volcker or Arthur Burns?'"

Nobody wanted to be the second coming of Arthur Burns — the chair whom Nixon had bullied into lowering rates. "I'd rather go in the books as a terrible Fed chair than as somebody who knuckled under," Powell told a reporter in autumn of 2018.[7]

Powell used a long-planned speech before the Economic Club of New York on Wednesday, November 28 to clear up lingering misconceptions over his "long way from neutral" comment. With a single generic observation in his speech — that the Fed's rate was now "just below" a range of estimates of the neutral rate — Powell relieved the pressure. Michelle Smith, who had handled communications strategy for every Fed chair since Greenspan, passed a note card to Powell after he wrapped up an obligatory question-and-answer session. *Up 528 points*, it read. The episode drove home the power of Powell's words and just how raw investors were growing about his policy intentions.

The Powell doctrine

As Trump's attacks piled up, Powell had started following four unwritten rules in public.

Rule 1: Don't talk about Trump.

The first rule led to uneasy laughter, blank stares, and awkward silences. At an October lunch with economists in Boston, Powell raved about the team he had assembled at the central bank, but he sat mute when the subject turned to Trump's criticisms.

Rule 2: When provoked, don't return fire.

At another on-stage interview, this one at the Dallas Fed in November, Robert Kaplan, the bank president, made a subtle reference to Trump's attacks. "One of the questions from the audience is, 'Gee, I read in the newspaper that you have been mentioned by political leaders over the last several months,'" Kaplan said to nervous laughter in the auditorium.

"That was very delicate, Rob," Powell responded.

Rule 3: Stick to the economy, not politics.

At that same interview, Powell pivoted to Rule 3 — stick to the economy. Asked about Trump's attacks, Powell answered that he was focused on low unemployment and stable inflation. "We don't try to control things we don't control," said Powell. "We try to control the controllable."[8]

Rule 4: Develop allies outside the Oval Office.

Congressional Republicans uniformly lauded Powell's demeanor — a clear sign that his outreach on Capitol Hill was yielding dividends. While he was waiting for a meeting during one such visit, a Republican lawmaker outside the Senate chamber walked up to Powell and told him,

"I just want you to know you've got a lot of support up here. More than you think." Another Republican grabbed him by the arm. "You don't have to say anything at all, but I want to give you some feedback," he said. "How you are handling this is brilliant. Exactly the way to go. Don't take the bait." Powell laughed and offered his thanks.

———

Inside the Fed, Powell's colleagues closed ranks around him. Clarida realized by October 2018 that if there was any space between him and Powell, the White House would try to drive a truck through it. He decided never to allow *any* daylight in public between them. CNBC reporter Steve Liesman once teased Clarida about beginning half of his answers during their television interviews with "As Chair Powell said."

Every time Trump took a swing at Powell, Powell's inbox exploded with supportive notes from reserve-bank presidents, corporate executives, and Wall Street luminaries. After watching one of his press conferences, Volcker sent him a congratulatory note, "which I never do," he said. "He handled himself very well. I told him so."[9]

In early December 2018, during the annual Christmas-tree lighting inside the Fed's marble atrium, Powell and Clarida treated central-bank staffers to a rare Christmas duet, with the chair playing guitar and Clarida singing. While presenting gag gifts to various department heads at the board, Powell pulled a lump of coal from a stocking and announced that it had arrived from an unnamed "DC postmark." Everyone broke out in laughter.

Tariff Man

Investors breathed a sigh of relief on Saturday, December 1, when Trump announced a trade truce after a high-stakes dinner with Chinese leader Xi Jinping during a summit of world leaders in Buenos Aires. Trump hailed an "amazing and productive meeting with unlimited possibilities" and agreed to delay some tariffs. "Relations with China have taken a BIG leap forward! Very good things will happen," Trump tweeted on Monday morning. The trade war was off. But on Tuesday, Trump reversed himself: "I am a Tariff Man," he declared on Twitter.

Market sentiment deteriorated. Gary Cohn told his former White House colleagues that the outburst had cost the president 2,000 points on his precious Dow, which tumbled from 25,826 on December 3 to 23,593 on Monday, December 17, the day before an important FOMC meeting was set to begin.[10]

At 8:30 a.m. that Monday, Trump lobbed a now-familiar demand at the Fed. "It is incredible that with a very strong dollar and virtually no inflation...the Fed is even considering yet another interest rate hike. Take the Victory!" he tweeted. The next day, Trump added that he wanted the Fed to stop shrinking its asset portfolio. (By the fall of 2018, the Fed was allowing up to $50 billion to roll off the portfolio every month.) "Don't let the market become any more illiquid than it already is," the president exhorted. "Stop with the 50 B's. Feel the market, don't just go by meaningless numbers."

Trump's public demand that the Fed not raise interest rates on the eve of its two-day FOMC meeting, when officials had widely telegraphed precisely such a rate increase, had no precedent. The chief economist at Pantheon Macroeconomics summed up the zeitgeist in a client note before the Fed meeting began: "Jay Powell does not want to go down in history as the Fed chair who was pushed around by an economically illiterate president."[11]

US economic data painted a still-bright picture. Sales at retailers and restaurants indicated the holiday-shopping season was off to a good start. The unemployment rate was holding at 3.7 percent — lowest in forty-nine years — with wages rising. On his Bloomberg data terminal, the ubiquitous Wall Street trading-desk tool, Powell could quickly call up bond-market pricing that showed investors still anticipated a rate increase — a green light to raise rates.

The December debacle

Ahead of the December gathering, only three of the twelve Fed bank presidents were opposed to raising rates, and none of them had a vote at the meeting. A couple of others wanted Powell to signal more clearly a time-out on future increases afterward. Some of the most respected economists on the committee, however — among them Chicago Fed President Charles Evans and New York Fed President John Williams — thought the Fed would need to keep raising interest rates, and that it was far too soon for Powell to signal any pause.

Powell huddled in his office with Williams and Clarida during a 1:30 p.m. meeting on Monday, December 17. Overhead was a replica of an antique chandelier from the Château Malmaison, which served as the last residence in France of Napoleon Bonaparte.

"Guys, it's not too late," Powell told the other two men. "We can pause at this meeting. We don't need to hike."

Between markets tumbling and the president's attacks, it felt like a lose-lose proposition. If the Fed scrapped its plans to raise rates, it would look like the markets — or Trump — were in control. "We're just now getting to the lowest estimate of neutral," Clarida told them. Clarida harbored doubts about continuing to raise rates above neutral in 2019, but that was a problem for another day. "If we can't get to neutral with the lowest unemployment rate in fifty years, with inflation above 2 percent, and with growth above its trend, when are we ever going to get to neutral?" he said.

Their verdict was clear: the rate increase was a go. Powell would announce a quarter-percentage-point rate rise, along with language suggesting that the Fed would consider a slower, more flexible path upward— a so-called *dovish* hike. None of it worked.

Markets fell modestly after the Fed released its 2 p.m. statement. Powell, appearing unfazed by the recent market convulsions, projected confidence at his press conference, saying that recent volatility had "not fundamentally changed the outlook." The comment kicked off a frenzy of selling. When a reporter asked Powell whether the Fed might abort plans to shrink the balance sheet, as Trump wanted, Powell tried to shut down such talk. He explained the committee's initial desire to keep "runoff on automatic pilot" and use interest rates to tighten the money supply.

Traders on Wall Street groaned. The *autopilot* talk spooked investors, who took it to mean the Fed was on some predetermined march to tighten monetary policy.

"Tone-deaf," said one analyst afterward.

Powell knew as soon as the press conference ended that he hadn't pulled off the so-called *dovish increase*. Reporters held up their phones to one another, the screens bathed in red. The Dow fell at one point by 513 points as Powell spoke. The 10-year Treasury yield slumped — a sign that bond investors were less optimistic about growth. In early November, yields had been as high as 3.24 percent. Now they hit 2.78 percent.

Just months after arguing against overconfidently relying on the unobservable estimates embodied by the "celestial stars," Powell had pushed ahead with a rate increase that held fast to those very estimates. It was one he would come to regard, with the benefit of hindsight, as a mistake. "Policy at this point does not need to be accommodative. It can move to neutral," he had told reporters that afternoon. Some critics worried that the Fed's determination to safeguard its independence or its fear of being viewed as reacting to the market swoon that preceded its meeting had led Powell and his colleagues astray, biasing them to pursue a policy path whose fundamental merit had weakened significantly.

The market rout continued over Thursday and Friday — although it was fanned by more political intrigue at the White House. Defense Secretary James Mattis shocked Washington by resigning after Trump unexpectedly ordered troops out of Syria. After that, in a pique over the funding of his border wall with Mexico, the president upended a bipartisan effort to avoid a government shutdown, which began that Saturday. It was the worst week for the stock market since the 2008 crisis: the Dow was down 16 percent that month, while the Nasdaq slid more than 20 percent — the threshold that qualifies as a bear market — from its late-summer highs.

Back in September 2017, a few days after his job interview with Trump, Powell had met with a former colleague from the Bush administration for breakfast at the ornate Mayflower Hotel in downtown Washington. William Heyman had worked with Powell on the response to the Salomon crisis in 1991 and was now the top investment executive at a large insurance company, which — like pension funds and other institutions that promised fixed returns over a long period of time — had struggled with the protracted low-rate policies in the wake of the 2008 financial crisis.

After mulling Powell's prospects to lead the Fed, Heyman gave him some advice: "If you get this job, you really have to try to normalize interest rates. And you have to do it until the market absolutely throws up all over you."

Mission accomplished.

Chapter Six

"BONEHEADS"

The government shutdown before Christmas 2018 forced Donald Trump to cancel his annual Palm Beach holiday in Mar-a-Lago. Stuck in Washington, he fumed to advisers that picking Jay Powell as Fed chair had been the worst decision of his presidency. Powell would "turn me into Hoover," Trump lamented, referring to the president who presided over the 1929 crash that started the Great Depression.[1]

Trump's popular TV show, *The Apprentice*, ended each week with his tagline "You're fired!" With markets cratering, a furious Trump asked advisers if he could fire Powell. This represented the nuclear option: it would shatter the illusion of an independent Fed once and for all. At one point, Trump instructed economic adviser Larry Kudlow to confer with White House lawyers on his removal authority. Kudlow and the lawyers reported back to Trump: you can't fire the Fed chair over an interest-rate dispute. The law said that any of the seven Fed governors could be removed "for cause," which courts had interpreted to mean dereliction of duty, not a mere policy dispute. But the statutes were ambiguous about whether this provision meant the governor serving the four-year term of the chair could be stripped of that position, allowing the president to demote Powell.

Both Mnuchin and Kudlow didn't need to be told that pushing the button on the nuclear option would accelerate the markets' tailspin. And Powell had made it clear internally that under no circumstances would he leave, meaning a constitutional crisis loomed if Trump wanted to go there. Kudlow also saw how Powell had assiduously courted lawmakers and figured Trump would hurt himself with the Senate if he tried to sack the Fed chair. Mnuchin and Powell texted back and forth over the holidays, as word of Trump's ire grew. Powell walked through how he had tried and failed to execute the dovish rate increase, and Mnuchin made clear he had Powell's back. *You have a really hard job*, he would tell Powell, playing peacemaker. And to Trump, Mnuchin would calmly say, *You're going to be very happy with him in the end.*

After word about Trump's unhappiness became public on Saturday, December 22, Mnuchin posted a tweet on his account, attributed to the president, that read, "I never suggested firing Chairman Jay Powell, nor do I believe I have the right to do so." On Sunday, Trump's newest chief of staff, Mick Mulvaney, appeared on ABC and said the president "now realizes" he cannot dismiss the Fed chair over a policy dispute.[2]

Later that day, Mnuchin released a bizarre statement that said markets were functioning properly and that he had called the heads of the nation's largest banks, who assured him they had "ample liquidity" to lend to consumers. It felt like overkill — the equivalent of being told, after visiting a doctor for a sprained ankle, that there was no reason to worry about cancer.

The sense of disarray added to market jitters the next morning, December 24, and the Dow dived another 650 points. After Mnuchin arranged a call with Powell and other financial regulators, the president tweeted, "The only problem our economy has is the Fed. They don't have a feel for the Market, they don't understand necessary Trade Wars or Strong Dollars or even Democrat Shutdowns over Borders."

On Christmas morning, Trump invited reporters into the Oval Office during a videoconference with soldiers overseas. Asked if Powell's job was safe, Trump offered weakly, "I have confidence in them," referring to the Fed. The next morning, Kevin Hassett, the chair of the Council of Economic Advisers, faced the same question. "Yes, of course, 100 percent, yes," Hassett said from the West Wing driveway. The Dow closed 1,086 points higher, up 5 percent. Trump called Hassett to congratulate him.[3]

Powell's pirouette

By January 2019, the December rate increase began to look like a mistake, corroborating Powell's earlier thinking about not relying too much on the stars. His colleagues at the Fed had to confront what appeared to be a new normal in the economy, one that didn't follow the rules suggested by the Phillips curve or other standard forecasting tools. Unemployment had fallen well below the natural rate, the magic break point at which it should send inflation higher. But inflation wasn't rising. If Powell was going to follow the evidence, he needed to change the Fed's traditional policy approach.

On the morning of Wednesday, January 2, 2019, Powell met in his office with Richard Clarida, with John Williams joining by phone from New York. They agreed that the Fed needed to signal a pause in its projected rate hikes. Powell would use a previously scheduled interview that Friday on a stage with Ben Bernanke and Janet Yellen to unfurl the pivot. Powell avoided any miscues by reading from prepared notes in response to an opening question. Softer-than-anticipated inflation readings would allow the Fed to be "patient," he said.

Always-attentive investors knew what this meant: the Fed was done raising rates for now. Markets rallied. Powell didn't have time to consult with the rest of the FOMC, but in the coming weeks, none of his colleagues registered a complaint.

During a January 10 speech in Manhattan, Clarida invoked an otherwise-awkward hypothetical to suggest that something fundamental was changing at the Fed: "Were models to predict a surge in inflation, a decision for preemptive hikes before the surge is evident would need to be balanced against the cost of the model being wrong," he said.[4]

Translation: *We're not going to rely so heavily on models.* For Fed watchers, it was astonishing to hear those thirty-one inelegant words come out of a Fed governor's mouth. Central-bank leaders simply don't go around hinting at their flaws.

At the conclusion of the Fed's January 30 meeting, Powell ratified Clarida's reevaluation of the old folk wisdom, making clear that even with unemployment well below most estimates of the natural rate, the central bank wasn't going to raise rates again unless inflation rose well above the Fed's 2 percent target. Powell was casting aside the Phillips curve — a historic shift for the Fed. Officials also announced plans to maintain a larger asset portfolio, meaning they would stop paring their Treasury holdings a few months later.

The Fed is an enormously conservative institution, one that rarely changes course as quickly and fundamentally as it did in January 2019. On two fronts — rates and the balance sheet — the Fed had made extraordinary U-turns. These course corrections were even more humbling than normal because they corresponded with what Trump had been loudly demanding.

Dinner with Donald

With Trump on the warpath after the Christmas Eve market freak-out, Kudlow and Mnuchin floated an idea: maybe Trump should break bread with the affable Powell? It was perfectly normal for presidents to meet with Fed chairs, but given Trump's behavior, the dinner risked fueling speculation that the central bank was being brought to heel. "If the conversation is a chance for the president of the United States to tell the chairman of the Federal Reserve how to run Federal Reserve policy, I'd just as soon not answer the phone," said Alan Greenspan.[5]

A dinner with Trump was the last thing Powell wanted. But Trump was the president, and Powell wasn't going to say no. In January he told Clarida that if the dinner went ahead, Mnuchin would attend — and that Powell wanted Clarida there as backup. On Friday, February 1, Clarida was packing for a business trip to Paris when Powell called. The White House dinner was on for the next Monday, which happened to be Powell's 66th birthday. Paris would have to wait.

Michelle Smith, the communications chief, presented a plan to both men during a meeting in Powell's office that Monday, February 4. It was a four-sentence statement that closely followed the Powell doctrine of low-key, apolitical, evidence-driven economic policy.

"My recommendation is, regardless of what they say [over dinner], this is the statement that we're releasing as soon as you walk out of the dining room," said Smith. Nobody knew how any meeting with Trump would go, but at least now they knew how it would end.

That night, Powell and Clarida arrived at the ornate Treasury Building in an armored SUV, took a private elevator up to Mnuchin's office, and met with the secretary in his dining room. Powell took the press statement from his breast pocket and handed it to the Treasury secretary. "This is not a discussion," Powell told Mnuchin. "We're informing you that we're releasing this statement after the dinner."

"It's OK, but obviously we'll need to show this to the president," Mnuchin responded.

It was an unseasonably warm winter day in Washington, but all three men were on edge as they made the short walk to the White House. Mnuchin and Powell were both nervous because the dinner could easily be a train wreck. Clarida had less to lose professionally, but was still uneasy because he was having dinner with the president in his private dining room. On the way up to join Trump in his residence, Mnuchin told them it would be the first meal he'd ever had in the family quarters.

Trump engaged in a few minutes of friendly chitchat, regaling his guests with buddy stories about Tom Brady and Bill Belichick, the quarterback and head coach of the New England Patriots, who had won the Super Bowl the day before. "They're big supporters of mine," Trump volunteered. He also recounted a recent round of golf he'd played with Tiger Woods and Jack Nicklaus, two of the sport's all-time greats. Knowing Trump does not drink alcohol, they all declined drinks when the staff offered them.

Powell took his seat at the dining table on Trump's right side, opposite Mnuchin. Clarida sat across from Trump, meaning that for the next hour he would have unbroken eye contact with the commander-in-chief. Trump did most of the talking. He peppered Powell with plain-vanilla questions that started out innocently enough. "What's your outlook for the economy?" Powell recited the same bland talking points he had offered after the recent FOMC meeting.

On a couple of occasions, however, the conversation veered into directions that made Powell and Clarida nervous. "Well, that's 2019," Trump would say. "What I really care about is your outlook for the economy in 2020." Mnuchin tried as best he could to drive the conversation back from the cliff's edge of election-year politics.

Trump summed up his frustration with the Fed at one point over their meal of charcoal-grilled ribeye and creamed spinach. "Look, I have been a businessman all my life," he began. "I'm at these rallies with 20,000 people. I get off the stage and I'm talking to the construction workers. And I just think you guys spend too much time looking at equations and models. I'm out there, and I meet everyday Americans. I have a sense for the pulse of the economy that you don't have because you spend all your time looking at models and stuff."

Powell and Clarida didn't say much in response. Even if Trump had a point, he was less interested in a thoughtful give-and-take about the economy than in making sure the Fed stayed out of the way of his reelection.

No one mentioned Powell's birthday as the dinner wrapped up. Instead, Mnuchin pulled the statement from Powell out of his pocket and said, "Mr. President, this is the statement the Fed would like to issue." It stated that Powell "did not discuss his expectations for monetary policy" and that the Fed would make its decisions "based solely on careful, objective, and non-political analysis."

Trump read it over twice without saying anything. Then, after a pause, he said, "That's OK."

Before leaving, Trump gave his guests a tour of the Lincoln Bedroom. If that dinner represented a détente, it would last just a few weeks.

"Act as appropriate"

By the spring, the president was demanding that the Fed undo its earlier rate increases by cutting rates, even though the economy appeared to be holding together. The Fed ignored Trump. On Friday, May 3, the Labor Department reported a surge of hiring in April that eased fears about a slowdown. Powell felt comfortable with the Fed's make-no-moves stance, but it would be the last time he felt that way for a long time.

Two days later, on a Sunday night, the president announced the first of two body blows to business confidence. Trade talks with China had broken down; in retaliation, the president imposed new tariffs. A few weeks later, and completely out of the blue, Trump threatened to slap new tariffs on Mexico if the country failed to enact tighter migration curbs — even though he had just signed an updated North American Free Trade Agreement. Business executives were left to wonder: If Trump could reverse himself like that, what was any signed agreement worth?

In May 2019, yields on ten-year government notes — which tend to go down when investors become risk-averse or pessimistic about growth — slid from 2.5 percent to 2.13 percent. When the long-term yield slips below the level of three-month Treasury bills, it creates a dreaded Wall Street dynamic known as the "inversion of the yield curve." Essentially, investors expect central bankers may need to lower short-term rates in response to a slowdown. Inverted yield curves have frequently preceded recessions by one or two years.

Before an early June speech at the Federal Reserve Bank of Chicago, Powell huddled with Clarida and Williams. They agreed on adding a key phrase to his introductory remarks: Powell pledged the Fed would "act as appropriate" to sustain the expansion. The markets heard "a rate cut is firmly on the table" and posted their biggest gains since Powell's January 4 pledge to be "patient."

In the span of five months, the Fed had shifted from raising rates to potentially cutting rates. In doing so, they knew that plenty of critics would claim they had changed course in the face of threats from the White House.

In a sense, Trump did get Powell to cut rates — by pursuing a trade policy that Wall Street and many large and small businesses hated. Powell feared that a darkening global outlook, clouded by trade policy, could lead borrowing costs to rise and other financial conditions to tighten if the Fed didn't cut rates. A broader slowdown in manufacturing, investment, and trade could spread to the much larger swath of the economy driven by consumer spending.

But not everyone on the Federal Open Market Committee agreed. That summer, Powell would face more division on the committee over how to respond to Trump's trade war than at any point so far. In July, Powell, joined by Clarida and Williams, argued for a "risk management" posture that justified cutting rates before economic data showed conclusive evidence of a slowdown. At FOMC meetings, Clarida would speak first during the policy discussion, and Williams would speak second to last, before Powell, to steer a consensus. They pointed to research that says when a central bank is faced with little room to lower interest rates because they are already close to zero, it should use what limited ammunition it has early and fast.

"The idea of keeping your powder dry, it's actually a mistake," Williams told reporters. "If you're worried about a negative shock or risk out there, you want the economy to be in a strong position when that shock hits."

Tough guy

Powell was moving toward a rate cut that summer, but not fast enough to satisfy Trump. The challenge for Powell was that once Trump publicly demanded a course of action, there was no way to prove the Fed was acting independently if the central bank ended up following that course of its own accord. When ABC's George Stephanopoulos asked Trump on June 14 if he worried that his demands were putting Powell "in a box," Trump responded, "Yes, I do, but I'm gonna do it anyway because I've waited long enough."[6]

On June 25, Powell tried to deflect speculation that he was following Trump's orders. "We have a very important job...and desire to play no role in broader political issues," Powell had said during a discussion in New York, with his adult children in the audience. "We're human. We'll make mistakes....But we won't make mistakes of integrity or character."

The next morning, Maria Bartiromo egged Trump on by asking him about Powell's response during one of the president's marathon telephone interviews on her Fox Business Network program. "He's trying to prove how tough he is because he's not going to get pushed around," Trump told Bartiromo. "Here's a guy, nobody ever heard of him before. And now I made him, and he wants to show how tough he is! OK, let him show how tough he is! He's not doing a good job, OK? Let me be nice about it."

Months earlier, after the February dinner, Kudlow had floated the idea that they formalize such a meeting. Once a quarter, Mnuchin, Powell, and Kudlow would meet with Trump to talk about the economy. Eisenhower and Kennedy had organized similar meetings with Chair Bill Martin. But Trump said no. He was too angry at Powell to share a room with him.

Fed officials did what they could to tune out the attacks. Throughout 2019, Randal Quarles, Trump's first pick for the Fed board in July 2017, would deflect Trump's indecorous attacks by placing them in a broader historical context. Quarles was married to Hope Eccles, a granddaughter of Marriner Eccles's brother. He reminded visitors how he used to tell his kids about the time that "Uncle Marriner" stood up to President Truman.

Powell had no interest in engaging in a tough-guy showdown with Trump. His overriding goal was to make sure the US economic expansion — which by July 2019 would be the longest on record — did not end on his watch. But a second, equally critical personal mission was coming into view: make sure the Fed as an institution survives the Trump years intact.

Other Trump appointees, including Attorney General Jeff Sessions and Defense Secretary James Mattis, resigned after it became clear they had lost the president's ear. For Powell, however, the decision could not be personal; the independence of the institution was at stake. At a congressional hearing that July, Representative Maxine Waters, the California Democrat who chaired the House Financial Services Committee, posed a hypothetical.

"Mr. Chairman, if you got a call from the president today or tomorrow, and he said, 'I'm firing you, pack up, it's time to go,' what would you do?"

The committee room fell silent.

"Well, of course I would not do that," Powell answered softly.

"I can't hear you," replied Waters in a singsong voice, prompting laughter from the gallery and Powell to crack a grin.

He spoke louder. "My answer would be 'no.'"

In private, Powell was even more explicit. "I will never, ever, ever leave this job voluntarily until my term ends under any circumstances. None whatsoever. You will not see me getting in the lifeboat," Powell told a reporter that spring. "It doesn't occur to me in the slightest that there would be any situation in which I would not complete my term other than dying."

After the FOMC meeting on July 31, 2019, the Fed announced it would cut rates by a quarter-percentage point. Days later, Trump ordered more tariffs on China, sending markets reeling. Long-term yields tumbled. Whatever reprieve the rate cut had offered was immediately erased.

Our bigger enemy

To relieve stress, Powell would ride his bike eight miles from his home in leafy Chevy Chase, Maryland, winding through Rock Creek Park to the Fed's stately headquarters in downtown Washington's Foggy Bottom neighborhood. His security detail trailed a few hundred yards behind him on electric bikes. After work he might fiddle on the guitar, with Pippa, his family's terrier, at his feet. Powell worked most weekends, cutting into his golf game. He kept abreast of the latest economic debates and animal videos on Twitter using a private account. Strangers sometimes stopped him in airports or restaurants to compliment his grace under fire. His wife, Elissa, had mostly put her film work on hiatus and chaired Chevy Chase's board of managers, where she had to sort out a small-town conflict in 2019 over complaints surrounding a neighborhood dog park. Otherwise, she tried to manage a home environment that was as stress-free as possible.

In tweets that summer, Trump blasted the "clueless" Powell as a "terrible communicator" with "no guts" who showed a "horrendous lack of vision" and led a group of "Boneheads." Trump demanded that the Fed cut its rate, then a little above 2 percent, by a full percentage point and resume Treasury-bond buying, something reserved for an extreme emergency. It reeked of desperation driven by stock-market declines amid a trade war that was going poorly for the president. "Doing great with China and other Trade Deals," Trump tweeted on August 21. "The only problem we have is Jay Powell and the Fed. He's like a golfer who can't putt, has no touch."

In late August, Powell returned to Wyoming's majestic Tetons for the Kansas City Fed's annual symposium. Hours before Powell's highly anticipated opening keynote, on Friday, August 23, Beijing said it would impose retaliatory tariffs on almost all US imports not already subject to duties. Trump's trade war was spinning out of control.

Powell knew there was only so much the Fed could do to help the economy if Trump kept ramping up a trade war, so he used his speech to deliver his most pointed warning yet about the risks to the economy. There were "no recent precedents to guide any policy response to the current situation," Powell said. The Fed could "not provide a settled rule book for international trade." He also signaled that another rate cut was likely at the Fed's next scheduled meeting in mid-September, calming markets.

A few minutes after Powell returned to his front-row seat, Trump fired back on Twitter. "As usual, the Fed did NOTHING!" said the president, who mistakenly thought the Fed had been meeting that morning to debate a rate cut. "Who is our bigger enemy, Jay Powell or Chairman Xi?" Later, Trump issued an even more bizarre tweet in which he "hereby ordered" American companies to prepare to leave China. Markets plummeted.

While attendees passed their smartphones back and forth, Powell sat Sphinx-like at the front of the wood-paneled ballroom adorned with antler chandeliers. Michelle Smith forwarded the tweets by email to Clarida, who wasn't within phone-passing distance.

"Ugh ugh," he messaged back.[7]

That evening, as Powell and his wife danced to a country-and-western band in Jackson Hole, a reporter on the White House lawn asked Trump if he wanted Powell to resign. "Let me put it this way," the president said. "If he did, I wouldn't stop him."

Fed listens

While Trump's Fed fight got all the attention, the biggest shift the Fed made in 2019 had nothing to do with the White House or the state of the economy. Just before he became chair, Powell decided he would initiate a review of the Fed's basic policy-setting framework. It was a bit unusual — daring, even — for the Fed, which had not done anything like it since formalizing its inflation target in 2012. Powell thought the Fed, having navigated past the political storms that followed the financial crisis and the use of quantitative easing, was finally in a reasonably sturdy position to crawl out from under its desk and confidently open itself up for examination. On Clarida's first day as vice chair in September 2018, Powell asked him to spearhead the project. Powell wanted to conduct a road show of sorts — a public listening tour, branded "Fed Listens," that was out of character for the cloistered central bank.

The premise was simple: Was the 2 percent target still viable if the Fed was going to be stuck more often with rates near zero?

The actual inflation rate had run below the 2 percent goal for much of the expansion. Some people inside and outside the Fed persuasively asked what the big deal was if inflation was at 1.6 percent instead of 2 percent? Inflation isn't perfectly measured anyway. For Powell, the concern was that they kept missing the target by undershooting 2 percent. Central bankers worried that households' and businesses' expectations of future inflation might slip lower and lower, becoming "unanchored," as economists put it.

Meanwhile, the listening tour in 2019 hammered home the benefits of lower unemployment. This goal represented half of the Fed's dual mandate but given the importance of the Phillips curve in guiding policy decisions, it often looked like officials treated it as the lesser of the two goals, subservient to the importance of low inflation. An hour-long panel of noneconomists stole the show during two days of academic presentations at the main research conference Clarida organized in Chicago in June 2019. "When I hear we're at full employment, that's not my reality. That's not my community's reality," said Juan Salgado, the chancellor of City Colleges of Chicago, which enrolled 80,000 mostly minority students. Powell, who took notes and asked questions, seemed to genuinely enjoy the sessions.

As 2019 drew to a close, the policy review seemed likely to deliver some important changes. At the time, the Fed didn't take into account when inflation had persistently run above or below 2 percent. Now, the Fed would take past shortfalls of that target into account by seeking modestly higher inflation during good times. In other words, the Fed would signal to investors that it would hold rates lower for longer after downturns.

An uneasy peace

The Fed had its disagreements — Powell faced several dissents from Fed presidents as he led colleagues to cut rates. But they were nothing compared with the atmosphere at the White House. Trump's summertime antics had generated furious pushback from the kitchen cabinet of executives who reported to him on the economy. At one Oval Office meeting in October, Kudlow arranged for a handful of outside advisers to deliver a warning: the president's trade war with China would jeopardize his reelection if he didn't quickly find a way to park it. US and Chinese officials began making progress soon after on a narrower set of trade talks.

By the end of October, the Fed had cut rates three times in 2019, and had signaled that further cuts were unlikely. The unemployment rate ended 2019 at 3.5 percent, a fifty-year low. It had been a bruising year for Powell, but the crucible strengthened his standing with elected officials in Washington and with his central-bank peers. Senator Jack Reed, a Rhode Island Democrat, saluted Powell's "steady hand" and apolitical approach before a dinnertime Chamber of Commerce address in Providence. Reed's warm introduction inspired the 750 audience members to give Powell an extended standing ovation.[8]

Stocks raced to new records after Washington and Beijing agreed to a "phase-one" trade deal that would provide an election-year truce. Investors sent the Dow to finish daily trading above 29,000 for the first time on January 15, 2020, when President Trump lavished praised on Chinese Vice Premier Liu He at a White House signing ceremony. When Trump spotted in the audience Kevin Warsh, the former Fed governor he had interviewed for the chair job two years earlier, he couldn't resist another dig at Powell. "I could have used you a little bit here. Why weren't you more forceful when you wanted that job?" Trump said. "I would have been very happy with you."

One week after the signing ceremony, on January 21, the Chinese government confirmed human-to-human transmission of a novel coronavirus after an outbreak in Wuhan, China, that had begun weeks earlier. That same day, the Centers for Disease Control and Prevention in Atlanta reported the first confirmed US case from a man in Washington State who fell ill four days after returning from Wuhan.

The virus had arrived.

Chapter Seven

INTO THE EMERGENCY ROOM

Every January, heads of state mingle with the titans of finance and industry in the Swiss alpine ski resort of Davos for the World Economic Forum's series of highfalutin, invitation-only seminars, meetings, and parties. As it has swelled in influence, the event has grown to attract celebrities and activists as well. In 2020, for example, central players such as European Central Bank president Christine Lagarde and financier George Soros were joined by climate activist Greta Thunberg and Bollywood star Deepika Padukone, an ambassador for mental health. The Big Idea in 2020 was "stakeholder capitalism," featuring seminars on gender parity and the technological arms race.

During a dinner-panel discussion on January 23, 2020, Treasury Secretary Steven Mnuchin spoke up during a discussion on climate change and trade. Why, he asked, had no one uttered a word about the most important issue then facing the world: the deadly new coronavirus that had shut down the most populous city in central China? Earlier that day Beijing had announced that it had banned movement in and out of Wuhan, the epicenter of a spiraling public-health crisis. Mnuchin told the dinner guests that he was anxious about what the hit to China's economy would mean for global growth — though he didn't think the virus would be a serious threat to the US economy or spread around the globe.[1]

If President Donald Trump, another star Davos attendee, shared any of these worries, he kept them well hidden. The president expected a historically strong economy to carry him to a reelection victory in ten months, and he was quick to downplay any and all threats to his prospects, including the novel coronavirus. "It's one person coming in from China, and we have it under control. It's going to be fine," he told CNBC's Joe Kernen.[2]

Trump spent more time during the interview harping on the Federal Reserve for raising interest rates too fast in 2018. "It was just a big mistake, and they admit to it," Trump said, even though the Fed had made no such admission.

One week later, on January 28, Fed Chair Jay Powell and his colleagues gathered to convene their first Federal Open Market Committee meeting of the year. At the customary press conference after the two-day meeting ended, Powell reviewed the previous year, patting himself on the back for avoiding a recession. "There are grounds for what I would call 'cautious optimism' about the outlook now for the global economy," he said. "And then comes the coronavirus."

At the end of that week, as White House national security advisers raised concerns about the spreading virus, Trump issued a nationwide ban on the travel of noncitizens who had been in China within the last fourteen days and were not immediate family of US citizens or permanent residents.

On February 5, the Senate voted to acquit Trump of two articles of impeachment. The president, now as focused as ever on the fall campaign, called Powell a couple of days later to berate him for refusing to keep lowering rates.

The following Tuesday, February 11, Powell testified on Capitol Hill, indicating that the Fed had no plans to change interest rates from their current range between 1½ and 1¾ percent. The economy was a bit of a mixed bag—Chinese stocks had slumped at the start of the month after an extended Lunar New Year holiday ended, but US markets were still largely shrugging off the virus. The United States had watched menacing flu threats largely blow away over the past two decades, including in 2003 with SARS and again with the H1N1 flu in 2009.

Yet just nine days later, after gathering in Saudi Arabia with finance leaders of the Group of Twenty, Powell knew this one couldn't be shrugged off.

"Wake up!"

Normally the Fed meets every six weeks or so — usually more than enough time to assess how the economy is performing and to decide whether to change interest rates or not. In between these meetings, economists patiently gather data. But the economic situation was worsening much more rapidly than normal. Nonetheless, during a speech and question-and-answer session with private-sector economists on Tuesday, February 25 — the day after Powell returned from Saudi Arabia and the same day that Kudlow would describe the virus as "contained...pretty close to airtight" — Clarida stuck to a Fed script that was quickly finding itself past its expiration date. "It is still too soon to even speculate" about how the virus would change the economic outlook, he said.

One week earlier, Daleep Singh had left his job as a senior strategist at a Brazilian hedge fund to join the New York Fed as the head of its markets group. He had moved from Goldman Sachs to the Treasury in 2011, where he rose quickly through the ranks. Just in his mid-forties, Singh had contacts and ex-colleagues around the world. What he heard from them was unsettling. One contact in China told him that sales at Adidas were down 85 percent in mid-February, and that not a single Jaguar car had sold in China that month. Then Singh heard from a trader in London that sea-freight traffic there had hit all-time lows. Oil markets were weakening.

After Clarida's remarks that Tuesday, Singh's text-message inbox blew up with hate mail from his former colleagues in finance. *The Fed is totally disconnected from reality*, they said. *Wake up!* One closely watched indicator of volatility, the Chicago Board Options Exchange's volatility index, or VIX — also known as the "fear index" because of how it tracks investor anxiety — surged to 27.85, a level last seen during the market tantrum at the end of 2018. For weeks, markets had paid close attention to daily case counts in Wuhan, but otherwise brushed off worries about the virus. Starting in late February, however, a simple dashboard of daily reports illustrated how investors were rapidly bracing for a global event that would be far more menacing:

Date 2020	Covid-19 Cases	Covid-19 Deaths	Dow Jones Average	VIX Fear Index
Tuesday, February 25	10	0	27,081 (↓879)	27.85 (↑ 2.82)

At a press conference the next night, Trump announced that Vice President Mike Pence would head up the administration's coronavirus task force. But if this was an effort to project level-headed composure, the president quickly walked all over that message. After Dr. Anthony Fauci, the longtime director of the National Institute of Allergy and Infectious Diseases, conservatively explained to reporters why one of several promising vaccine candidates might not be available for at least a year, Trump offered his own fantasy. "It's a little like the regular flu that we have flu shots for, and we'll essentially have a flu shot for this in a fairly quick manner," he said, reminding Americans that the seasonal flu killed more than 20,000 people each year. "View this the same as the flu."

At that time, there were only 15 recorded cases of coronavirus in the United States. "The 15 within a couple of days is going to be down to close to zero," Trump said.

Date 2020	Covid-19 Cases	Covid-19 Deaths	Dow Jones Average	VIX Fear Index
Wednesday, February 26	15	2	26,957 (↓124)	27.56 (↑ .29)

"This is why we're here"

Shortly after she returned from Amsterdam that week, Fed governor Lael Brainard relayed to Powell her assessment that the virus was going to hit the US big-time. Powell agreed. Even if the rest of the government didn't quite realize yet what their role should be, Brainard and Powell found themselves increasingly aligned about the dangers ahead and the scale of the potential challenges. It was times like these when people really counted on the government to deliver, Brainard told Powell. "This is why we're here."

The daughter of an American diplomat, Brainard was born in Hamburg, Germany, and grew up on both sides of the Iron Curtain in Europe during the Cold War after her father took a post in Warsaw. She later cited the stark difference in living standards between Western Europe and communist Poland as having fostered her interest in economics. Brainard described life in Poland as grim, with high rates of alcoholism and an economy "suffocated under a heavy state apparatus."[3] The most successful parts of the economy were farming and small business enterprises that had "the least amount of red tape and the greatest role for individual initiative."[4]

Brainard graduated from Wesleyan University and Harvard, where she earned her PhD in economics in 1989. In 2009, the registered Democrat was tapped by Tim Geithner to serve as the Treasury's top diplomat. The office for her Treasury post had been restored to look as it did when President Andrew Johnson occupied it in 1865 while waiting for Abraham Lincoln's widow to leave the White House. Brainard accepted an appointment to be a Fed governor in 2014.

Some chafed at her impatient attitude and her reluctance to do the sometimes-dull administrative work that came with being a governor. Other staff initially regarded her as an apparatchik. Sometimes Brainard would retreat to her office during coffee breaks rather than mingle with other FOMC members. But as she settled into the job and listened to feedback, some coworkers noted a marked shift in her attitude. She established herself as someone with solid economic chops and keen instincts on how to set monetary policy. Once Powell became chair, she had taken on many of the low-key assignments that she had initially showed less interest in doing.

Powell's lack of formal training in economics and the record number of four vacancies on the board gave Brainard an opening to play a more influential role in policy than in her early years, when Janet Yellen was chair. Even though Brainard had frequently dissented on votes to ease financial regulations under Powell, they had more in common than outsiders realized. Both had very high expectations of themselves and the staff that worked for them, and they both excelled at digesting and synthesizing lots of information.

———

Powell figured that with such an infectious and disruptive virus, once there were six cases in New York City there might as well be 60 or 600. Schools and offices would close. How long the affliction would last was anyone's guess, but the hit to aggregate demand from all these people withdrawing from normal life would be enormous. His daughter's spring graduation from Princeton would probably be canceled. After talking to a friend who was a National Basketball Association executive, Powell wondered if there would be any professional games in three weeks.

Powell imagined an increasingly likely scenario: desolate shopping malls, kids home from school early, the TV playing reruns of past NBA finals. This was looking less like Y2K — the classic example of the government over-preparing for a calamity that never materialized — and more like a significant and sustained shock to the economy.

The Fed was facing two distinct economic problems. As workplaces shuttered and global supply chains became squeezed, the first was a jolt to the economy's capacity to produce goods and services, or its supply side. Lower interest rates couldn't do much about that. But the Fed could help alleviate the second problem, a demand shock, in which households and businesses hold off on spending or investment. Lower rates might not immediately boost demand, but they would help ease financial conditions for households and borrowers, which would reduce the risks of an abrupt financial shock.

At 4:45 p.m. on Thursday, February 27, Powell called Clarida, who had been meeting with faculty and students at Yale University, and for the first time discussed whether they needed to take some stronger action.

Date 2020	Covid-19 Cases	Covid-19 Deaths	Dow Jones Average	VIX Fear Index
Thursday, February 27	15	2	25,766 (↓1,191)	39.16 (↑11.6)

"Act as appropriate"

On the morning of Friday, February 28, after his weekly breakfast with Mnuchin but before a round of phone calls with his international counterparts, Powell decided to issue a statement signaling that the Fed was ready to cut rates. After conferring again with Clarida and Williams, they concluded it should say, in effect, "We are awake to what's happening." He began calling reserve-bank presidents to give them a heads-up. Nearly all supported it.

At 2:30 p.m. the Fed released Powell's terse, four-sentence policy statement. This had happened only once before — following the stock-market crash on Black Monday in October 1987. Although the fundamentals of the economy remain strong, "the coronavirus poses evolving risks to economic activity," the statement read. "We will use our tools and act as appropriate to support the economy."

There they were again — the words *act as appropriate*. The prior June, Powell had used those three words to put rate cuts on the table. Thomas Laubach, who as director of the Fed's monetary-affairs division was the most senior adviser to Powell on interest-rate policy, had warned that any such statement was likely to lead markets to expect a rate cut before the FOMC's next scheduled meeting, on March 17 and 18. Cutting rates in between meetings is rare and reserved for especially delicate moments, including during the 2008 financial crisis and after the 9/11 attacks. The Fed refers to them as *unscheduled meetings*, but the press inevitably would label them *emergency meetings*.

The unexpected attempt to calm investors led to a furious rally in the minutes before markets closed at 4 p.m., but by then the Dow had still fallen 12.4 percent — a drop of more than 3,500 points — for the week, the worst slump since the 2008 financial crisis. That afternoon in his office, Powell reviewed what the Fed's next steps would be if the central bank found itself with rates back at zero and the balance sheet growing again: head to the Hill, join forces with Mnuchin, and bang the table for fiscal relief.

North Carolina Congressman Patrick McHenry, who spoke periodically with Powell and Quarles in his capacity as the top Republican on the House Financial Services Committee, was struck by how the Fed — with no medical experts on its staff — was initially more alert to the problems brewing. "They were on the leading edge of the government in terms of awareness about what was coming," he said.

Date 2020	Covid-19 Cases	Covid-19 Deaths	Dow Jones Average	VIX Fear Index
Friday, February 28	15	4	25,409 (↓357)	40.11 (↑ .95)

If aliens invaded

After Pence took over the coronavirus task force, Mnuchin and Kudlow joined to provide perspectives on the economic implications of virus-mitigation measures. But Trump and Kudlow maintained that the Fed, not the rest of the government, could provide whatever economic response was necessary — a position they would stick with through early March. Their stance struck Fed officials as a dangerous and silly one. If swaths of the economy shut down, interest-rate cuts would provide only the most marginal benefit.

Moreover, the Fed's rate was still historically low, in a range from 1½ to 1¾ percent after the three cuts that officials had made from July to October 2019. In each of the past two downturns, the Fed had had room to cut by five percentage points before hitting zero, which was nowhere near possible now.

In Hong Kong, the government unveiled a one-time cash payment of $1,284 to every resident after measures to halt the coronavirus tipped the city's economy into a recession. The White House, by contrast, had given its blessing to an $8 billion funding bill working its way through

Congress. Even though this was more than three times the $2.5 billion the administration had requested, it was a comically small amount. The US economy generates about $2 billion an hour, and this paltry sum amounted to $24 per American.

When he got off the plane from Riyadh the previous Monday, Powell wondered whether they would have to cut rates at their March meeting. After releasing his four-line statement just five days later, on Friday, he wondered if they could wait even another nineteen days. Time was speeding up. Everything that had happened over the past week had confirmed his worst fears about what was unfolding. If the Fed was going to have to make an emergency cut, it might as well go now, Powell concluded. The only question was how to sequence it.

As it happened, the US was taking its turn in 2020 as chair of the Group of Seven nations. (The other members were Canada, France, Germany, Italy, Japan, and the United Kingdom.) Mnuchin told Powell that weekend that he would convene a meeting of G7 finance ministers by telephone early on the morning of Tuesday, March 3. Powell decided that if the Fed was going to cut, it made sense to lower rates in connection with that meeting. When word of the G7 call leaked out on Monday, investors raced to conclude that there would be big fireworks — the kind of coordinated rate cut by central banks that had occurred in October 2008. The Dow surged nearly 1,294 points, or 5.1 percent, the biggest one-day percentage gain since March 2009 and the biggest point advance on record.

At a meeting with pharmaceutical executives at the White House that Monday afternoon, Trump brushed off a question about whether the White House should be readying any economic stimulus by pointing to the big gain in the Dow that was underway. But Mnuchin didn't have any fireworks planned, and neither did many of the other finance ministers or central bankers. After all, only the central banks in the Anglosphere — Canada, Australia, and the United Kingdom — had any real room to cut rates.

That night at 7 p.m., Powell and around twenty Fed officials in Washington convened in the Fed's Special Library, the small, dark conference room lined with bookcases across the hall from the big boardroom. They sat in front of videoconference screens showing reserve-bank presidents who called in from across the country. Cleveland Fed President Loretta Mester, in London for a speech, joined by phone at midnight local time. Randal Quarles called in from the Fed's branch in Salt Lake City, Utah, where he spent his weekends.

The staff gave a quick overview of how the economic outlook was deteriorating. Stacey Tevlin, director of the research-and-statistics division, presented a new bad-case scenario that projected a modest recession with a rise in the unemployment rate to 6 percent. It would prove a vast understatement. There was plenty of precedent for dealing with the failure of a big bank or hedge fund, a surge in layoffs, or a natural disaster that temporarily pinched growth in one region of the country — but virtually none for a coast-to-coast infectious disease. It was hard for economists and other policymakers to grasp just how suddenly and dramatically the economy was slamming to a halt.

Powell explained his reasoning for calling the FOMC together. He had hoped they would've been able to wait until at least their April meeting to cut rates, but that wasn't a reasonable expectation any longer. The number of confirmed coronavirus cases in the United States had surpassed fifty across more than seven states, and eleven deaths had been confirmed. The virus was a material risk to the economic outlook, he said, and the Fed needed to send a clear signal that it understood the significance of what was happening and that it would move decisively to counter a tightening of financial conditions.

Then Powell unveiled his proposal — a half-point cut in the federal-funds rate, to a range between 1 percent and 1¼ percent — to be announced at 10 a.m. the next morning, a few hours after the G7 call. Powell felt the odds were still decent that the US could avoid a recession, but the Fed needed to do whatever it could to improve those odds. *The world is looking to us to do this*, said Powell, *and it's the right thing to do right now.*

A couple of reserve-bank presidents cautioned against overreacting. When the Fed does something surprising or unusual, there's a potential to send a signal that shakes rather than inspires confidence by fueling a *what-does-the-Fed-know-that-we-don't?* dynamic on Wall Street.

Normally, Fed officials don't spend much time worrying about this because everyone generally has access to the same official economic data as do the economists at the Fed. But now medical developments, not economic data, were driving decisions. Things were moving so quickly that misinformation abounded. Memos circulated on Wall Street that the Fed was receiving confidential CDC briefings (it wasn't) and that the Fed had a better picture of the virus threat than the public (it didn't). *Had it been up to me,* thought Quarles, *a half-point cut was too much.* But he stuck by a promise he had made to share his candid advice privately while supporting whatever Powell chose to do publicly.

The meeting lasted around an hour, and the vote was unanimous. For procedural reasons, Powell waited to cast his vote until the next morning so they could withhold their announcement until after the G7 call. A few hours after the Monday meeting ended, at 10:30 p.m. in New York, Australia's central bank announced a quarter-point cut in its interest rate to ½ percent, a record low.

At 1:30 a.m., Trump flagged the decision on his Twitter account in another grievance-laden diatribe against the Fed. "Jerome Powell led Federal Reserve has called it wrong from day one. Sad!"

Date 2020	Covid-19 Cases	Covid-19 Deaths	Dow Jones Average	VIX Fear Index
Monday, March 2	72	11	26,703 (↑1,294)	33.42 (↓ 6.69)

On Tuesday, Mnuchin's G7 call began at 7 a.m. and lasted just twenty-three minutes, ending with a perfunctory statement that pledged readiness to take action. For markets, it was a big nothingburger. Mnuchin was testifying in front of a congressional panel at 10 a.m. when the Fed announced its rate cut, which sent whispers of *Holy shit!* through the committee room on Capitol Hill. Mnuchin, who had been given a heads-up about the half-point rate cut that morning by Powell, looked surprised as he held up his iPhone displaying a breaking news article on the decision.

At the same time, Clarida was at a meeting of G7 deputy finance ministers and governors in a windowless hotel conference room on Baltimore's waterfront. It would turn out to be the last in-person gathering of international finance officials for more than a year. Clarida read the statement to the assembled ministers as soon as the Fed released it, and a soft gasp filled the room.

Since Alan Greenspan had begun announcing Fed rate changes in 1994, the FOMC had approved rate cuts in between scheduled meetings on only four other occasions — during the collapse of the gigantic hedge fund Long Term Capital Management in 1998, ahead of the 2001 recession, and twice during the 2008 financial crisis.

Steven Englander, a Yale-trained PhD economist who headed research on currency-market trading at Standard Chartered, was on the Asian investment bank's New York trading floor when the announcement hit the newswires. "It was a 'holy fuck' moment for markets," he said. "People were saying, 'What's going on here? Their meeting is two weeks away. There's nothing obviously bad, and they're doing something they've only done before in emergencies.'"

Markets rallied for about fifteen minutes after the announcement. A few European central bankers teased St. Louis Fed President James Bullard: "If aliens invaded the planet," they joked, "Washington's first response would be to cut interest rates."

"More easing and cutting!" Trump declared in a tweet around 10:45 that morning.

At a hastily arranged press conference fifteen minutes later, Powell explained that no matter the immediate market reaction, he felt compelled to act to prevent borrowing costs for large companies and small businesses from widening further. With negative headlines about the virus likely to grow more alarming, the best the Fed could hope to do was to short-circuit the potential for financial markets to seize up. "A rate cut will not reduce the rate of infection. It won't fix a broken supply chain. We get that," Powell said.

By day's end, whatever optimism had greeted the Fed's cut was followed by fear. The ten-year Treasury yield dipped below 1 percent for the first time ever as investors sought its safe haven. Stocks gave up more than half of the prior day's record gains, closing down nearly 800 points. The drop revealed the limitations of interest-rate cuts and underscored Powell's view of the recklessness of Trump's let-the-Fed-deal-with-it stance.

Powell was right — defending against a pandemic demands a wide range of reactions, from public-health policies to Congress to governors and mayors. But some commentators deemed the Fed's move panicky: too much, too soon. Larry Summers, who had served as Bill Clinton's Treasury secretary and a senior economic adviser to Barack Obama, argued that the central bank's overreaction was scaring people more than the virus was. "They would have been much better advised to move more slowly," he said in a television interview. "Sometimes a weapon in reserve is more potent than a weapon fired off to no great effect."[5]

Back in Baltimore, the deputy finance ministers wrapped up their day's meeting with a tense and glum dinner. Officials at the Bank of Canada, who were preparing to cut interest rates at a regularly scheduled meeting on Wednesday, had considered moving their announcement up by twenty-four hours to coincide with the Fed's decision but decided against it to avoid signaling a bigger emergency. Tobias Adrian, a senior IMF official, pulled Clarida aside to offer his own two cents: "You guys know if this gets any worse, you're going to have to do a hell of a lot more," he said.

Date 2020	Covid-19 Cases	Covid-19 Deaths	Dow Jones Average	VIX Fear Index
Tuesday, March 3	114	14	25,917 (↓786)	36.82 (↑3.4)

Preparing for the worst

Just nine days after Powell returned from Riyadh, the Fed — and the country, for that matter — was deep in unknown territory. Policymakers' personal lives would soon be upended in ways that are uncommon during an economic crisis. During the 2008 financial crisis, the Fed's governors and presidents didn't get much sleep, but they weren't worried about family members or colleagues being hospitalized — or even dying — from a little-known, extremely contagious virus. They couldn't do a thing to improve the shaky public-health response or to mitigate the impact that an invisible contagion might have in driving fear among investors or consumers. After a year of wondering how Trump's impulsive policy-by-tweet might affect the economy, they now had to worry about his coronavirus-denial mindset.

The slow federal government response alarmed Boston Fed President Eric Rosengren, the longest-tenured of the twelve reserve-bank presidents. He had been getting updates on the medical situation from a former Boston Fed director who was a hospital executive, among other local experts. Rosengren had also been hearing concerns from his daughter, a doctor in Connecticut. A late-February strategy meeting for senior managers at the Boston-area biotech firm Biogen Inc. turned into a super-spreader event. Two weeks after the meeting, the state's health department reported that seventy patients presumed or confirmed to be infected in Massachusetts had links to the Biogen meeting.

All this grim news led Rosengren to begin stocking up on N95 masks, nonperishable food, and other supplies for his family. The Boston Fed ordered employees not to travel to a growing list of countries with outbreaks, guidance that went beyond the CDC's directives. At a meeting on Wednesday, March 4, with Boston Mayor Marty Walsh, Rosengren told Walsh that the mayor would be forced to shut down the city "pretty soon," which seemed to surprise the mayor.[6]

Rosengren's bleak health outlook colored a similarly miserable economic forecast. "When you start sending everybody home, it's pretty clear that's going to have a big ripple effect on the economy," Rosengren explained later. "My own views were that we were going into a very serious problem. If you're allowing people on planes, it's just a matter of time until the virus hits our shores. And so we should have been very concerned."

That Friday, Rosengren joined five other reserve-bank presidents at a conference in New York — though virus fears moved him to skip out on a dinner the night before. He told Boston Fed employees to start working from home the next Monday. During Rosengren's conference talk, he warned that the public-health impact of the coronavirus would overwhelm the Fed's traditional tool kit. So Rosengren floated a provocative idea: changing the Fed's governing charter in order to give the central bank the latitude to directly buy a broader range of assets, including corporate bonds.

Fed officials are about as receptive to amending the Federal Reserve Act as they are to a root canal without anesthesia. The expanded capacities might improve their ability to execute monetary policy, but opening up the act meant Congress might shoehorn in all sorts of other changes the Fed wouldn't want. The existing law restricts the central bank to buying Treasury securities, government-guaranteed mortgage bonds, and short-term municipal debt. But central banks in Japan and Europe, where rates had been pinned near zero for years, had already embarked on larger bond-buying programs, including corporate debt.

It was a headline-grabbing proposal. Rosengren had opposed all three of the Fed's rate cuts the year before out of concern that lower rates were fueling aggressive risk-taking that could inflate dangerous bubbles. Now here he was standing before a handful of other reserve-bank presidents, arguing for broad new authorities to backstop lending markets. *Wow,* thought Chicago Fed President Charles Evans, who was sitting in the audience. *That's different.*

Rosengren later offered his rationale. "It was clear we were going to hit the zero lower bound. It was clear we were going to do QE [quantitative easing] in some size. And at that time, it was already clear that the most efficient thing would be if we could actually purchase other types of securities."

Events were proving his point in real time. Despite a positive report on February employment that morning, the benchmark ten-year Treasury yield dropped to another all-time low of 0.7 percent. After the 2008 crisis, the Fed had stimulated the economy by pushing long-term rates lower — an approach that wouldn't be very effective if the rates were already almost at zero.

Rosengren also included a plea in his speech for Congress and the White House to step up. "Maybe we're asking monetary policy to do too much," he said. "In a very low-interest-rate world, we should spend a lot more time thinking about how fiscal policy could do its job."

Date 2020	Covid-19 Cases	Covid-19 Deaths	Dow Jones Average	VIX Fear Index
Friday, March 6	445	26	25,864 (↓257)	41.94 (↑ 2.32)

By the weekend, at least six US governors had declared states of emergency, with more than 400 confirmed cases across thirty states and twenty-six deaths. Stanford University said it would move its classes to virtual instruction. Worse, testing capacity was falling dramatically short of demand, with just 1,583 tests completed by the CDC and 5,861 including public-health labs. By contrast, South Korea, with one-sixth the population of the US, was conducting 10,000 tests *per day*.[7] One consequence was that there were far more cases of the virus than were being detected. Americans were watching confirmed case numbers in horror when, in reality, the situation was significantly worse.

While leaving an especially sobering meeting of the president's coronavirus task force that weekend, Mnuchin turned to Kudlow and said, "This thing's coming here, and it's coming hard and big."

Kudlow looked him in the eye and said, "I'm afraid you're right."

Chapter Eight

MELTDOWN

On Sunday, March 8, Dallas Fed President Robert Kaplan took his five-year-old son to his first basketball game — the hometown Mavericks played the Indiana Pacers in front of 20,000 fans at the American Airlines Center. The Mavs lost a close one, 112-109. Three days later the entire league shut down — neither team would play again until the end of July.

As the game ended, the Dallas Fed's top energy analyst called Kaplan with a heads-up: Russia and Saudi Arabia had failed to agree on the oil-production cuts the market had anticipated that weekend. It was horrible timing. The resulting oil-price war was sure to push indebted energy drillers across the US mid-continent to the brink of bankruptcy amid growing tension on Wall Street.

Until that point, markets had operated relatively smoothly despite big daily swings in the price and volume of stocks and bonds being traded. As coronavirus restrictions began hitting workplaces, a new fear was in the air: How would Wall Street banks and dealers function as they began moving traders to remote locations or even sent them home altogether? The oil-price war essentially handed a fifty-pound weight to financial markets already hanging by a thread.

"If we only had to deal with covid, it would have been, as we found, very challenging. But people would've had some time," said Kaplan, who had spent twenty-three years at Goldman Sachs and nine years at Harvard Business School before he became Dallas Fed president in 2015.

"What that Sunday-night decision [by the Russians and Saudis] did is accelerate the stress to now because energy is a key part of the credit market and the surprise announcement" rippled through credit markets.

With global demand for crude oil plunging as more of the world joined China in locking down, oil-producing nations faced two choices: reduce the amount of oil they pump to support existing prices, or continue to pump and slash prices. The Saudis chose the latter as part of a gambit to steal market share from Moscow. Fears of a glut immediately cascaded through Asian financial markets when they opened late Sunday.

Strains multiply

At 6:15 the next morning, New York Fed President John Williams left his downtown Manhattan apartment and headed over to his office to join a virtual conference of central bankers. Normally the meeting would have taken place in Basel, Switzerland, but travel restrictions had shut that down. Powell joined from his office in Washington. They all braced themselves for what was about to hit — which proved to be every bit as bad as they anticipated.

Because so many oil companies had issued lots of junk bonds — debt with less-than-investment-grade ratings — the stress on energy companies was never going to stay confined to their industry. Fund managers might be stuck with billions of dollars in virtually unsellable energy-firm bonds. As a result, the borrowing costs for hundreds of companies that financed with junk debt would go up.

Due to the large amounts of debt that companies had taken on to pull oil out of the ground, the price war unleashed a wave of selling on Wall Street that went well beyond energy companies. US stocks fell hard enough at the 9:30 a.m. opening bell to trigger the circuit breaker — a cooling-off period devised to prevent a rerun of 1987's Black Monday market avalanche — for the second time in twenty-three years. Trading was frozen for fifteen minutes, after which the rapid sell-off continued. Crude oil prices slid 30 percent. The yield on the ten-year Treasury dropped below 0.5 percent, another all-time low.

The financial panic created a global dash for US dollars. At 12:15 p.m.

that Monday, Williams and Lorie Logan, the New York Fed's veteran market authority, dialed into a meeting to discuss with Powell, Clarida, and staffers in Washington what was happening in the markets and to outline next steps. Logan's team was seeing increased selling of US Treasury securities by central banks from Brazil to Mexico, which were racing to raise dollars that could be used to defend their currencies. European central banks and the Bank of Japan — which had strong national currencies — were also racing for dollars to make sure *their* commercial lenders could meet local demands for the US currency.

Powell and his top lieutenants separated proposals for dealing with the panic into three buckets based on how quickly they could be enacted. The first bucket consisted of making more of the short-term loans known as repurchase agreements, or "repo loans," very rapidly. Basically, the Fed lends cash to approved broker-dealers, such as JPMorgan, Barclays, Wells Fargo, and Citigroup. These big banks then lend the money to hedge funds and other institutions in exchange for super-safe collateral such as US government debt. This exchange adds a special type of electronic cash, known as reserves, into the financial system. The additional cash in the economy is supposed to grease the wheels of finance.

As part of its reversal of the balance-sheet runoff in 2019, the Fed had started supplying more repo loans that September after concluding the central bank had drained too many reserves from the system. Now they contemplated launching a more aggressive operation — more lending with twenty-eight-day terms, instead of the traditional overnight or two-week loans.

The second bucket was for items that could not be announced immediately but might be feasible to deploy later in the week. This included what are known as US dollar "swap lines," under which the Fed lends dollars to foreign central banks for fixed periods. Those central banks can then lend to their own local banks to repay dollar-denominated obligations. In exchange, the Fed would receive an equivalent loan of the foreign currencies. The swap lines would help slow the international dash for dollars.

The third bucket contained proposals that would not be ready to announce or implement anytime soon.

The final agenda item posed the question: "Does the FOMC need to do anything before next Wednesday?" Wednesday, March 18, would mark the conclusion of the scheduled two-day FOMC meeting. The idea of doing a second emergency rate cut after the prior week's half-point cut had no precedent. Powell and Clarida were hoping they wouldn't have to seriously consider that option.

The Dow closed down 7.8 percent that Monday, falling 2,013 points. It was the worst percentage decline since 2008, and the first time the index had ever lost more than 2,000 points. All eleven sectors in the S&P 500 were down, led by energy, which slid 20 percent. The eleven-year bull market in stocks was nearly over. Oil prices dropped the most since the Gulf War in January 1991. The thirty-year Treasury yield fell below 1 percent for the first time, settling at 0.938 percent. The VIX surged at one point that day to 62, its highest level since December 2008.

Around 5 p.m., Powell sent Clarida and Williams a note alerting them that sensible Fed watchers and other analysts outside the building were projecting a rate cut to zero before March 18. Powell said that wasn't his inclination, but it showed how rapidly the ground was shifting.

If there was a silver lining to the deepening rout, it was that markets were forcing Trump and lawmakers on Capitol Hill to take the potential economic fallout more seriously. At a tense Oval Office meeting that Monday, White House advisers debated how to design a relief package, while Trump unleashed a scathing tirade at Treasury Secretary Steven Mnuchin for not doing more to pressure Powell to cut rates.[1]

Date 2020	Covid-19 Cases	Covid-19 Deaths	Dow Jones Average	VIX Fear Index
Monday, March 9	1,061	35	23,851 (↓2,013)	54.46 (↑12.52)

Getting fiscal

The following day, Trump, Kudlow, and Mnuchin joined Senate Republicans for their weekly policy lunch. The president had seized on the idea of passing a ninety-day moratorium on payroll taxes, which would allow employers to stop withholding the 6.2 percent tax that represents the employee's share of Social Security taxes. The idea went nowhere. "I've got to think about that," said South Carolina Senator Lindsey Graham, a staunch Trump ally. "The money that that costs, could it be better applied to sectors of the economy that are hit?"[2]

Senate Majority Leader Mitch McConnell announced Mnuchin would negotiate on behalf of Republicans with House Speaker Nancy Pelosi, who the president was refusing to speak with since the impeachment weeks earlier. The president was becoming a bystander in the response to the oncoming economic crisis. After the meeting, he gave a vague appraisal to reporters: "There's a great feeling about doing a lot of things."

The previous week, Jason Furman, a former top economic adviser to President Obama who now taught at Harvard, had written a column in *The Wall Street Journal* making the case for a big stimulus package — far beyond what Democrats or Republicans were contemplating. The centerpiece of his comprehensive $350 billion proposal called for one-time payments of $1,000 for all taxpaying US citizens or residents, and $500 for every child. A top House Democratic lawmaker invited Furman to brief the entire Democratic caucus on Wednesday, March 11.

Furman's concern over the virus had only escalated. Harvard had announced the night before that students would move to all-remote instruction. Furman found himself in despair over the comparatively leisurely attitude that greeted him among Democrats on Capitol Hill. Some lawmakers told him they agreed something big needed to be done, and that's why they would bring forward an infrastructure bill — in May, two months away. *Everyone's blaming the virus,* said another lawmaker, *but isn't all this concern really about OPEC and the stock market?*

To hammer home his point that Congress would need to spend much more money, Furman led with epidemiology, not economics: *Virus infections are doubling every three days in the United States and Europe,* he explained. *The US is maybe a week behind Europe, at best. Look at the curve in Italy and Spain,* he said. *It's growing exponentially.*

Unless Congress stepped up, Furman told the lawmakers, he thought what loomed was scarier than — and likely to be worse than — the financial crisis of 2008. Addressing Oregon's Ron Wyden, the top Democrat on the tax-writing Senate Finance Committee, Furman asked him: *Don't you understand that 500,000 people are going to die?*

History would prove him correct. But nobody in the room was ready to believe it.

The legislators were shaken when Furman finished, but after he left, Pelosi seemed to shoot down his idea of sending out checks. The massive fiscal-policy stimulus that Furman imagined would not be arriving immediately. A combination of political dysfunction, inability to grasp the severity of the problem, and overreliance on the Fed's ability to manage economic problems meant the ball was still in Powell's court.

Date 2020	Covid-19 Cases	Covid-19 Deaths	Dow Jones Average	VIX Fear Index
Tuesday, March 10	1,497	37	25,018 (↑ 1,167)	47.30 (↓ 7.16)

The panic begins

The whole point of global financial markets is to move money to where it's needed, when it's needed. And US Treasury securities (commonly called Treasuries), which are backed by the full faith and credit of the world's superpower, are the ultimate "risk-free" asset. They are used as a benchmark to set the prices of tens of trillions of dollars of other financial instruments. They're used to finance the US government. They're used as an investment and hedging instrument. And they're used by the Fed to implement monetary policy. As a result, one of the most fundamental obligations of the central bank is to make sure that this risk-free asset is completely liquid — meaning investors can trade it for cash virtually instantaneously, anytime they wish.

The safety of Treasuries usually makes financial markets self-stabilizing. Most of the time, when investors get bad economic news, they buy Treasuries. As other investors follow the traditional flight to safety, bond prices rise. Treasuries are the perfect place to weather storms, a hedge that makes money. But on Wednesday, March 11, that traditional relationship began to unravel, threatening to unleash a catastrophic breakdown through a much broader set of funding markets. If Treasuries aren't safe, a global financial panic is virtually guaranteed.

That morning, news broke that Boeing planned to make use of the full amount of a $13.8 billion lending facility — a prearranged credit limit that the company had not come close to exhausting — as soon as Friday. Air travel had ground to a halt, and Boeing and the airlines were facing the near-total collapse of their revenues. Investors took the announcement as an act of desperation, sending the plane maker's shares plunging. Wynn Resorts and Hilton Hotels followed Boeing's move, converting their credit to cash in case they needed it to maintain operations. As revenue vanished, more companies began to wonder if they would have access to new financing, so they began borrowing from their existing credit lines to sock away dollars to pay workers and bills.

"Typically, we think about [borrowing from] these types of corporate facilities as having real negative stigma," said Beth Hammack, the Goldman Sachs treasurer responsible for overseeing the bank's $1 trillion balance sheet. But the emerging pandemic was different. This, said Hammack, "was a moment where if you were a corporate treasurer, you seemed to be almost negligent if you weren't drawing on those facilities, and so that put a strain on the banking system, as well as on the corporate bond markets."[3]

With so many companies tapping into their credit lines at the same time, Wall Street banks were facing cash pressure. Analysts at the New York Fed saw the availability of term funding — loans between banks and other financial institutions of more than a few days — begin to dry up. There just wasn't enough cash to go around.

In Dallas, Robert Kaplan was meeting with a group of investment executives when he stepped out of the room to speak by phone with the head of a large private-equity firm. News had just crossed the wires that private-equity firms, including Blackstone and the Carlyle Group, were directing their portfolio companies to draw on their lines.

"What are you doing?" Kaplan asked one of the executives. "Is this true? You understand it's all over the press."

The executive sheepishly said they hadn't issued a formal directive, and they certainly didn't intend for any such instruction to spill into public view. *Too late*, Kaplan thought. *The damage is done here, and you've created a panic.*

Generally speaking, companies draw on these backup lending sources only when they're panicked about day-to-day cash needs, such as making payroll.

Bank CFOs were nervous about what was happening, too. If everybody draws down their loans at the same time, banks must scramble to bolster their balance sheets. For the week ending March 11, banks reported a $27 billion increase in new commercial and industrial loans, or a 1 percent increase, nearly all of which reflected companies drawing down their lines. Such lending jumped by another $142 billion, or 6 percent, for the week after that — the largest weekly increase since the Fed starting publishing such data in 1973.

What seemed prudent created fear. And as in all the worst financial panics, the fear quickly became a self-fulfilling cycle.

Investors were soon selling everything they could. Bond prices were falling in tandem with stocks, sending yields higher on longer-dated government bonds. Investors' actions spoke for them: *We need cash so urgently, we're going to sell our Treasuries.* During the scramble for dollars, Treasuries were no longer serving as the market's traditional shock absorbers, leading portfolio managers to sell whatever they could. The dash for dollars fed on itself.

"There was nowhere to hide. There was no safe haven," said Daleep Singh, head of the New York Fed's markets desk. "What was truly the most frightening part of 2020 for me was how Treasury yields were spiking higher at the time that equity markets were plummeting. This was an un-hedge-able risk from a market perspective."

Unwinding trades

There was another stress on the Treasury market: the breakdown in a popular arbitrage trade by hedge funds called the "basis trade." The trade exploited tiny pricing differences in the interest-rate market, and firms used lots of borrowed money in the overnight "repo" markets to make these trades profitable. It was normally very low-risk. But the unusual market volatility had turned the trades into big money losers, leading hedge funds to liquidate their positions. Hedge funds faced margin calls, which meant they had to post more collateral, and this triggered even more selling of Treasury securities at the worst possible time. Federal Reserve economists later pinned these trades as responsible for nearly $173 billion in Treasury sales in March.[4] Investors who might normally have taken advantage of the arbitrage opportunities created by such extreme dislocations couldn't do so because they were unable to borrow money to place new trades.

As the waves of Treasury selling initially began, staffers at the New York Fed saw a potential recurrence of what had happened in the repo market the prior September. The Fed's next step was to expand—again—the amount of repo loans it would make available. That afternoon, Logan's team sharply boosted the total amounts it would lend to $500 billion. Even if markets didn't immediately take the Fed up on the larger volume of loans being offered, they figured, providing clarity to investors about the central bank's intentions to stabilize markets might boost confidence. But the announcement made little difference that day. Money couldn't get through the pipes.

The Fed wasn't alone in failing to soothe markets. In London, the Bank of England made an emergency rate cut that morning, bringing interest rates to the lowest level in the bank's 325-year history. The cut was announced alongside a wider package that included a big government-spending boost.

"This is a big package. It is a big deal," said the bank's governor, Mark Carney, whose term was set to expire four days later. Stocks on

London's FTSE 100 initially rallied, but only briefly, then closed at a four-year low.

Banking bandwidth

David Solomon, Goldman's chief executive, began March 11 bumping elbows — instead of shaking hands — with lawmakers on Capitol Hill, where he addressed a bipartisan coalition that had lobbied the White House for more relief funds. "He didn't sugarcoat it," said Congressman Josh Gottheimer, a New Jersey Democrat. "But the big picture was comforting."[5]

Solomon delivered a similar message in a meeting with bank executives in the White House Cabinet Room that afternoon. "We'll get through this, but it's going to require some navigation on the part of all of us," he told the president. The CEOs took turns encouraging Trump to provide more relief — for the temporarily unemployed, for small businesses, and for the health-care sector.

Bank of America CEO Brian Moynihan put a positive spin on his sales pitch. "Between testing and building up the hospitals.... If we can take care of those things, this thing will crack pretty quickly," he said.

Was the message getting through to Trump? He nodded his agreement, then parroted the part of Moynihan's observation he liked: "If we get rid of the problem quickly, everything solves itself. We don't need stimulus."

The meeting broke up at 4 p.m. Executives checked their phones to see that the Dow had closed down another 5 percent. Having suffered a 20 percent decline since the February 12 high of 29,511, the eleven-year bull market that began after the 2008 financial crisis was now officially history. Since its inception in 1896, the Dow had never gone from an all-time high to a bear market in such a short span. More ominously, bond prices had also fallen in line with stocks, sending yields on the thirty-year Treasury to 1.49 percent from 1.3 percent the day before and from 0.98 percent on Monday. Citigroup's stock dropped 8.6 percent.

During a 5 p.m. conference call with Powell and Williams, Clarida flagged a Bloomberg story that said the unwinding of the basis trades was intensifying the unusual strains in the Treasury market. There's a kernel of truth there, he said. Even though Clarida thought he was familiar with that whole corner of the rate-arbitrage market, his initial reaction was that the unwinding trades would blow over in two days. In New York, Logan and Williams began preparing to sharply ramp up the cheap-money repo loans the Fed would make available the next day in the hope that banks would begin moving more cash through the system.

Locking down

Before the afternoon Cabinet Room meeting with the banking executives, Mnuchin found himself on the losing side of a debate in front of the president in the Oval Office over whether to halt European travel to the United States. Earlier that day, the World Health Organization had declared a global pandemic. Deborah Birx — an Army doctor and former US global AIDS coordinator who had recently been tapped as the coronavirus task-force coordinator — argued that every case stopped from entering the US would prevent new clusters of hundreds of cases.

Mnuchin argued strenuously against such a ban. "This will create a depression," he warned. "It's going to crush the airlines. It's going to crush Boeing!" Mnuchin continued, "Forget about ball games! Forget about campaign rallies!"[6] The Treasury secretary, who preferred to be called "Steven," was the only person making these arguments, even if others in the room were privately sympathetic.

"So it's everybody versus you, Steve," Trump said.

As the meeting ran beyond its allotted hour, they reconvened in the Cabinet Room, with Pence leading the discussion. Birx demanded to see Mnuchin's data. "I have the data to show we're going to go well above a quarter-million deaths, if we're lucky," she said. "We'll be at 250,000 deaths if we take strong action, now. What data do you have?"

Mnuchin was grasping for some kind of plan that would avoid such an overreaction. *Couldn't we protect the elderly and at-risk populations, sequester them from everyone else?* Others in the room dismissed the notion out of hand. *How are you going to do that — put them in hotels?* Someone chimed in, "Isn't that a little bit like putting them on cruise ships? How's that going?"

Anthony Fauci had warned that things were about to get much, much worse, according to an account in *The New Yorker:* "There's no place in America where it's business as usual. By the time you mitigate today, we're three weeks late."[7] In a bad flu season, 60,000 Americans might die. Now they were looking at a virus with a mortality rate twenty times greater than that.

Trump reconvened the task force after the meeting with the bankers to discuss how he would break the news. Mnuchin had been dispatched to notify the CEOs of the major US airlines about the newest travel ban. At 9 p.m. that night, during a rare and somber Oval Office address, Trump said he would ask Congress to take emergency action so Americans "impacted by the virus can stay home without fear of financial hardship." But the only part anyone remembered was his announcement of a thirty-day ban on people *and cargo* coming from Europe, which would begin that Friday at midnight. The cargo ban was stunning because it meant that some of the $1 trillion in annual trade with Europe would have to be paused. Futures markets tumbled. Aides quickly corrected the president to note the ban didn't include restrictions on US citizens. Trump also issued a correction to his speech on Twitter an hour later to say the ban didn't apply to cargo.

The Utah Jazz and Oklahoma City Thunder had been set to tip off at the Chesapeake Energy Arena in downtown Oklahoma City an hour before Trump addressed the nation. After a thirty-seven-minute delay, a voice came over the loudspeaker to say the game had been postponed: "Take your time in leaving the arena tonight and do so in an orderly fashion. We are all safe."

Fans would later learn that Jazz center Rudy Gobert had tested positive for the virus. Less than an hour after the game's postponement, the

NBA announced the entire season was being suspended indefinitely. The next day, Disneyland said it would close on Saturday. The theme park had done so only twice in its sixty-five years: once after the 1963 assassination of President John F. Kennedy and again after the terrorist attacks of September 11, 2001.

America was locking down.

Date 2020	Covid-19 Cases	Covid-19 Deaths	Dow Jones Average	VIX Fear Index
Wednesday, March 11	1,915	43	23,553 (↓1,465)	53.90 (↑6.6)

Chapter Nine

TURNING THE KNOBS TO 11

E very week, Treasury Secretary Steven Mnuchin and Jay Powell had a standing breakfast meeting that alternated between their respective official dining rooms. Over the past two years, Powell had heard over and over — not directly from Mnuchin — how Trump's tempest over the Fed spilled back onto the secretary, whom Trump blamed for recommending Powell. Trump's dressing down of the Treasury secretary had become an Oval Office routine before the pandemic. Through it all, Mnuchin had never come to Powell and asked him for a favor to help appease the president's concerns. As far as Powell was concerned, Mnuchin had had his back through it all. That had allowed for a greater degree of trust in their relationship than would be apparent publicly.

On the morning of Thursday, March 12, the usually punctual Mnuchin was running late. At 8 a.m. he was sitting outside the Eccles Building in an idling black SUV with tinted windows, hashing out the contours of the next virus relief package on a phone call with House Speaker Nancy Pelosi.

Mnuchin knew Pelosi to be a shrewd and unflappable negotiator. He also recognized she had helped the Bush administration steer its way through an unpopular bank bailout at the height of the 2008 financial crisis. And now Mnuchin, the son of a successful New York banker, and Pelosi, the daughter of a Baltimore political patriarch, were responsible for putting together the government's response to the spreading crisis. After the Senate GOP meeting with Trump had flopped, the president had delegated responsibility to Mnuchin, with Senate Majority Leader Mitch McConnell's grudging acquiescence.

The incipient market meltdown gave fresh urgency to Mnuchin and Pelosi's effort. They had spoken twice on Wednesday about the parameters of what was becoming a $192 billion aid package that included free coronavirus testing, increased funding for food stamps, and fourteen-day paid sick leave for workers affected by the pandemic. Their morning call would be the first of eight between the two on Thursday, with Mnuchin also regularly updating House Republican leaders and Trump.

Pelosi hadn't met with the president since the prior autumn, when she stormed out of a foreign policy meeting at the White House after Trump hurled insults at the Democratic leader. Trump frequently derided her in public as "Crazy Nancy," but their feud had reached a new low in February. Trump, livid over his impeachment by the House and fresh off a Senate acquittal, refused to shake her hand at his State of the Union speech. Standing behind Trump afterward, Pelosi tore up her ceremonial copy of his remarks in front of the packed chamber. The icy relations between Trump and Pelosi contributed to concerns in financial markets that the urgently needed fiscal relief might be slow to materialize, if it came at all.

If Congress and the White House were going to get anywhere responding to the looming economic disaster, it would ride on Mnuchin and Pelosi.

Like Pelosi, Powell was persona non grata with the president, but he had a constructive relationship with Mnuchin. Once Powell and Mnuchin finally sat down to coffee, fruit, and yogurt that morning, their discussion turned to worst-case contingency plans. During the 2008 financial crisis, Ben Bernanke had broken the seal on a little-used but powerful provision from Section 13, subsection 3 of the Fed's charter. This provision, dubbed *13(3)*, allowed the central bank to lend broadly during a crisis if five of the seven Fed governors vote in favor of creating such a lending facility. The Fed can invoke this authority only if it finds "unusual and exigent circumstances."

Even though the Fed wasn't authorized to purchase riskier assets such as corporate bonds or toxic mortgage assets directly, it could invoke special lending powers if it deemed circumstances were "unusual and exigent." It could then create a limited-liability corporation that would, in turn, purchase the risky assets.

The emergency-lending programs had been controversial during and after the 2008 crisis — so much so that Congress, in the 2010 Dodd-Frank financial regulatory overhaul, had slapped new curbs on the Fed's ability to use them. Never again could the Fed use its "unusual and exigent" powers to bail out individual banks or financial institutions, as it had done with Bear Stearns and AIG. Congress instead required such lending to be broadly based, meaning any terms had to apply to at least five institutions.

Lawmakers also required the Treasury secretary to sign off on any new 13(3) programs. In addition, because the Fed believed it was not allowed to sustain lending losses, the Fed was likely to seek assurances that the Treasury would cover losses if it purchased securities or loans that weren't already government-guaranteed, including corporate bonds or auto and credit-card debts that had been bundled and resold as securities.

"As things got bad, we started thinking about what were the tools that we had without congressional action," Mnuchin said.[1]

The task of preparing the lending backstops fell to Fed governor Lael Brainard. She had spent the early part of March shaping the Fed's physical posture to virus risk, including canceling travel and limiting the number of people permitted to enter the Fed's buildings. Powell knew Brainard also shared his activist monetary approach to the oncoming storm.

At the Treasury ten years earlier, Brainard had distinguished herself while working behind the scenes with European officials to design key elements of a strategy to resolve banking crises on the Continent. During one meeting of finance-ministry officials at the height of that crisis, an attendee recalled how Brainard had told foreign counterparts what their objectives should be. "She went around the table and pointed her finger,

'We want you to do this, this, this,'" the attendee said. "It was really quite extraordinary. They were taking notes, and they were going to do it."

That week, Powell asked Brainard to join him alongside Richard Clarida and John Williams as the policy-forming team for the foreseeable future — the Troika would become known as the "troika-plus-one." She would become one of Powell's most trusted lieutenants during the Pandemic Crisis.

Battlefield medicine

Following a budding market meltdown, Wednesday night's speech by Trump had thoroughly disappointed investors. They were looking for more specifics about how Washington would help workers and businesses. Instead the headline had been the European travel ban, which together with the NBA's season suspension had helped clarify the unimaginable economic losses that were in store.

Nerves on Wall Street Thursday morning were further stretched because it wasn't clear how work was going to get done. Firms began rolling out business-resilience plans that had been ordered up after the September 11, 2001, attacks and refined after 2012's Superstorm Sandy knocked out critical infrastructure in lower Manhattan, closing exchanges for two days. CME Group, which operated the trading floor at the Chicago Board of Trade, announced it would close the floor after business ended on Friday, the first major US exchange to take such a precaution. The fall in the S&P 500 was so swift that a fifteen-minute trading halt was triggered just minutes after the opening bell, with shares down by the 7 percent limit.

At 8:30 a.m. on Thursday, Clarida sent a "draft plan" to Powell, weaving various threads into a possible road map for the coming week's Fed meeting. It called for slashing the federal-funds rate to near zero and making essentially unlimited amounts of overnight and short-term financing available to broker-dealers.

In addition, Clarida proposed cutting to near zero the discount rate, a separate lending rate that the Fed charges banks to borrow directly from the central bank at its discount window. The Fed hadn't taken this step even during the 2008 financial crisis. Over the past few decades, the discount rate had become largely symbolic because banks avoided the discount window except at times of extreme distress. This, though, could be one of those times, and the Fed wanted to encourage banks to use it. Finally, Clarida recommended at least $500 billion in purchases of Treasuries, which markets would immediately see as a return to the large-scale bond buying, or quantitative easing, that had been so controversial one decade earlier. Clarida suggested buying $60 billion per month through the end of the year, perhaps concentrating the purchases in the least actively traded off-the-run securities, or Treasury bonds and notes issued before the most recently issued bond or note of a given maturity, that were gumming up the market.

Clarida had returned to his home in Westport, Connecticut, one week earlier for what he thought would be a weekend stay, but he remained there as health concerns mounted along the Northeast corridor. Clarida's home office doubled as the studio where he had recorded an album of original folk-rock music, *Time No Changes*, a few years earlier. On March 12 he logged into a Fed-issued HP laptop — the only way he could communicate on the Fed's secure email and video systems — from his sound-studio-turned-office and joined a meeting with Powell, John Williams, and senior staff. As they debated the merits of larger Treasury purchases, some voiced hesitation over how, exactly, they would describe the rationale for such large purchases. Wouldn't investors call this *quantitative easing*?

Inside the Fed, those words referred to purchases designed explicitly to hold down long-term interest rates to spur the economy, but that wasn't really why they were needed right now. There was broad agreement that the Fed would need to step into the market in a bigger way, but Williams and others had been reluctant to commit to buying longer-dated bonds. The Fed could justify the bond buying by citing the need for market functioning, but Clarida worried that, if market functioning was restored quickly, the Fed's stated rationale might compel them to stop buying when Clarida wanted to keep going.

Frustrated with the incremental response and their reluctance to give a larger headline number for the overall purchases, Clarida rallied the group to get past their concerns about the semantics.

"I don't care if they call it fucking QE," he said.

As it turned out, the markets were becoming so dysfunctional that no branding exercise was necessary. The Dow was down 2,250 points.

Just a few blocks from the stock exchange, Lorie Logan's team at the New York Fed proposed two big changes to how the central bank might intervene in the market. First, they would offer essentially unlimited repo loans, using a big headline number. With Powell's approval, they would now offer $500 billion worth of three-month loans later in the day, with two additional offerings of $500 billion on Friday. Altogether they would pledge to put $1.5 trillion in cash into the system, plus $1 trillion per week in one-month loans after that. But just because the Fed made more money available to bank dealers didn't mean those firms were prepared to lend it out.

That's where the second change came in. Logan, the market veteran at the New York Fed, had already been authorized by the FOMC to buy $60 billion per month in Treasury bills, or securities with maturities of up to one year, to restore reserves that had fallen too low the prior September. Now she was proposing to buy Treasuries of longer maturities. The market for thirty-year Treasury bonds was under severe stress amid continued sales. Traders were finding that the prices being quoted on their Bloomberg screens for certain securities weren't matching what dealers were actually willing to pay. The world's most liquid bond market was drying up.

To make these purchases, Powell invoked a little-noticed provision in the FOMC's annual directives to the New York Fed that allowed him to "undertake transactions...in order to appropriately address temporary disruptions of an operational or highly unusual nature in U.S. dollar funding markets." Officials had added this emergency authorization in 2013, after Superstorm Sandy. Powell felt that such a move required at least consultation with the voting members of the FOMC, so he, Clarida, and Williams divvied up calls to the other eleven reserve-bank presidents.

The New York Fed announced its plans in a terse statement at 12:30 p.m., after which the Dow pared some of its morning losses, regaining 1,000 points. Yet the results of the Fed's first $500 billion repo offering at 1:45 p.m. showed that banks had taken up just $78.4 billion in funding. To Williams's surprise, unlike during the September reserve shortage, more Fed funding wasn't fixing the problem. If the Fed made cheap cash available but banks wouldn't lend it to customers, it suggested these lenders were trying to conserve their balance sheets.

The dismal scientists

After the 2008 financial crisis, Bernanke had tasked four economists with building a new division focused on the stability of the financial system. The Fed had hundreds of PhD economists across its divisions of research and statistics, international finance, monetary policy, and banking regulation. But until then it had never dedicated a unit to monitoring potentially destabilizing threats lurking in the shadowy corners of Wall Street — the very dangers that had caught the central bank off guard.

Andreas Lehnert, a fifty-one-year-old economist who had become the division's leader in 2017, was drawn to the study of disasters. On the bookshelf in his home office was a series of books about how people die in national parks — *Death in Yosemite, Death in the Grand Canyon, Death in Yellowstone* — along with others in the wilderness-catastrophe genre. There were titles on how to run a big inner-city hospital, on the ill-fated *Challenger* launch decision, and a copy of *Why Buildings Fall Down*. Lehnert had always been a voracious reader — so much that his parents once locked up his books because they feared he was spending too much time with them. They came home one day to find him reading the phone book and studying various dialing codes. Lehnert's love for the dismal science blossomed when his dad, who worked for Phillips Petroleum in the northeast Oklahoma city of Bartlesville, brought home a copy of the *Economist* magazine. Lehnert couldn't put it down.

Lehnert had started at the Fed in 1998 and became a top research economist on the mortgage market in the run-up to its boom and bust, but he had almost quit before rising through the ranks. Some research he had conducted on the benefits of adjustable-rate mortgages found its way into a speech to a group of credit-union executives by then-Chair Alan Greenspan. The remarks caused a backlash from the powerful housing-finance lobby. Lehnert, dismayed that he had brought controversy upon "the Maestro," offered his resignation during a staff meeting. "Nonsense," said Greenspan, waving his hand. "It's just politics."

Every January, Lehnert picked a theme for the year to help frame the work of his threat-division staff, which had grown to around fifty people. During a previous year, his team had in fact done a round of planning related to a pandemic. But they hadn't seriously envisioned broad stay-at-home orders that bring economic activity to a grinding halt, inducing a massive collapse in output or the extreme demand for cash. Instead they had examined the risks that higher deaths — so-called *excess mortality* — could strain life-insurance companies.

For his 2020 theme Lehnert had chosen "crisis management," reflecting his concern that his group was losing some of its institutional memory around the operations, logistics, communications, and understanding of the Fed's crisis-fighting tool kit. Just a few weeks into the year, plans for a dress-rehearsal planning session were interrupted by the Covid-19 live-fire exercise.

The Tools Memo

By late February, Lehnert's team began sending a comprehensive summary of each day's financial developments to the Fed board with an eye toward where the financial system could break down quickly. Even though a million different things can go wrong in markets, there are relatively few choke points where the financial system can rupture. They focused on different funding markets to spot signs of stress in one area spilling into another.

Lehnert had also started pulling together a Microsoft Word document he called the Tools Memo, a loose collection of ideas that the Fed could pursue if things deteriorated dramatically. His memo included emergency lending operations that the Fed had used during the 2008 crisis. It contemplated restarting a backstop for short-term corporate IOUs (called commercial paper), which companies use to finance their day-to-day business operations, and short-circuiting another run on money-market mutual funds, which many investors treat as a cash equivalent. Because the Fed's emergency measures from 2008 had remained so politically controversial, however, he wasn't sure if he should be preparing to rev up the programs from the Tools Memo.

Lehnert got his answer at a planning meeting that Thursday morning.

Following his breakfast with Mnuchin, Powell gathered with staffers in a converted conference room that, until the 1970s, had been the formal dining room in the Eccles Building. Staffers presented the pros and cons of intervening more aggressively in markets. Central banks, cautious by nature, don't attract risk-takers; central bankers prefer to take time to see if one, two, or three days of wild market swings might fade. What's more, taking bold steps sometimes risked bailing out sophisticated investors who had knowingly made highly leveraged, risky bets. It was the same "moral hazard" rationale used to argue against the bailout of the Bank of New England in 1991. *It's not the Fed's job to keep them from losing money,* one Fed staff director warned. *Are we really going to go bail out hedge funds that knew they were taking on more risk when they invested in off-the-run Treasury securities?*

Before too long, Powell intervened. The US was facing a synchronized shutdown of the world's major economies. *This is a once-in-a-lifetime global historical disaster,* he said. "We have these tools," Powell said, "and if we don't use them to their fullest extent, I don't know how I'll be able to look back and explain to the public why we didn't do that in this situation. It's different from all the other situations we've been in."

When Lehnert walked out of the old dining room, he left behind any doubts about how aggressively to calibrate his coordinates. *OK,* he thought, *we're turning all the knobs to 11.*

"Not here to close spreads"

That same morning, in a gleaming forty-five-story tower that juts into the Frankfurt skyline, the European Central Bank was deliberating its next response to the virus. Europe had been hit harder and sooner by the corona-virus than the US. Deaths in Italy had already surpassed 1,000. Unfortunately, ECB president Christine Lagarde had fewer tools to spur growth than did Powell. While Fed officials had been worrying for years that low interest rates would give them less firepower to combat an economic contraction, the ECB's rates were already below zero, at -0.5 percent. As a result, the ECB voted against cutting rates into more deeply negative territory, settling instead on a package of bond-buying stimulus measures.

At 9:30 a.m. New York time, Lagarde sat down for a press conference to announce the ECB's rescue package. Eight years earlier, she had watched Mario Draghi make one of the most successful speeches ever by a central banker. In July 2012, economic strains on the euro threatened to break apart the union, with some betting that Italy and Spain would return to using the lira and peseta as yields soared on their euro-denominated bonds. "Within our mandate, the ECB is ready to do whatever it takes to preserve the euro," Draghi had told a London audience. Then he paused, adding a dramatic flourish: "And believe me, it will be enough."

When news hit the wires, traders pushed the eject button on trades shorting the euro. Those three words — *whatever it takes* — became iconic because they conveyed Draghi's implicit promise that if no investor would buy Italy's or Spain's bonds, the ECB, able to print as many euros as it wished, would do so in their place. It calmed markets and strengthened the euro without the ECB's taking any explicit action.

Lagarde, a former French finance minister who had served as head of the International Monetary Fund for eight years, succeeded Draghi as ECB president on November 1, 2019. She inherited a fractured committee of European central bankers, with especially fierce opposition to Draghi's expansive policies coming from Germany, the bloc's largest economy. Like Powell, Lagarde was trained as a lawyer, not an economist. Lagarde had been frustrated by the inability of European governments to form a cohesive joint response of fiscal actions, which put more pressure on the central bank.

Her press conference that morning featured a gaffe that was almost the mirror image of Draghi's *whatever it takes* moment. One reporter asked her what the central bank could do for especially hard-hit nations such as Italy, where sovereign-debt bond yields were soaring compared with Germany, widening the spread over the latter's relatively risk-free bonds.

"We are not here to close spreads," said Lagarde. "This is not the function or the mission of the ECB. There are other tools for that, and there are other actors to actually deal with those issues."

The blunder stunned investors. One French economist called it "the opposite of *whatever it takes*." Italian bond yields spiked immediately, and the comment drew a swift rebuke from Rome.

Lagarde tried to clean up her comment in a CNBC interview a few hours later. "I am fully committed to avoid any fragmentation in a difficult moment for the euro area," she said. But between the virus and the US travel ban, the damage had been done. The pan-European Stoxx 600 index fell 11 percent on Thursday, its worst one-day drop ever.

By the end of Thursday, March 12, 2020, the Dow Jones Industrial Average had fallen 10 percent, or 2,352.6 points, a bigger drop than any of the worst days of the 2008 financial crisis. The index had posted larger losses only three other times: on Black Monday in 1987 and on October 28 and 29, 1929, during the crash that would usher in the Great Depression. More ominously, the prior day's pattern of falling bond and stock prices continued, rippling out to other asset classes.

The economic scenario unfolding forced investors to confront a calamity worse than 2008, one verging on the 1930s. Millions could lose their jobs if businesses were forced to close and people hunkered down at home.

Date 2020	Covid-19 Cases	Covid-19 Deaths	Dow Jones Average	VIX Fear Index
Thursday, March 12	2,592	52	21,200 (↓2,353)	75.47 (↑21.57)

Have you heard of TALF?

Powell fired off an email to Clarida at 6 a.m. on Friday, asking him if he thought it still made sense to cut rates that weekend rather than wait until the following Wednesday's FOMC meeting.

"Yes to Sunday," Clarida wrote back. The priority now was to fine-tune their basic message after having lowered rates to zero: *We've done a lot and expect a good outcome but, of course, are prepared to do more.*

At 9 a.m. that morning, a top monetary affairs official sent around the latest proposal from the FOMC to Powell and his lieutenants: a cut in the fed-funds rate to near zero and $100 billion in Treasury purchases per month until at least December.

In another early-morning note, Clarida queried Powell and Williams on whether the Treasury would be willing to put up money for emergency lending programs from a special purse available to Mnuchin. "Let's do hope we don't get to that point!" Clarida added parenthetically. Powell responded that Mnuchin was already on board.

If the Fed was going to buy riskier assets, it would need the Treasury or Congress to protect the central bank from losses. No law said that explicitly, but the Fed's own internal policies required making only those loans it was confident would not incur losses. The Fed could offset defaults by charging high fees, but if the fees were too high and no one borrowed, the effort would be wasted.

Asking Congress would be messy and time-consuming, so the most attractive source of funds in a pinch resided in something called the Exchange Stabilization Fund, or ESF. Technically, the roughly $90 billion in the account was supposed to be used for Treasury intervention in currency markets. Congress and the Roosevelt administration had created it in 1934 to stabilize the value of the dollar after the US went off the gold standard. But at the height of the financial panic after the collapse of Lehman Brothers in 2008, the Treasury Department announced it would temporarily guarantee more than $3 trillion in deposits in certain money-market mutual funds using $50 billion from the ESF. The Treasury acted without congressional approval, and Congress later formalized the guarantee and reimbursed the ESF. But it also forbade the Treasury from ever using the ESF to provide such a guarantee again.

By the end of that second week in March, New York Fed markets executive Daleep Singh began reaching out to Mnuchin's top staffers: *Have you all heard of TALF? There's this whole alphabet soup of lending facilities we launched in 2008 and 2009. We're brushing up on all of that,* Singh offered, *and maybe you should too — especially the parts in which the Treasury provides equity to the Fed to absorb losses.*

During the 2008 crisis, the Treasury had provided $20 billion from the bank-bailout fund to the Fed for one particular lending program known as TALF. The Term Asset-Backed Securities Loan Facility was controversial because it offered cheap loans with which pension funds, hedge funds, and other distressed debt investors could buy up riskier securities such as credit cards, auto loans, and commercial-property mortgages. It was a bid to revive markets for such debt that operated largely outside the banking system, with the Fed helping private-sector players to rehabilitate these markets.

White House economic adviser Larry Kudlow had been quietly pushing the idea of Treasury-Fed lending facilities for more than a week — first with Mnuchin and later with Trump, who was still fixated on interest rates. The supply, not the price, of credit was the issue now, as it is in almost all financial panics. While Mnuchin appeared to be initially skeptical such lending operations would be necessary, the potential magnitude of economic disruptions was increasing by the day, and congressional leaders quickly realized the targeted relief bill he was negotiating with Pelosi would not be enough.

"The first inning was the $8 billion bill. This is the second inning," Mnuchin said during a CNBC interview before markets opened on Friday, March 13. The top priority in that next inning, he said, would be relief for airline companies and small and midsize businesses.

The TV hosts asked Mnuchin about rumors of markets being shut down. Those rumors "are ridiculous," Mnuchin responded. "We intend to do everything we can to keep markets open."

CNBC's Jim Cramer asked Mnuchin how closely he would be working with Congress and the Fed, reminding him that Roosevelt's Treasury secretary (Henry Morgenthau) and his Fed chair (Marriner Eccles) had worked "hand in hand" before and during the Second World War. Mnuchin did his best to reassure markets that the White House would not shrink from the moment. "Whatever we need to do, whatever the Fed needs to do, whatever Congress needs to do, we will provide liquidity, and this will be an entire whole-of-government approach led by the president," he said.

When the discussion turned to the 22 percent market rout on Black Monday in October 1987, Mnuchin tried to paint a contrast. "I was a young trader in 1987, and that was a much scarier time than it is today, OK?"

No one was going to confuse Mnuchin the cheerleader with Draghi's *whatever it takes,* but someone from the administration was finally providing a measured message to reassure markets — one that the combative Trump seemed incapable of delivering. That morning, Mnuchin pointed to the Fed's $1.5 trillion in bank-lending offerings as "unprecedented." He alluded to rolling out other lending programs — notwithstanding the limits Congress had placed on them.

Turning to the challenges that banks could face as more companies drew on their credit lines, Mnuchin encouraged them to seek emergency loans, if needed, from the Fed's discount window: "They should feel free to draw from the discount window. That's another great source of liquidity for them to lend to companies."

The interview wrapped up just as stock markets opened, with the Dow racing up 1,025 points in the first few minutes of trading.

Shortly after Mnuchin had calmly pledged a "whole-of-government approach led by the president," Trump launched another Twitter missive attacking the Fed. "The Federal Reserve must FINALLY lower the Fed Rate to something comparable to their competitor Central Banks. Jay Powell and group are putting us at a decided economic & physiological disadvantage. Should never have been this way. Also, STIMULATE!"

The last-taxi problem

The New York Fed had started sending its staff home on Wednesday and Thursday. On Friday, Lorie Logan rode to the bank's headquarters on Maiden Lane in a car that Williams had arranged to spare her the subway commute from the Upper West Side. Taking public transportation now seemed like an unnecessary infection risk.

The latest data on Treasury market trading painted a dire picture. The bid-ask spread — the difference between the lowest asking price and the highest offered price for the thirty-year Treasury bond — was reaching levels more than six times its recent average, something last seen in the 2008 financial crisis.

Yet 2020 wasn't 2008. The earlier financial crisis started in credit markets — namely, for riskier mortgage products — and spread inward over many months from this periphery to the center of the financial system via banks and short-term funding markets. Now a panic brought on by a dash for cash amid pandemic-induced economic closures risked spreading from the inside out, in a matter of hours and days. Countless markets, such as those for government-backed mortgage securities, were priced in reference to Treasury securities. If the Treasury market broke down, so would all these other markets.

"Our market is now completely closed," one Colorado mortgage banker told *The Wall Street Journal* that evening. "There is no offer to buy any [government-backed] mortgage product of any type."[2]

If homeowners couldn't lock in their mortgage rate, they weren't going to be buying houses or refinancing. Normally when the Fed cuts rates, it ignites a wave of refinancing that immediately reduces monthly payments for households, like a tax cut. But if the Treasury market wasn't working, efforts to make loans cheaper by cutting rates would have no impact.

Markets were experiencing an enormous shock to *liquidity* — a catch-all term that refers to the cost of quickly converting an asset into cash, or vice versa. By mid-March, everyone with liquid assets wanted to hold fast to them. No one wanted to buy risky assets, even if they looked cheap, because no one knew where asset prices were headed. Why grab a shiny object only to discover it's a sharp knife?

"It was absolutely one-way traffic, and everybody was a seller. Everybody. Just raise cash," said Christopher Vogel, a veteran trader who headed the rates and currency division at TD Securities, an arm of a large Canadian bank. "Anything near 99, 98, 97, 96 cents to the dollar? We'll take it. The redemptions we saw were fierce, and the buying hands were in the pockets."

The result: sell Treasuries.

"When cash is dear, you sell what you can, which may not necessarily be what you want," said Hammack, the Goldman Sachs treasurer.[3]

The 2008 crisis had brought a major regulatory overhaul from Congress — the Dodd-Frank bill that focused on reducing the risks posed by large, systemically important banks, often referred to as those "too big to fail." But this crisis was one the architects of the bill hadn't envisioned: all the banks were fundamentally sound, but a system-wide shock — the pandemic — led every bank dealer to make the same decision and say, "Conserve cash."

Economists and regulators referred to this as "the last-taxi problem." Upon pulling into the train station at midnight, a tired traveler is delighted to find a single taxi idling at the cabstand. After hailing the driver, the passenger is informed that this taxi can't go anywhere due to a local ordinance mandating there always be at least one taxi at the station. A similar dynamic was unfolding with the big banks, which had larger cash reserves but were reluctant to use them because of their own risk-tolerance rules. Even though banks had fortified their balance sheets for a moment like this, a crisis was nevertheless the last moment in which they wanted to take steps that might weaken them.

Investors recognized that banks had built cushions of capital to withstand a serious shock, but now were refusing to deploy them. To boost liquidity, a financial institution can draw down its reserves, seek additional short-term debt in bond markets, or sell assets to generate cash. But if multiple institutions are doing this at once, a positive feedback loop can form, raising borrowing costs and driving down asset values in a way that squeezes businesses or institutions that weren't facing any initial liquidity crisis. If banks, in turn, reduce the amount of loans they make available to customers, and businesses can't get bank loans or short-term loans in credit markets, they might default on other loans and be forced to lay off workers.

On Thursday, the Fed had thought it could fix the liquidity problem by supplying lots of cheap funding to dealers. Once it was clear that money was not moving through the system, officials realized they needed to do something different — and quickly. "We had this huge one-way flow that was trying to get through the system, and the system wasn't going to be able to handle this in the very near term," said Williams. "The diagnosis changed very quickly to say we've got to somehow get in and pull out assets that are, in a way, clogging up the system."

On Friday morning, Clarida had pointed to cries for help from Wall Street in an email to Powell and Williams: "We are in the season of maximum special pleading from hedge funds and asset managers who are taking losses on credit bets and cash futures Treasury arbitrage," Clarida wrote. Any whiff that the Fed was rescuing traders whose bets were getting slaughtered could cause an uproar. "[T]o state the obvious it is not our job to insure them against loss," said Clarida. Instead he suggested keeping "focus on market function issues which are correlated with but not the same as funds unwinding / losing money."

Using the authorization Powell had provided on Thursday to purchase $80 billion in Treasuries over one month, Logan proposed buying $37 billion in the span of a few hours. The New York Fed had never bought more than a few billion in Treasury debt on any particular day. It required the bank, with its personnel fanning out to work from multiple remote locations or from their homes, to conduct multiple auctions in one day at sizes that had never been done before. Nonetheless, the New York Fed announced the program at 10 a.m.: "These purchases are intended to address highly unusual disruptions in the market."

In Washington, Powell was busy preparing for Sunday's emergency Fed meeting. An hour after the New York Fed's announcement, he sought Clarida's input on how they should communicate the rationale for their asset purchases. Clarida was more concerned about making sure they announced a large total volume of purchases, not just a smaller monthly commitment. "Whatever we call it I do think it is important in what we announce Sunday that we put a headline number on outright T purchases (at least 500 bil?) vs keeping the month by month optionality in terms of how much we buy and for how long we buy."

Another key prong of the Fed's action plan fell into place that morning: the dollar-swap lines offered to foreign central banks. Because so much global financial activity depends on the use of the dollar, a scramble for dollars by investors abroad—Japanese insurance funds that bought dollar-denominated US corporate bonds or Mexican and Turkish companies that had borrowed in dollars—risked greater financial distress. These foreign investors might seek to unload assets to raise cash at the worst possible time. When turmoil hit markets earlier that week, Logan and Beth Ann Wilson, head of the Fed's international finance division in Washington, had initiated talks with five central banks—the Bank of Japan, European Central Bank, Swiss National Bank, Bank of England, and Bank of Canada—about increasing the frequency of dollar-swap loan offerings, extending the terms to several months, and lowering the price. "All agreed that conditions in dollar funding markets had deteriorated," Wilson wrote.

The Fed would be going all-in—on interest rates, the balance sheet, market function, bank liquidity, and global dollar funding.

Stocks closed sharply higher on Friday, fueled by a late rally that powered the Dow to a 2,000-point gain on hopes that Mnuchin and Pelosi would agree to their down payment on virus-related relief.

Just as markets were rallying, Trump held a Rose Garden press conference in which he officially declared the pandemic a national emergency: "Two very big words." He announced plans to surge the production of testing kits, and he tried to project calm. "We'll remove or eliminate every obstacle necessary to deliver our people the care that they need and that they're entitled to. No resource will be spared," he said.

Mnuchin announced he had reached a deal with Democrats that evening, the product of eighteen phone calls that day with Pelosi. The House bill sailed through on a 363-40 vote shortly after midnight.

Date 2020	Covid-19 Cases	Covid-19 Deaths	Dow Jones Average	VIX Fear Index
Friday, March 13	3,450	57	23,185 (↑ 1,985)	57.83 (↓ 17.64)

The right to remove

Even though stock markets reversed most of Thursday's fall, bond markets were still badly messed up. After hitting a low of 0.98 percent on Monday, the yield on the thirty-year Treasury had risen for four straight days, to 1.56 percent at Friday's close, the opposite of the traditional flight-to-safety pattern. The same was true for the ten-year note, which closed at 0.94 percent, up from Monday's low of 0.54 percent. More ominously, pressures were bubbling up in new markets, particularly the $1.1 trillion market for ultrashort-term corporate debt known as commercial paper.

Lael Brainard briefed Powell and the Troika at 8 a.m. on Saturday about how soon the Fed might be able to respond to the turmoil in the commercial-paper markets. She had formed a team with staffers from Lehnert's division in Washington and Singh's team in New York to prepare a new version of the Commercial Paper Funding Facility, one of the most novel "unusual and exigent" operations that the Fed launched in October 2008. But it would not be ready to fly by Monday.

Meanwhile, Powell reached out to Mnuchin to see if the Treasury would be able to commit money from the ESF to backstop losses, something the department hadn't provided for in 2008. Mnuchin, who had a deep understanding of short-term funding markets and the implications of any freeze, didn't need to be convinced. *Whatever you need,* he told Powell.

Central banks in other democracies were undertaking coordinated actions to shore up confidence. Bank of England Governor Mark Carney had appeared alongside Rishi Sunak, the UK chancellor, that Wednesday after both men unveiled a one-two punch of interest-rate cuts and stimulus spending. "There is no reason for this shock to turn into the experience of 2008 — a virtual lost decade in a number of economies — if we handle this well," said Carney, who was set to leave office at the end of the week.

The Canadians unfurled a similar unified action on Friday afternoon. Finance Minister Bill Morneau invited Bank of Canada Governor

Stephen Poloz to appear alongside him in Ottawa at a press conference where he planned to announce a big fiscal package. Poloz was at first concerned that such a joint appearance might undercut the appearance of central-bank independence. But after discussing it with the bank's governing council, the Canadian central bankers not only greenlighted the joint press conference but talked themselves into having Poloz announce a surprise rate cut at the same time. It all happened so fast that the press conference almost didn't start on time; the bank had to rush to furnish Poloz with the French translation of his opening remarks.

On Saturday morning, Mnuchin joined Trump, Pence, and the coronavirus task force for an Oval Office meeting. At a press briefing afterward, Mnuchin stood behind Trump, who sported a dark blue baseball cap emblazoned with *USA* in big white letters. A reporter asked the president why he kept attacking the Fed: "If you feel so strongly about it, why don't you dismiss the Chairman? Or do you think you're powerless to do so?"

"No, I think I have the right to do that, or the right to remove him as chairman," answered Trump. "He has, so far, made a lot of bad decisions." When Powell heard about the exchange later that day, he was slack-jawed. Trump had been goaded into saying that yes, he would push the button on the nuclear option when markets were maximally raw.

Trump unloaded his familiar complaints about Powell, among them that US yields were higher than German ones. "We have some tremendous opportunities right now, but Jerome Powell is not making it easy," said the president.

Trump had been told he couldn't fire Powell, so he broached an idea that sat in a legal gray area — demoting Powell. "I have the right to remove," Trump insisted. "I'm not doing that. I have the right to also take him and put him in a regular position and put somebody else in charge. And I haven't made any decisions on that."

Reporters shouted more questions. Trump turned and exited the room.

Chapter Ten

BAGEHOT ON STEROIDS

By Sunday, March 15, 2020, Jay Powell had spent two weeks immersed in an expanding two-front war. He had tried to treat a budding financial panic with more and more extreme monetary measures, but the crisis kept spreading. Worse, this disaster was one that the Fed had been designed to confront. It stood powerless to address the other force on the economy — a public-health emergency.

Normally central banks — large, bureaucratic organizations staffed with academics — move ploddingly and carefully because the economy itself changes gradually. But there was no precedent for what was happening now. Faced with an unknown, invisible enemy, Americans were hoarding toilet paper, bleach, and Lysol disinfectant wipes. Had they had known the scale of the problems overwhelming the financial sector, they might have queued up at ATMs instead.

Powell had called the Federal Open Market Committee together for its first emergency cut thirteen days earlier. On Thursday, March 12, its members met again via video conference for a quick update on the series of ominous developments unfolding in financial markets. They were just days away from their regularly scheduled meeting, but Powell decided they couldn't wait. Market strains were too intense.

At 10 a.m. that Sunday morning, Powell convened a second emergency meeting, this one in the Fed boardroom. In his agenda, Powell had proposed not just a rate cut but also a package of actions designed to show the Fed's commitment to the overwhelming force necessary to meet the moment. Financial panics are psychological as much as anything else. The Fed needed to convince investors that the central bank would not permit a growing health emergency to spiral out of control.

A couple dozen staff and two other Fed governors attended in person. Mindful of the growing health hazards, they left alternating empty chairs around the table. Before and after the meeting, they awkwardly maintained physical distancing, as people around the world were learning to do. Lael Brainard, recognizing the need for Powell to remain visibly healthy at all times, had misgivings about holding the meeting in person, even at a reduced capacity.

A black SUV ferried Richard Clarida, still at his home in Connecticut, on the hour-long drive to the New York Fed's fortress-like castle in lower Manhattan. The city streets struck Clarida as deserted. Inside the building, Clarida gathered with New York Fed President John Williams in his wood-paneled conference room, where they were joined by senior advisers, including Lorie Logan, manager of the Fed's $4.6 trillion portfolio of bonds and other assets.

Logan had weathered two other crises at the New York Fed, which sat a few blocks from the World Trade Center towers. After the buildings fell the morning of September 11, 2001, Logan and her colleagues sought refuge for a few hours in the basement of the iron-barred, neo-Florentine fortress on Liberty Street. The basement, sunk eighty feet into the bedrock of Manhattan Island, houses a vault filled with hundreds of thousands of gold bars belonging to nations around the world. The New York Fed acts as the eyes and ears on Wall Street of the central bank and conducts all the financial-market transactions on the system's behalf.

At some point that afternoon, Logan and a colleague returned upstairs to check on markets, escorted by bank security. The phones were ringing off the hook on the deserted trading floor. Banks were calling asking for direction on potential lending operations, but no one was there to answer. And in 2008, Logan had curtailed her maternity leave to help deal with that financial crisis.

Randal Quarles also joined the Sunday morning meeting virtually. Quarles had left DC to spend the weekend at home in Salt Lake City, and again drove to the San Francisco Fed branch located in the Utah capital.

Along with Clarida and Quarles, the rest of the committee appeared via video conference — their images arranged in a *Hollywood Squares–*style grid displayed on giant projection screens hanging from the Fed boardroom's twenty-six-foot-high ceilings. During the Second World War, US and British military officers had used the boardroom — at that time one of the largest air-conditioned rooms in Washington — to plan the Allied invasion of Normandy. Now the people inside were hoping to end a different kind of battle, but one with equally far-reaching international implications.

The meeting that morning was unusually somber, but Powell set an unfamiliar brisk pace. Instead of the normal two days of leisurely deliberations, Powell wanted to announce their plan at 5 o'clock that very afternoon; the Fed's strong commitment would therefore be released before the start of business in Asian markets.

They began with a briefing from Logan, who ran through the range of total dysfunction in financial markets. Volatility was hitting all-time highs amid a breakdown in the Treasury market. Normally Treasuries are a safe haven, fostering a predictable pattern in which bond prices rise, bringing down yields, when stocks fall. But the opposite was happening now, with stocks and bond prices both falling, calling into question the "risk-free" status of Treasury securities. One segment of the market for older Treasury bonds had ceased to function effectively. Other markets for corporate debt, municipal bonds, and exchanging foreign currencies for US dollars likewise showed signs of breaking down.

Instead of the usual finely tuned and rigorously debated economic forecast, the staff forecast sketched out just two illustrative scenarios: one where the economy would start to rebound in the second half of the year, and a second where the economic recession would be so lengthy that the economy would not begin to exit it until sometime in 2021. The uncommonly poor visibility on the future was at the heart of the storm in financial markets. What was gross domestic product going to be? No one knew. What would happen to corporate earnings? No one knew.

In addition to proposing a one-percentage-point rate cut, which would drop the Fed's short-term rate to near zero, Powell outlined even bigger salvage measures. Its most audacious component by far would authorize Logan's team to purchase at least $500 billion in Treasury securities and at least $200 billion in mortgage securities. They would cut the discount rate for emergency loans the Fed could extend to banks to a quarter percentage point, making such borrowing more generous than it had been in the 2008 financial crisis. They would activate the network of relatively inexpensive dollar "swap" loans with five other central banks, making it easier for foreign firms to borrow in the US currency. And they would announce regulatory guidance encouraging banks to use cash buffers to support continued lending to businesses and households.

With the Treasury market melting down, Powell faced little opposition to these market-stabilizing measures. Everyone around the table that day realized the economy was entering a wrenching upheaval. But they were divided over how their interest-rate setting should address it. A few of the reserve-bank presidents and two of the governors were afraid Powell's proposed rate cut would backfire. Quarles and another Fed governor, Michelle "Miki" Bowman, weren't convinced that monetary policy was going to help solve the economic problem at hand. It wasn't going to reopen stadiums and arenas. Once rates were at zero, they were likely to stay there for a long time, creating new challenges for the banking system.

Loretta Mester, a PhD economist and opera buff who had become president of the Federal Reserve Bank of Cleveland in 2014, opposed cutting by a full percentage point; she argued for a milder half-point reduction. The larger cut would leave the committee no room to cut rates later if the economy needed more help. "The lack of liquidity in the financial markets was a real first-order problem, and that was really where I thought our focus should be," recalled Mester.[1] They could always come back later to cut rates more, she argued, once markets were working again.

At the heart of the debate was whether it made more sense to conserve ammo or fire it all up front. But there was also the possibility that, by taking extreme action, the Fed would unnerve people, actually worsening the panic. The Fed had cut rates just twelve days earlier. What was so bad, investors might ask, that the Fed couldn't wait a few more days for its regular meeting to announce the cut? What did it know now, investors might wonder, that it didn't know a fortnight ago?

"We're trying to get our decision made by 5 p.m. on a Sunday," said St. Louis Fed President James Bullard. "This is going to be somewhat shocking to markets. You're moving up a decision that could have been made only three days later."[2]

A few skeptics had gone to Powell for reassurances before the meeting. *We'll support this,* they told him. *But if the virus emergency passes quickly and turns out to be a false alarm, give us some assurance we'll raise rates reasonably quickly to get those cuts back.* Thinking there was a good chance precisely that would happen, they told Powell, *We're going to look like we've really overreacted here.*

It was an easy promise for Powell to make. *There's no way that's going to happen here,* he thought.

Powell's top lieutenants strongly backed his proposal. Widespread social distancing, thousands of canceled events, and restrictions on large gatherings were now "a fact of life that will be with us for some time," said Clarida, the Fed's vice chair. "Life and economic activity are being disrupted to a degree not seen since at least 2001, and perhaps not since 1918."

Speaking from his suspended screen, Clarida voiced concern over how the recent boom in business debt could exacerbate a downturn. "Some companies will go under. Many will be downgraded. Investment firms will liquidate with the proceeds they pay out, fleeing to [the] safety of Treasuries, dollars, and bank reserve deposits in our coffers."

But at that still-early juncture, Clarida thought maybe the Fed's response could help the economy avoid two consecutive quarters of shrinking output — the technical definition of a recession. "It is actually rather unusual for policymakers to be able to identify in real time a truly exogenous shock that, if not confronted, would in itself push the economy into recession," he told his colleagues. "Today we face such a shock."

Clarida acknowledged the concerns around the table about subsequent shocks with fewer tools to respond. "Against that argument is the recognition today that Covid-19 poses a clear and present danger to the economy," he said. In other words, what was the point of saving ammunition when such a fierce enemy was already storming the ramparts?

Brainard spoke strongly in favor of a "three-pillar strategy" to 1) restore functioning in the Treasury market and short-term funding markets, 2) provide maximum monetary easing, and 3) ensure that banks knew regulators wanted them to dip into their cash buffers to keep lending to businesses and households. Brainard also foreshadowed emergency lending programs that she was finalizing with the New York Fed to backstop markets for the short-term corporate IOUs called commercial paper.

In the same vein, Williams thought the committee needed to show complete conviction that the central bank intended to fix the Treasury market. This wasn't a time to take a sequential approach that risked surprising investors (who already expected the Fed to take rates down to zero) and miscommunicating about the Fed's resolve. "The question is always, 'Do you do things in pieces? Do you do some gradualism?' And in a situation like this, you don't want to be half-hearted," Williams said later. "You wanted to be a strong force and as decisive as possible."[3]

After four hours of debate that day, Powell secured broad support for his shock-and-awe package of rate cuts, bond purchases, dollar loans, and bank guidance. Mester cast the lone dissenting vote in favor of a smaller cut. Powell adjourned the meeting at 2:40 p.m. and prepared to conduct a brief news conference by telephone a few hours later.

Powell knew the stakes. More would need to be done. There would be emergency lending programs to shore up critical short-term corporate-borrowing markets. Problems were spreading to a corner of the financial markets known as money-market funds, which invest in short-term corporate and municipal debt holdings. But by going all-in and early, Powell hoped the Fed could inspire a degree of market confidence that would buy officials a few more days of breathing room.

At 5 p.m. on Sunday, March 15, 2020, the US Federal Reserve issued a 663-word statement that announced the rate cuts and Treasury purchases. It began with two typically terse and detached sentences: "The coronavirus outbreak has harmed communities and disrupted economic activity in many countries, including the United States. Global financial conditions have also been significantly affected."

To insiders, however, it was the equivalent of bright bold red letters: THE MARKETS ARE A TOTAL SHITSHOW.

The Most Improved Player award

Donald Trump had just finished another grim afternoon briefing with the coronavirus task force and was walking down the hallway leading to the White House briefing room, with scientists and policymakers trailing behind. An adviser yelled out, "Tell him that Powell just cut the rate to zero."

Trump stopped, turned his head, and flashed an expression of genuine surprise. "Well, here's an amazing thing."

The president paused for a second before cutting the tension. "Jay Powell gets the Most Improved Player award." Everyone laughed.

At 5:15 p.m., wearing a bright sky-blue tie, Trump stepped to the podium in a crowded White House briefing room and led off with the Fed's announcement. "As you know, it just happened minutes ago...and I want to congratulate the Federal Reserve," the president began. "I have to say this: I'm very happy. And they did it in one step. They didn't do it in four steps over a long period of time."

Earlier that day, Trump had spoken to the CEOs of Walmart and other large grocery stores, where the conversation turned to supply chains and panic hoarding by a nervous public. But Trump, obsessed with lowering interest rates his entire presidency, seemed awestruck by the Fed news and encouraged everyone not to go overboard stockpiling groceries, household cleaners, and paper goods. "People shouldn't go out and buy. We're going to all be great. We're going to be so good. We're going to do — what's happened with the Fed is phenomenal news."

Meanwhile, huge swaths of American life were coming to an abrupt halt. New York City and surrounding counties announced schools would close the next day, joining the nation's second-largest system in Los Angeles, which had announced its own closures two days before. More governors were shutting indoor dining at all restaurants and bars. The CDC recommended that events involving more than fifty people be canceled, or postponed for at least eight weeks.

After a few minutes, Trump left the podium without taking questions, still preoccupied by the rate cut. "It's a tremendous thing that took place just now... I don't know if that's ever happened on a Sunday before," he said. "But I would think there are a lot of people on Wall Street that are very happy."

Donald Trump, who had wanted zero interest rates in the worst way, was getting all of that and more.

Lift every limit and lend

That same Sunday afternoon, Sophia Drossos had taken her children to get crepes — a good excuse to get out of their apartment on the Upper West Side of Manhattan for an hour — when she saw the alert on her phone about the monetary barrage. As Drossos, a consultant at a Wall Street hedge fund, digested the announcement, she thought, "This is going to be the turning point." The Fed was quickly undertaking purchases of huge amounts of debt.

"I had never seen a Fed decision like that. It was their full-court press on the market, covering all different angles," said Drossos, who had started her career as a markets analyst at the New York Fed in 1997 before becoming a top currency strategist at Morgan Stanley.

She immediately thought of Donald Kohn, a Fed economist who had been a top deputy to Alan Greenspan before being named vice chair under Ben Bernanke. Following the collapse of the Twin Towers, Kohn had issued firm instructions to one of Drossos's bosses: "I want you to lift every limit and lend — whatever is needed."

The advice had stuck with Drossos for the past nineteen years. *Lift every limit and lend.* That's exactly what it felt like the Fed was doing now, yet investors' initial reaction was one of fear, not comfort.

When Drossos heard about the Fed statement, the New York Stock Exchange would not open for Monday trading for another sixteen hours.

But investors could still bet on the expected value of stocks in so-called after-hours markets. At 6 p.m. — one hour after the Fed's massive monetary infusion — the after-hours markets tumbled by 5 percent, hitting their automatic shut-down limit. Drossos struggled to make sense of it — who would be selling on a day when the cavalry is arriving? "And it wasn't just the cavalry — they were rolling out the howitzer!"

Uncertainty about the coronavirus response was a major factor straining markets: How would trading operate if the virus started spreading like wildfire around the US financial infrastructure in New York? When was Congress going to step up with broader relief measures for furloughed workers and idled industries? And how quickly were healthcare authorities going to get ahead of the exponential rise in virus cases?

"This was a week when we weren't just worried about financial markets. We were worried about the functioning and operating of government, about day-to-day society," said Drossos.

The mother of three had started stockpiling cases of water bottles when ordering groceries from the FreshDirect delivery service. When she read a headline that suggested Governor Andrew Cuomo was thinking about shutting down New York City, she told her husband she needed to make one last run to Zabar's, the neighborhood's iconic food store. Drossos made sure their car was full of gas, and she pulled out cash from the ATM.

The Fed had never cut rates at two consecutive emergency meetings. During his 6:30 p.m. conference call with reporters, Powell emphasized the necessity for the Fed's unprecedented action to return markets to more normal, liquid functioning. "That is an essential part of our job. That is actually the thing that central banks were originally designed to do, to provide liquidity to financial systems in stress, so we take that job very seriously."

Andreas Lehnert, the "Tools Memo" crisis-management czar, sat through the eerie meeting wondering when it would end so he could get back to his office and finish up work on the emergency-lending facilities his team had been racing to finalize.

At the end of the long day, Clarida dashed off a note of encouragement to Powell for inspiring his colleagues to move so quickly. Powell responded at 6:56 the next morning: "Focus turns 100% now to liquidity, where we may have a lot to do!" There was no time to stop and reflect.

Powell braced for a rough trading day on March 16. Even after the Fed's head-spinning series of break-glass-in-case-of-emergency actions, international markets had seen huge losses overnight. Stocks had been pounded in Asia and in early-morning trading in the United States, but nothing had prepared him for the horror show that soon nearly froze Wall Street. Powell began working that day from his home office, a wood-paneled room lined with bookcases and five of his guitars. Inside the television set was usually tuned to CNBC or Bloomberg TV, almost always with the sound off. His desk was an old library table from the living room of his childhood home just a few blocks away.

When US markets opened in New York at 9:30 a.m., a red bar on CNBC flashed an alert: The Dow Jones Industrial Average had plunged 10 percent, by 2,250 points. The decline halted trading for fifteen minutes.

Powell and his colleagues had gone all-in, but the virus was unleashing a financial panic they couldn't quell. "It was a frightening economic time. The system was much more broken than it was during the 2008 financial crisis," said Mnuchin.[4]

———

It was an all-out panic. "There were obviously a lot of investors who had pressed the button for the sell order on Monday, and it didn't seem to matter what the Fed had announced [the previous] night," said Nathan Sheets, a former Fed and Treasury economist. "A universal meltdown."

Who, Drossos wondered now, is being forced to sell?

Bridgewater Associates, which managed $160 billion, was one candidate. That weekend, Bridgewater founder Ray Dalio conceded the world's largest hedge fund had been wrong-footed during the turmoil, with its flagship fund down 20 percent. "We did not know how to navigate the virus and chose not to because we didn't think we had an edge in trading it," Dalio told the *Financial Times*. "In retrospect, we should have cut all risk."[5]

That could explain the heavy selling despite the Fed's growing commitment to stabilize markets. "I got really spooked at that thought," said Drossos, "because I know how big they are, and I know it's not just them."

On the trading floor of TD Securities, across from the Museum of Modern Art in midtown Manhattan — recently shuttered by coronavirus protocols — traders sat staring at their screens, not trading. "Markets were frozen," said Christopher Vogel. "They were locked." The former Marine tried to keep a cool head while repeatedly tapping the *F9* button on his computer to refresh the profit-and-loss figures for his team's trading positions. "I kept saying, 'Wow, I've got a lot of US Treasuries, and I'm really down an awful lot of money,'" he said.

Unusual and exigent

Since the 19th century, central banks have been guided by the principle that in addition to preserving a stable currency, they should serve as lenders of last resort to stabilize the financial system during a panic. The British journalist and economist Walter Bagehot authoritatively codified how to stop a run in his 1873 book, *Lombard Street*. His work dissected in plain language how the Bank of England successfully fought London's Panic of 1866, and his advice remains as applicable to modern markets — where billions of dollars are transacted at the stroke of a key — as it was 140 years ago. It remains a Bible of sorts for central bankers.

Bagehot argued that financial panics could be stopped early if the central bank lent freely to solvent firms against good collateral. Put all the money in the window to show depositors there was no need to pull out their cash. If necessary, these loans could be expensive — carrying a "penalty rate" — to discourage overuse.

"A panic, in a word, is a species of neuralgia, and according to the rules of science you must not starve it,"[6] Bagehot wrote. "The holders of the cash reserve must be ready not only to keep it for their own liabilities, but to advance it most freely for the liabilities of others. They must lend to merchants, to minor bankers, to 'this man and that man,' whenever the security is good. In wild periods of alarm, one failure makes many, and the best way to prevent the derivative failures is to arrest the primary failure which causes them."

When Congress created the Fed in 1913, the central bank could lend to other businesses only through banks. But in July 1932, as banking failures during the Great Depression deepened a credit crunch that starved businesses of working capital, Congress blurred the line between monetary and credit policy by inserting an obscure provision into a highway-construction bill that radically expanded the Fed's potential lending spigots. This provision — the 13(3) powers requiring "unusual and exigent circumstances" — gave the Fed special authority to use its powers to create money out of thin air and to designate any of the twelve reserve banks to purchase assets from or make loans to corporations, individuals, or partnerships outside the banking system that the Fed regulates.

From 1932 to 1936, the Fed used its 13(3) authority sparingly: It made just 123 loans worth a meager $1.5 million — around $28 million adjusted for inflation in 2020. The largest included a $300,000 loan to a typewriter manufacturer and $250,000 to a vegetable grower.[7]

By the 1950s, the Fed was ready to get out of this business altogether. "It is good government as well as good central banking for the Federal Reserve to devote itself primarily to...guiding monetary policy and credit policy," Chair Bill Martin told lawmakers in 1957.

Congress granted the Fed's wish the following year. It repealed the authority to make working-capital loans and ceded that job to the fledgling Small Business Administration. The original "unusual and exigent" authority stayed in place, but the Fed wouldn't break the glass on its emergency lending authority again until March 11, 2008, when Lorie Logan and her colleagues at the New York Fed launched a securities-lending operation to address the funding riptide that was bringing down investment bank Bear Stearns. Even then, markets were so raw that the Fed didn't even publicize the fact that the board had unanimously invoked the "unusual and exigent circumstances" clause. Public knowledge that such an extreme weapon was being deployed for the first time in seventy-two years might simply have exacerbated market convulsions.

Once the glass was broken, however, the Fed invoked the emergency-lending measure two more times that week, and Chair Ben Bernanke relied heavily on the 13(3) authority again after the failure of Lehman Brothers on September 15, 2008. More controversially, the Fed also used the "unusual and exigent" exception to rescue the failed but massive insurance company AIG. (Bank of America and Citi got credit guarantees through the same emergency lending, though the two big banks never required any actual funds from the Fed.) By November 2008, outstanding credit under these programs exceeded $700 billion.

The lending ended up being less risky than skeptics feared. The Fed didn't lose any money on the programs, and in fact turned a profit. The programs also proved relatively easy to shut down after the financial crisis ended.

"This is a bad one"

The 2008 financial crisis also demonstrated that the Fed, using some clever legal work-arounds, wasn't as constrained from purchasing assets as many initially thought. The Federal Reserve Act restricts the central bank to purchase only government debt, government-backed mortgage securities, and short-term municipal bonds. But the program known as the Commercial Paper Funding Facility had shown that the Fed could creatively sidestep these restrictions by again invoking its "unusual and exigent" authority. By October 2008, the market for commercial paper was deteriorating. To purchase these otherwise ineligible securities, the Fed could create an "unusual and exigent" lending program in which a designated reserve bank — in this case, the New York Fed — forms a new corporate entity that purchases commercial paper. The only catch was that Fed officials had to be confident they wouldn't lose money, which could invite harsh scrutiny from lawmakers.

The idea that invoking "unusual and exigent" circumstances would spook investors, as the Fed had feared twelve years earlier, felt quaint by March 2020. Even if the monetary weapons remained politically controversial, many on Wall Street believed they had provided Bernanke with the big guns needed to beat back the 2008 crisis. By Monday, March 16, 2020, the Fed had fired most of its other munitions, but markets were still dropping. Investors and other market watchers wondered when the Fed would deploy its "unusual and exigent" response.

Larry Kudlow teased a forthcoming announcement on the White House lawn a few minutes before noon on Monday. "The Fed has enormous power, enormous power," he said. "And it looks like they're going to start using it in connection with the Treasury Department and the president."

Later that afternoon, at 3:20, President Trump returned to the White House briefing room to deliver an uncharacteristically sober report about the risks facing the nation. He encouraged all Americans, even the young and healthy, to work or attend school from home if possible. "Avoid gathering in groups of more than ten people," he said, reading off a sheet. "Avoid discretionary travel. And avoid eating and drinking at bars, restaurants, and public food courts. With several weeks of focused action, we can turn the corner and turn it quickly."

Reporters pelted Trump with questions: *How long might this virus mess last?* "People are talking about July, August, something like that... Could be longer than that," the president said. "This is a bad one. This is a very bad one. This is bad in the sense that it's so contagious."

Markets were already getting pounded, and they fell further that afternoon as Trump spoke. The president was still at the podium at 4 p.m. when trading closed for the day. The Dow Jones Industrial Average had fallen 2,997 points — nearly 13 percent. It was the largest point decline ever, the second-largest percentage decline since Black Monday in October 1987, and worse than any single trading day during the Crash of 1929. Treasury yields, thankfully at least, fell that day after the Fed bought $40 billion in government debt, setting another record. The bond rally was a welcome break from the ominous pattern that had emerged the prior week. But borrowing costs for almost every other asset — mortgages, corporate debt, municipal bonds — were rising, and that was if credit was even available.

Critics again pounced on the Fed for screwing up. "There's a problem with both what the Fed did and what the Fed did not do," said Mohamed El-Erian, the former Pimco executive who had been in the running for Clarida's job. The central bank "should have been more laser-like focused on areas of market failures...and then followed up with more general-interest rate cuts when that can have an impact."[8]

The Fed's emergency cut hadn't done anything to provide immediate relief or to buy time for the central bank to deliver reinforcements. Powell's initial reaction — *Oh, hell* — quickly gave way to a more stoic attitude of *OK, let's just keep going.* He didn't regret anything they had done, but he knew right away that restoring markets would require bolder actions. Markets were now looking for much, much more from Congress and the White House, in the form of a comprehensive relief package. Most important, the country needed its public-health system to demonstrate it was getting its hands around the unfolding health emergency.

Of course there was an additional "unusual and exigent" angle to 2020's Pandemic Crisis — the fast-moving virus. The sort of market pressures that had built over many months in 2007 and 2008 were now being uncorked in mere days. What's more, the Fed was closed. When they left the Eccles Building following their emergency meeting on Sunday night, a senior staffer suggested to Powell that it was probably time for them to start working from home. Powell and his lieutenants battling the financial problems would no longer have the luxury of camping out together in conference rooms stocked with coffee and Diet Cokes to strategize tactics.

Powell watched that catastrophic Monday play out from home, surrounded by his books and guitars. He had no need for his Fed office's formal fireplace, chandeliers, or large mounted black-and-white prints of photographs by Sebastião Salgado. With a television tuned to CNBC and a specially configured laptop to access his Bloomberg data terminal, Powell fielded calls from central-bank counterparts abroad, lawmakers, Mnuchin, and his Fed team, who were likewise in the process of retreating to their home offices. But it was another reminder of how invasive this crisis was.

That same Monday, Lorie Logan had arrived at the New York Fed before 6 a.m. to find unsecured lending rates still uncomfortably high. Even though the Fed had set its new rate target between zero and ¼ percentage point, the fed-funds rate was trading at the top of that range or even above it. The data told Logan there were still significant pressures in funding markets. Those strains were spilling into the rapidly deteriorating market for commercial paper. If businesses couldn't roll over their loans, they could face new questions about how they were going to make payroll or finance daily operations. It was becoming more expensive for the highest-rated American businesses to borrow money for three months at a time than it was for the US government to borrow for ten or even thirty years. To meet the demand for cash, money-market funds were selling more commercial paper, saddling Goldman and JPMorgan Chase with more inventory than they wanted.

Fed officials in New York and Washington were racing to finalize a reboot of 2008's Commercial Paper Funding Facility, freeing them to buy three-month debt from firms with solid credit ratings. Mnuchin, an astute reader of the Fed's proposed term sheets, needed no background explanation of what was happening in the market. But he thought that the Fed should charge slightly higher rates than it had done in 2008. He approved $10 billion from the Treasury's war chest — the Roosevelt-era Exchange Stabilization Fund (ESF) — to cover losses on such loans. Fed officials were relieved to avoid a messy debate over whether they were taking on too much risk. Fed and Treasury officials agreed to price the facility with a penalty rate that was 2 percentage points above an overnight-borrowing benchmark. It would be a recurring issue in which the Treasury, rather than the Fed, pushed for higher rates or more restrictive terms.

Another challenge loomed. The Treasury's ESF had, at best, $90 billion in fiscal firepower available. Fed officials were already looking down the runway at other emergency-lending programs that might be needed.

"I think we all understand there is only so much in that pot," Clarida told Williams after a conference call with Powell and the Fed's general counsel, Mark Van Der Weide.

Late on Monday, the nation's eight largest banks reported that they had borrowed from the Fed's discount window — not out of panic, they maintained, but as part of a broader effort to ease the public stigma of such borrowing. Fed presidents also began urging smaller banks to seek help at the discount window, but many of those banks were concerned about the reputational risk. To obscure which banks may have been taking emergency loans, the Fed stopped its weekly reporting of district-by-district borrowing amounts.

Date 2020	Covid-19 Cases	Covid-19 Deaths	Dow Jones Average	VIX Fear Index
Monday, March 16	7,449	102	20,188 (↓ 2,997)	82.69 (↑ 24.86)

Sending checks

Nothing grabs the attention of leaders of both parties in Washington like a stock-market crash. By the morning of Tuesday, March 17, stocks had fallen 32 percent in just five weeks. By comparison, the market slid 54 percent over a considerably longer 18 month period from 2007 to 2009. Now, senators and their senior staffers saw how the Fed had shot everything it had to shoot — and how, on Monday, the markets had tanked anyway.

At 10:45 a.m. that day the Fed launched the Commercial Paper Funding Facility, and Mnuchin announced his approval of $10 billion to backstop such lending. It was the first 13(3) lending program since the 2008 crisis, and the first to require the Treasury secretary's approval.

About an hour later, Mnuchin joined Trump to brief reporters at the White House. Utah Senator Mitt Romney had endorsed Furman's earlier proposal to send $1,000 to every American, and now Mnuchin threw the White House's support behind the scheme. "We're looking at sending checks to Americans immediately," Mnuchin said. "Americans need cash now, and the president wants to get cash [out] now. And I mean now, in the next two weeks."

The news lifted market sentiment, which rallied throughout the day amid signs that Congress and the White House would speed up work on a relief bill that could top $1 trillion. "It is a big number," Mnuchin told reporters a few hours later, after leaving a briefing with Senate Republicans. It would get a lot bigger still.

The White House had begun pulling together an initial package that included $50 billion for the airline industry and up to $500 billion in grants for small businesses. Democrats, meanwhile, were putting together proposals that would extend the amount of time that laid-off workers could collect unemployment insurance.

At a lunch with Senate Republicans, Mnuchin delivered ominous and blunt warnings. The Treasury secretary privately voiced worries that the economic fallout they were facing could be worse than 2008. To drive home his point, he warned lawmakers that without sufficient action, the unemployment rate could hit 20 percent. It was a breathtaking assessment. Since the Labor Department's official unemployment survey began in 1948, the rate had hit 10 percent only twice — once during Volcker's recession in late 1982 and early 1983, and for just one month after the financial crisis, in October 2009. An unemployment rate of 20 percent meant nearly 27 million Americans who had been working the month before would find themselves out of a job.

Mnuchin's sobering calculation became public later that evening — infuriating Trump — but markets were already surging over the prospect of more spending from Congress. The Dow climbed 1,000 points, or 5 percent. Wall Street's better mood briefly cracked the door open for blue-chip companies to raise cash. Companies issued around $28 billion in debt on Tuesday after having sold none on Monday. Exxon sold $8.5 billion in debt and Pepsi raised $6.5 billion. As soon as the debt markets felt open, Goldman Sachs hit the market. But the costs to borrow for even the best names in business were rising. Goldman, for example, raised $2.5 billion in ten-year debt with an interest rate 3 percentage points above a government rate that Tuesday. By contrast, one month earlier it had raised $2 billion in ten-year money at a rate just 0.95 percentage points above a government rate.[9]

Breaking the buck, déjà vu

Despite the rallies in markets and investor optimism, worrying trends were growing beneath the surface. Treasury yields began rising sharply on Tuesday. Were investors selling US Treasury debt because they worried an explosion in government borrowing would send rates even higher? Possibly. But the magnitude of the increase seemed unusually large and more reminiscent of the volatility seen the previous week.

Stresses were spreading to money-market mutual funds, accounts that millions of Americans assume are safe places to store cash. That wasn't always right. In 2008, one fund that had invested heavily in the short-term debt of Lehman Brothers sparked a panic when it told investors its shares were worth a few pennies less than the customary $1. This particular fund had "broken the buck," something investors thought impossible. The move threatened to spark runs on other "prime" money-market funds that invested in short-term corporate debt, forcing the government to step in. Not only would savers get run over if other investors raced to withdraw money from funds, but large US companies that relied on money funds to buy their commercial paper could also find themselves in a big pinch. The Boston Fed, which had special expertise in the area — many of the largest mutual funds are based in New England — had rolled out yet another "unusual and exigent" program that loaned money to banks in order to buy commercial paper from money-market funds, bailing them out.

Piecemeal reforms enacted by the Securities and Exchange Commission after the 2008 crisis had been insufficient, Boston Fed President Eric Rosengren had warned. Now the same problem was back. At the end of February, the money-market mutual funds that invested primarily in commercial paper had held $1.1 trillion in assets, of which $620 billion belonged to large, institutional investors. Holdings by those investors had fallen 12 percent, or $80 billion, since March 4. Money funds had seen larger outflows in past periods, but this redemption wave was notable for its speed and lack of warning. Soon Rosengren was getting calls from many of the large mutual funds, saying they were at risk of runs. "They were worried that they were going to break the buck," he said.[10]

Rosengren began sending flares to officials at the Fed board as well as the New York Fed, and he pulled together veterans from the 2008 crisis to design a newer version of their initial rescue operation. "The question was did we think we could skate through? And did we really want to be bailing out prime money-market funds again?" Rosengren said. "There was a fair amount of back and forth, but it became clear that this really wasn't about the money-market funds. You couldn't transact in short-term credit markets at all."[11]

"Fiscal news driving better markets, but still big concerns over MMFs," Powell wrote in a 3:31 p.m. email to Clarida.

"Think big"

With dozens of staffers working on getting the emergency-lending facilities, Powell turned his attention to making sure that Congress knew what the Fed was doing. Powell's concern was that lower rates and backstop lending programs couldn't begin to truly address the underlying problems caused by a steep drop in demand. In 1933, John Maynard Keynes wrote to President Roosevelt explaining that the economy needed more spending, not easier credit. The latter, he said, was like "trying to get fat by buying a larger belt."[12]

Now, Powell added his voice to the chorus calling for more relief spending. No longer able to physically wear out the carpets on Capitol Hill, however, he hit the phones. "Think big. Interest rates are low," he told House Speaker Nancy Pelosi during a 2 p.m. phone call.[13]

Powell spoke with another eight lawmakers who were managing the next bill that was taking shape. Regardless of the lawmaker's party or position, Powell's message was the same: This is the big one. Whatever fiscal support you can provide, do it now, and do it in the form of grants, not loans. The Fed's lending powers could help businesses, cities, or states for a few weeks or months, but ultimately it was Congress that had the power to spend and to help individuals and families.

These senior lawmakers were receptive, but they harbored their own parochial concerns. Pelosi, for example, was worried that state and local governments were about to get clobbered. Municipal borrowers, including hospitals, were being swept up in Wall Street's much-bigger retreat from anything remotely risky, and the San Francisco Democrat worried they would be unable to borrow at a time when they were being forced to spend more money. Lockdowns would only exacerbate the hit to their revenues. Mnuchin was floating a proposal to delay tax filing by three months, from April 15 to July 15, which threatened to create huge strains on states that normally relied on their tax coffers to fill up over the coming month. Now they were facing a shortfall at a time when they could barely borrow.

"Think big and help our states," Pelosi told Powell, "because they are taking a big bite of this wormy apple, and they need much more in terms of resources."[14]

As it turned out, Powell was already thinking big. Republican Senator Pat Toomey and other lawmakers had expressed some support for bulking up the Treasury's purse so that the Fed could lend against riskier assets. With more money to backstop losses, the Fed could take the basic idea behind the Commercial Paper Funding Facility and apply it to the $9.3 trillion market for corporate debt and the $3.9 trillion market for municipal borrowing.

Extending more safety nets under huge swaths of lending markets would help, but it would also cross all sorts of red lines. Even back in 2008, the Fed had ruled out intervening in the municipal market. Unlike the market for corporate debt, the municipal-debt market is incredibly fragmented, creating more operational challenges. And it was a political minefield — one littered with 535 potential detonators. Lawmakers who sit on the very committees that oversee the Fed could raise uncomfortable questions: *Why are you buying securities from that congressman's district but not mine?* Or *Why are you buying the debt of this predominantly White school district at a lower rate than the debt of this predominantly Black school district? Why are you favoring blue cities over rural red counties?* And what would happen if a city that borrowed from the Fed defaulted?

The Fed habitually stays away from policies that could put the institution in politically difficult positions. Neither Powell nor any other official ever wanted to demand that a city or state raise taxes or cut the pay of police or firefighters to secure or repay a loan. Nonetheless, Lael Brainard, whom Powell had tapped to oversee all of the emergency-lending programs, thought the fast-moving Pandemic Crisis left the Fed no choice. She lobbied forcefully for the Fed to suck it up and cross those red lines.

Wading into the corporate market created separate challenges. Powell and his colleagues had raised concerns in recent years about the risks piling up from growing business indebtedness. And by backstopping the corporate market, the Fed would expose itself to the same critiques it had faced after the 2008 financial crisis — that it was helping big borrowers while doing nothing for the little guy.

Powell agreed with Brainard. He thought the crisis was going to require the Fed to take action it was not comfortable with. Powell believed the Fed needed to be more open-minded about which red lines it was willing to cross.

"What do you think?" Powell asked Clarida during a phone call that evening.

Clarida had reservations about all this lending but suggested they could price the backstops at a penalty rate, following Bagehot's dictum, in order to incentivize states, cities, or businesses to seek first to borrow elsewhere.

"We're gonna have to do it," Clarida responded. "This shock is something that no one could have anticipated or insured against. But we need to do it right."

———

Powell's willingness to break boundaries underscored a great irony of the crisis. For years, almost every news article introducing Powell noted that he lacked a PhD in economics. Now, the Fed was being led by a former

lawyer with deep experience in corporate finance and considerable political skills at a moment when the Fed was being plunged into dicey questions of law, corporate finance, and politics. He may not have been an
economist, but Powell's background almost perfectly suited him to the
moment.

"Most economists who are central bankers would say, 'Monetary policy isn't the right tool here' or, 'We need to be cautious given that we're
central bankers, think of the long-term effects,'" said Randal Quarles, the
vice chair for bank supervision. "Someone with Jay's background is going
to approach things more by saying, 'OK, well, what's the problem we're
facing? How can we address that? How can we make that happen?' That
was the approach he took. I think that's why he was more willing to think
about things that many central bankers would say are almost off the table
even if they are technically possible."

Quarles had initially resisted some of Powell's efforts to expand the
Fed's response. "I take events as demonstrating that Jay was clearly right.
Indeed, almost any Fed chair would have done much less and moved
much more slowly."

In fact, Powell's actions over the last two weeks of March surprised
some of the people who know him best. "I don't think of him as a river-
boat gambler or anything, but it was an unusually forceful thing to do. Is
he the guy who's really going to have the chutzpah to do it?" said one long-
time friend of Powell's. "And he did, and he pushed everybody else to
do it."

Powell, meanwhile, was entertaining conversations with lawmakers
about what to do for businesses that couldn't borrow in the capital markets. Two Republicans were proposing to give small businesses access to
much larger loans from the Small Business Administration. But that program wouldn't reach middle-market businesses — those too small for the
capital markets but too big for small-business loans. Senator Mark Warner, a successful businessman and moderate Democrat who had been
governor of Virginia, began crafting a proposal for the Fed to make funds
available directly to these businesses.

Powell urged Mnuchin, Senate Majority Leader Mitch McConnell, and others to make grants as widely available as possible rather than rely on loans from the Fed. But Mnuchin already had a lot on his plate. He was asking Congress to authorize a grant program for the airlines and cargo carriers. Moreover, Democrats didn't trust the Trump administration. They feared a loan program run through the Treasury Department might steer loans to politically favored groups.

That led to a second great irony of the Pandemic Crisis. Lawmakers had slapped the Fed's wrists for using its lender-of-last-resort tools in 2008, imposing curbs to make those authorities more democratically accountable. Their message could be summed up along the lines of "Don't do this again, Fed."

Now the senior leaders of both parties were sending a different message. "Fed, do something, and fast."

This was going to be Bagehot — on steroids.

Date 2020	Covid-19 Cases	Covid-19 Deaths	Dow Jones Average	VIX Fear Index
Tuesday, March 17	9,577	126	21,237 (↑ 1,049)	75.91 (↓ 6.78)

Chapter Eleven

MONEY ALMOST STOPS

Wednesday, March 18, was a nightmare.

Jay Powell woke up to see Treasury yields continuing to climb higher, even though stock futures suggested markets would plunge at the opening bell. It looked like a return to the perplexing dynamic of a week earlier. When Treasury yields went in the opposite direction of stocks, they lost their ability to serve as a hedge, absorbing market ups and downs. Powell shot off a note to colleagues at 6:58 that morning: *What's up with the ten-year yield?*

Thomas Laubach, the monetary-affairs division director, weighed in via email about the risks that market dysfunction was returning. Reports of increased fiscal spending "is a good explanation for yields up, but not for stocks down." It didn't make sense, he said. "Maybe still some of the issues that bonds have lost some of their appeal as hedges for stocks?"

If the jump in long-term rates was a "rational response to higher supply, that's one thing," Powell wrote back. "If it is a sign of Treasury market liquidity again disappearing, that's something we would need to address."

Powell had been rushing out some of the Fed's most extreme tools on a daily basis, but none of it seemed to be working. With virus infections rising, the public-health situation was only going to get worse. That was sure to intensify market panic. A health crisis would become a financial crisis, which would in turn vastly amplify the ensuing economic crisis.

Canary in the coal mine

The US Treasury market is considered the world's largest and most liquid bond market. The second-largest and second-most liquid is called the "agency MBS market" — mortgage-backed securities guaranteed by the government. That market offers a key channel through which the Fed influences the economy because its changes to short-term rates ripple through to mortgage rates. But the agency MBS market was now caught in the same riptide of economic uncertainty as the Treasury market. In both, sellers were unloading securities, driving prices down and yields up.

Scott Simon, who had retired a few years earlier as the head of investing in mortgage- and asset-backed securities at Pimco, called Clarida, his former colleague. The pooled-mortgage investment vehicles known as REITs (shorthand for "real estate investment trusts") were imploding. Do you realize, Simon said urgently, that these firms are canaries in the coal mine? Even though the companies are small, their challenges shouldn't be ignored, he warned, because they were emblematic of pressures across the world of investment-grade and government-guaranteed bond funds. Bond funds that own the debt of the safest big companies also came under pressure as investors sold those assets to raise cash.

If you don't fix the market for top-rated bonds, Simon told Clarida, "It will get away from you."

A new frenzy was gripping all sorts of markets: mortgage REITs, money-market mutual funds, open-ended mutual funds that invested in corporate bonds — the list kept growing.

"Hell is coming"

So far, most Americans were stocking up on toilet paper, not paper money. But officials at the Fed's cash-management services were working overtime to make sure ATMs and banks could stay well stocked in case more people decided they needed cash in hand. Minneapolis Fed President Neel Kashkari heard from one banker who had fulfilled a $600,000 withdrawal in cash from a customer. A Bank of America branch on Park

Avenue and 52nd Street, a few paces from the headquarters of asset-management giant BlackRock, temporarily ran out of $100 bills.[1] "The Federal Deposit Insurance Corporation is reminding Americans that FDIC-insured banks remain the safest place to keep their money," the regulator said in a statement Wednesday. In bold letters, the agency added, "Since 1933, no depositor has ever lost a penny of FDIC-insured funds." The last thing the country needed was pictures of Americans lining up — six feet apart — at ATMs.

The Fed prepares for these kinds of surges in demand. In March the amount of paper currency circulating in the economy increased by $70 billion, or around 2.5 percent. The Fed was getting the equivalent of 700 million hundred-dollar banknotes into the economy in a matter of weeks, a magnitude not seen since the run-up to the Y2K scare before January 1, 2000 — an event for which officials had months to get ready.

Kashkari, a veteran of the 2008 crisis, urged calm in a *60 Minutes* interview he taped that day. "If everybody gets scared at the same time and they demand their money back, that's why the Federal Reserve is here," he said.

Did Americans need to take cash out of the bank? "You don't need to. Your ATM is safe. Your banks are safe. There's enough cash in the financial system. And there's an infinite amount of cash at the Federal Reserve," he said.

Others warned of the potential health hazards of money hoarding. The Colorado Bankers Association advertised how a single dollar bill could have changed hands 1,000 times, making it home to 3,000 different bacteria. "Keeping cash in the bank is a prudent defense against contamination," the trade group said.

During an emotional, twenty-eight-minute live interview after noon on CNBC, billionaire investor Bill Ackman called for a thirty-day shutdown of the economy. "Hell is coming," he said. "We need to shut it down. Shut it down now." He then described how, one month earlier, he had gone to the bank and taken out a large amount of cash.

The Dow tumbled as Ackman spoke, dropping as much as 2,000 points — to levels that nearly wiped out the gains achieved by the soaring markets that had typified Trump's presidency. The plunge triggered another market-wide fifteen-minute trading halt shortly before 1 p.m.

The headlines got worse. Detroit's top three automakers announced they were ceasing production at all plants. The US closed its border with Canada. Marriott announced plans to furlough tens of thousands of workers.

Daleep Singh, the markets desk chief at the New York Fed, was still being inundated with messages from contacts urging a shutdown to trading. "It was sheer, unadulterated panic, of a magnitude that was far worse than in 2008 and 2009. Far worse," said Singh, who had spent the 2008 crisis on the interest-rate desk at Goldman's trading floor in London. The idea of shutting down markets was especially discouraging. "It was a profoundly un-American thing to contemplate, to just shut everything down, and almost fatalistic — that we're not going to get out of this."

Mnuchin said he never considered closing the markets. "It would have been an absolute worst-case scenario. And the question for me is once you close the markets, opening the markets becomes really difficult. We saw the same thing after September 11," he said.[2]

"We are not doing enough"

The market meltdown showed investors were going deeper into liquidation mode. The Dow closed down 1,338 points, or more than 6 percent, while oil prices dropped to levels not seen since the months after the 9/11 attacks. More ominously, Treasury yields lurched higher. Foreign governments desperate to raise dollars were among the biggest sellers, and they dumped more than $100 billion over the first three weeks of March, a record.

Clarida spent the day working the phone. After markets closed, he sent Williams and Powell a note outlining an agenda for their next discussion. "Realize its hectic all around but we should try to talk this afternoon/tonight," he said. They needed to "step up size of our Treasury / mbs [mortgage-backed securities] purchases given ongoing supply hitting market beyond what it is absorbing."

Moreover, the mortgage-backed-securities market was "getting hit" with REIT liquidations, and Wall Street dealers weren't able to absorb the sales, Clarida reported. Finally, he passed along word that reserve managers at foreign central banks, desperate to grab dollars, were selling holdings of Treasuries.

"We are hearing same," Williams wrote back minutes later.

New York Fed asset manager Logan had published plans earlier that week to purchase $40 billion in Treasury securities per day, thinking her team would begin to reduce those purchases once they regained control of the market. But on Wednesday the New York Fed went the other way, upping the purchases to $45 billion. Williams reported that now they were preparing to increase them again, to $50 billion on Thursday. To provide sellers of agency MBS with the cash they desperately needed, the New York Fed was also considering revamping the way it settled those transactions on the fly. "Looks promising," Williams wrote. "Lorie will send update shortly."

Clarida replied immediately: "I think we may need to go much bigger on T [Treasury] purchases than 50 — sell-off today indicates to me we are not doing enough."

Because foreign governments maintain bank accounts at the New York Fed, Logan could see which countries were dumping Treasuries in a desperate bid to supply dollars back home. Reported Logan from the New York Fed after 5:30 p.m.: "We are hearing significant selling from reserve managers." Everyone was still dumping Treasuries, including foreign central banks.

Logan suggested devising a new lending program that would allow those countries to temporarily swap their Treasuries into dollars, which could relieve a key source of pressure on the Treasury market. Otherwise the Fed would have to continue buying larger and larger amounts of US debt to stabilize the Treasury market.

"Move as quickly as possible"

The Fed had long been known as the "lender of last resort" — the institution that could move quickly enough and forcefully enough to rescue

America's financial markets in the middle of a panic. But it had resisted becoming the backup lender to the entire world. On March 18, 2020, it jettisoned any lingering reservations.

In 2008, the Fed had temporarily (and somewhat grudgingly) extended its dollar-swap network to nine additional central banks. Powell emailed the FOMC at 5:48 p.m. to seek its sign-off. "In light of escalating pressures on [overseas dollar] markets, within the next hour or so we will be sending you materials to support a notation vote on extending the swap lines again to these 9 central banks....I apologize for the short notice, but things are moving very rapidly...and there is an urgent need to move ahead with these swap lines. I ask you to move as quickly as possible on this."

Other central banks had ramped up their emergency measures Wednesday. With strains spreading through financial markets in London, the Bank of England had announced plans earlier that day to provide unlimited amounts of financing to commercial-paper markets.

Shortly before 6 p.m., Clarida heard from Philip Lane, a former student of his who one year earlier had become the chief economist of the European Central Bank. The ECB would announce in around an hour, just before midnight at its headquarters in Frankfurt, a new €750 billion ($818.7 billion) bond-buying program aimed at shielding the Eurozone economy from the virus. The Pandemic Emergency Purchase Program sent a strong signal that Europe's lender of last resort would stand behind embattled governments, particularly in Italy and Spain. Those countries, already hard hit by the virus, had seen borrowing costs soar in recent days, fueling concerns of a rerun of the sovereign-debt crises that had gripped the Continent nearly a decade earlier. Clarida informed Powell and Williams of the decision, which had been reached during an unscheduled, late-night conference call.

Then at 6:16 p.m., Clarida urged even more-aggressive purchases in a note to Powell, Williams, and Logan. "We are all hearing...that T market is still not functioning — the sell off today in tandem with a down day in stocks and widespread reporting of hedge fund and reit liquidation indicate to me we should seriously consider upping the size of our daily operation — real rates are doing the surging — break evens have collapsed to all-time lows," he said. "[W]ith foreign selling on top of domestic we have more to do."

Clashing with the comptroller

Powell didn't respond for a few hours because he was in the middle of another mess. The Fed was racing that evening to finalize its backstop of the money-market mutual funds, which would be run by the Boston Fed and for which Mnuchin would provide another $10 billion in funding. The Boston Fed wasn't going to be ready to launch the program until early the following week, but officials concluded they needed to attempt a soft open by announcing that the program would be online soon. "That was explicitly to prevent the money funds from closing on Friday, Saturday, Sunday, Monday. We did not have an additional day," said Rosengren.[3]

But the announcement ran into a problem in the form of Joseph Otting, who headed the Office of the Comptroller of the Currency. The Federal Reserve shares responsibility for regulating the nation's banks with the OCC and the Federal Deposit Insurance Corporation. The OCC, established in 1863, is an independent bureau within the Treasury Department that charters and regulates national banks and federally chartered branches of foreign banks. Because the Fed's money-market-fund backstop was going to run through the banking sector, it needed the OCC to waive regulatory capital rules. Banks would borrow from the Boston Fed and use the money to purchase assets from money-market funds, pledging those assets as collateral for their Fed loans.

There was a hitch: the Fed needed the OCC to waive the requirement that banks have capital to absorb potential losses on these assets. If the value of the assets declined, the Fed — which held them as collateral against the loans — took the risk, not the banks. For all practical purposes, these loans presented no risk to the banks regulated by the OCC.

Otting, the head of the OCC, put his foot down: No, he told Fed vice chair Randal Quarles, he would not waive the capital rules.

Mnuchin and Otting were friends and former business partners. Mnuchin had hired Otting in 2010 to lead OneWest Bank and, in 2017, had tapped him to lead the OCC. Now, with money-market mutual funds at risk of accelerating a panic, Otting was telling the Fed he couldn't help. Quarles and Powell enlisted Mnuchin to intervene and wrestle his former business partner to the ground.

On a phone call that Wednesday night, Otting reiterated his rigid stance against relaxing the rules on how the Fed could support banks: "I'm not doing it." He worried about being forced to compromise capital standards in the national banking system in order to deliver relief to parts of the market outside his purview.

Mnuchin couldn't believe what he was hearing. The secretary sounded exasperated.

"What do you mean you're not doing it, Joe?" Mnuchin said. "This is a matter of national security we're talking about." After some back-and-forth, Otting eventually acquiesced.

Rosengren didn't think the Fed had any time to spare, and the standoff with the OCC risked delaying the Fed's announcement. "We already knew there'd be widespread closure of money-market funds if we waited any longer," he said later. The Fed announced the program at 11:30 p.m.

One Washington analyst summarized the speed at which the Fed was moving in a report the next morning titled, "The crisis that doesn't sleep." A Wall Street economist similarly remarked, "Midnight announcements tell you there was an urgency to put a safety net under the system."[4]

Sharp deterioration

Responding to Clarida's emails at 9:18 p.m., Powell asked if they needed to raise the headline number of Treasury purchases. "That's one option given the increase in T supply," Clarida wrote. But for now he was more concerned about getting control of the ten-year Treasury bond, to restore confidence in the world's safest investment.

When they spoke by phone that evening, Powell sounded exhausted for the first time since the crisis had accelerated two weeks ago. He asked for a debrief on the dysfunction in the Treasury and mortgage-backed-securities markets. Clarida told him it appeared to be a perfect storm—massive selling by foreign investors (including overseas central banks) on top of hedge funds and other investors unwinding their positions. Negative Treasury-bill yields offered greater evidence of a panic flight to cash.

Throughout the day, Clarida had been repeating one question to his staff: "Is this working?" Now he acknowledged the obvious to Powell: "Our purchases are massive, but they're not working." Rates on the most recently issued Treasury securities continued to diverge from older issues, an important danger sign that the Fed's purchases were falling short.

Powell sighed. "Are you saying we should move to yield-curve control?" he asked. Yield control would mean buying as much debt as necessary to achieve a certain yield—an open-ended commitment the Fed had not made since the Second World War.

"I'm not recommending it now, but failure is not an option," Clarida responded. "So at a minimum, we've gotta do more, and we've gotta get the ten-year yield under control."

Because so many other instruments are tied to the ten-year yield, Clarida thought, *getting rates low and suppressing volatility would have huge dividends for mortgage markets, corporate borrowers, and others.* He floated the idea of selling short-term Treasury bills, which had negative yields, to purchase more longer-dated notes and bonds.

Around 10:15 p.m., Logan sent out a mixed update. "Market participants are reporting that our purchases are having a positive effect, and we also see some of this in the data," she reported. "However, most market participants have suggested that heavy volatility and selling flows are swamping these positive effects." Given that, the New York Fed had already gone public that evening with plans to purchase $100 billion over the next two days. That would put the Fed on pace to purchase $225 billion in just one week of the "at least $500 billion" approved by the FOMC the previous Sunday.

"We are considering whether we could increase tomorrow's operations further, for example to $75 billion in total," Logan continued. "However, this would be a very large amount to purchase in one day. We think it can be achieved, but the risk is that we are...forced to accept very unfavorable (high) prices in the operation." Clarida had no concerns about paying too much.

If senior officials were comfortable with those risks after a planned discussion on Thursday morning, Logan added, "The team is prepared to act quickly after our discussion."

Logan moved on to address mortgage markets. The Fed's purchases had been helping, "but today's deterioration in conditions was sharp. As a result, we are planning to pull forward additional purchases." Moreover, the Fed's systems are built to settle purchases for mortgage securities about a month in the future — the standard trading convention for those bonds — but the rates to finance these sales were extremely high. Logan's team had rapidly explored changes to trading-and-settlement procedures to complete transactions within days, something the central bank had never done before. "There are operational risks here, but I believe they are worth taking," she wrote. "We aim to conduct $10 billion in such purchases tomorrow. We will do more if needed on Friday."

Finally, Logan turned to overnight money markets, which were settling down. Demands for cash by some banks had led the fed-funds rate to stay at the high end of its range, and Logan warned that the fed-funds rate might still print at the top or above the top of its range. "There are plans in place to call these banks to encourage them to use the discount window going forward rather than pay such high rates," Logan said.

It was a bleak picture. *We're toast*, Clarida thought to himself before retiring after midnight.

In the coming days and weeks, he would adopt a different analogy to tell his family how he felt that night: "We are in a jumbo jet at 30,000 feet in the worst storm in seventy-five years. Our instrument panel [the Treasury market] has gone dead, in both ways: We don't believe what they're saying, and when we push this button it doesn't do what we think." Despite massive interventions over the previous seventy-two hours, the Treasury market simply wasn't functioning properly.

And, catastrophized Clarida, *we are running out of fuel because we can't keep doing these lending programs if we run out of Treasury money. Not only do we have to stabilize the plane, we've got to land it in a fog and gale-force winds. We've got to find an airport, land the plane on a dark runway, then make sure it does not skid off into the ocean.*

Date 2020	Covid-19 Cases	Covid-19 Deaths	Dow Jones Average	VIX Fear Index
Wednesday, March 18	12,934	152	19,898 (↓ 1,338)	76.45 (↑.54)

Triage

Powell emailed Clarida first thing the next morning, March 19, unspooling his latest thinking. *We've got to go bigger on Treasuries and mortgages,* the Fed chair said. The global riptide meant markets were on the verge of collapse, said Powell, and he asked Clarida again for his thoughts on yield-curve control. At 11:30 p.m. the night before, Australia's central bank had rolled out its own yield-curve-control program by committing to buy government debt in whatever amounts were needed to hold near zero the yields on debt with maturities of up to three years.

Then Powell vented another brainstorm: Should the Fed come up with a 13(3) facility that would purchase existing corporate bonds? This was a step beyond their earlier idea of buying newly issued debt. With a little bit of support from the Treasury's war chest in the Exchange Stabilization Fund, Powell thought they could preannounce the whole thing and then increase the amount of funding available if and when Congress passed the relief package that was coming together on Capitol Hill. That strategy allowed them a shot at maximizing any benefit. *Now is when something is needed,* Powell wrote.

At 8 a.m. that morning, Logan briefed senior officials on the proposal to increase their Treasury purchases from $50 billion to $75 billion that day. Powell and the board agreed. It was a staggering multiple of anything they had ever done before. The Tea Party, conservative economists, and other groups had launched searing criticisms of the Fed during the controversial second round of quantitative easing. Now the Fed was going to buy *in one day* what it had bought *in one month* back in 2010 and 2011.

The Fed announced the expansion of its dollar-swap-line network at 9 a.m. So far that week, the central bank had loaned $112 billion to the European Central Bank and another $32 billion to the Bank of Japan. By funneling dollars overseas, the massive commitment was becoming one of the Fed's most significant and least-noticed expansions of power. Stabilizing foreign dollar markets would be critical to avoiding even greater disruptions to global markets that were spilling back to the US economy.

In South Korea, for example, big brokerages were trying to raise dollars to meet margin calls. They had previously borrowed money to buy billions of dollars of derivatives tied to stocks in the US, Europe, and Hong Kong. As stocks plunged, however, lenders were demanding that the brokerages put up more cash. The scramble for dollars pushed the Korean won to its lowest level in a decade against the dollar on March 19. These lending lines "may be the most important part of the international financial stability safety net that few have ever heard of," said Andrew Hauser, the Bank of England's top markets official.[5]

Like other expanded authorities, the swap lines created new political problems by pushing the Fed from domestic monetary policy into foreign policy. What if the president or the secretary of state ordered the Fed to extend a swap line to a country that the Fed believed might be too risky? (This was no mere hypothetical: over the coming weeks, the government of Turkish President Recep Tayyip Erdogan would appeal to the Fed and the State Department for access to a Fed swap line. Washington refused.)[6]

In theory, countries could turn to the International Monetary Fund for financial support, but those petitions were for particularly dire scenarios and in wealthier, more advanced economies, they carried a stigma. In South Korea, for example, there was a joke that *IMF* stood for *I'M Fired*.

Date 2020	Covid-19 Cases	Covid-19 Deaths	Dow Jones Average	VIX Fear Index
Thursday, March 19	17,540	203	20,087 (↑ 188)	72 (↓ 4.45)

"Lamps are going out"

Around 11:30 a.m. on Friday, Clarida sent Powell two charts from his Bloomberg terminal. One showed the implied volatility of two-year Treasury yields one year ahead. It had reached its lowest level for the past several years, a sign of how markets didn't expect the Fed to change interest rates. But implied volatility for ten-year rates at the same one-year future point had hit levels not seen since 2013. "Highest since taper tantrum!" exclaimed Clarida. He was concerned the Fed was buying too many government securities with short and intermediate terms, and not enough long-term debt.

"Our 200 plus bil aimed at restoring better function to off-the-run Treasuries has failed," he said in a note later that evening.

Municipal-debt markets, which finance schools, hospitals, transportation systems, and more, were seizing up. Even though most states have balanced-budget requirements that prevent them from running deficits the way the Treasury does, revenues tend to be lumpy and don't generally arrive when bills are due. Issuing debt helps the states smooth out these cash-flow challenges. That week, municipal-bond prices cratered as investors pulled a record $12.2 billion from mutual and exchange-traded funds that invest in municipal bonds.

"It sucks," said Hazim Taib, chief financial officer of the Connecticut Housing Finance Authority. "A market that is supposed to be liquid and functioning is no longer liquid and functioning, so if you want somebody to buy your bonds you have to pay through the nose."[7]

In response, Powell proposed that the Fed accept short-term municipal debt in both the Commercial Paper Funding Facility and the Money Market Mutual Fund Liquidity Facility. Powell asked his fellow governors to approve the change on Friday at 9:20 a.m. The Fed announced the expansion less than two hours later. It represented another foray across red lines that Ben Bernanke hadn't been willing to cross in 2008, when Fed officials considered but rejected the idea of purchasing muni securities.

Stocks slumped another 4.5 percent that Friday — the Dow had fallen more than 10,000 points since February 12. New York joined California and Illinois in ordering the state's workforce to stay home. The US closed its borders with Mexico and Canada to nonessential travel.

"The lamps are going out all across the economy," said the title of a report from JPMorgan chief US economist Michael Feroli.[8] The bank had cut its forecast for annualized growth in the first quarter to negative 4 percent and in the second quarter to negative 14 percent, the worst contraction in living memory. Goldman Sachs warned that more than 2.25 million Americans might claim jobless benefits the following week, shattering the previous record of 695,000 set in 1982.

One bright spot for the Fed, the ten-year Treasury yield fell to 0.92 percent — a notable decline, and a sign that the Fed's purchases of securities were helping. But lower yields were of little use if cities, states, and companies couldn't borrow, and corporate-bond markets were nearly frozen. Conditions had deteriorated to the point where officials feared only the most cash-rich companies (think Google or Microsoft) would be able to borrow in capital markets — and at huge premiums. Once that happened and every CFO and investor saw such cruddy prices being offered for high-quality names, it would reset the broader market, forcing weaker firms to pay astronomic sums.

Date 2020	Covid-19 Cases	Covid-19 Deaths	Dow Jones Average	VIX Fear Index
Fri, Mar 20	23,640	273	19,173 (↓ 913)	66.04 (↓ 5.96)

"Fear is the most contagious disease"

Berkshire Hathaway was among the best-off companies in America, sitting on some $124 billion in cash and Treasury bills because, as Warren Buffett later explained to shareholders, "We don't want to be dependent on the kindness of friends, even, because there are times when money almost stops. And we had one of those, interestingly enough... around the day or two leading up to March 23."

Most companies, of course, didn't keep the kind of cash on hand that Berkshire did because, as Buffett explained, CFOs all over the country "had been taught to maximize returns," which meant they relied on debt — commercial paper, bank lines of credit, and corporate bonds. As the crisis unfolded, "We got to the point where the US Treasury market, the deepest of all markets, got somewhat disorganized. And when that happens, believe me, every bank and CFO in the country knows this — they react with fear. And fear is the most contagious disease you can imagine. It makes the virus look like a piker." By the weekend of March 21, the financial system was "very close to having a total freeze of credit to the largest companies in the world who were depending on it," Buffett concluded.[9]

"Recent measures are not enough to restore confidence and stability," wrote two analysts at Deutsche Bank in a report published Sunday, March 22. "More is needed and we argue that the Fed now needs to deal with the corporate bond market directly." Trading conditions suggested the investment-grade corporate-bond market "is as good as broken now."[10] Congress needed to approve new authorities, they wrote, to allow the Fed to buy corporate debt. Most companies just didn't have resources for revenues to fall to zero and stay there.

Powell told colleagues at the end of that trying week that he felt like they were swimming after a speedboat. The ad hoc approach in rolling out the 2008-era playbook was critical, but the way they were doing it, Powell quipped, made the Fed look like a one-armed paper hanger. Markets were coming unglued so quickly that everything they did to make things less bad was not getting the job done. And needless to say, the country wouldn't have a chance against the virus if the financial system caved in on itself.

The weekend offered a chance to finally get ahead of the meltdown. Powell ordered Lehnert's team to work through the weekend preparing a series of term sheets that would, in painstaking detail, explain what additional red lines the Fed was prepared to cross.

Chapter Twelve

*"GET IN THE BOATS
AND GO"*

On Friday, March 20, President Trump gave his daily press conference in the White House briefing room to reporters, who left every other seat empty as a health precaution. Trump had just finished touting the antimalarial drug hydroxychloroquine — a possible "game changer" — when a question caught his full attention.

After pressing the president about being unrealistically positive, Peter Alexander, White House correspondent for NBC News, asked, "What do you say to Americans who are scared, though? 200 dead. 14,000 or so sick. Millions, as you witnessed, who are scared right now. What do you say to Americans who are watching right now who are scared?"

"I say that you are a terrible reporter," responded Trump without hesitating. He gestured for the next question before deciding he wasn't done.

Jabbing his finger at Alexander, Trump unloaded: "I think that's a very nasty question, and I think it's a very bad signal that you're putting out to the American people."

Alexander gestured at himself with his mouth open and an exaggerated look of incredulity. "The American people are looking for answers and hope, and you're doing sensationalism," said Trump.[1]

The president was right: The American people *were* looking for answers and hope — as were the battered markets — but they wouldn't get it from hydroxychloroquine. They needed it in part from a major relief package that Congress had put together with lightning speed over the past seventy-two hours. Trump, however, continued to be mostly a spectator during the most consequential legislation of his presidency.

"The Doom Loop"

Normally in a crisis, the senior brass from Treasury and the White House might solicit ideas from Congress. The ideas that emerge aren't always that good. After listening thoughtfully, administration officials might say, "Those ideas are OK, but here's what we're actually going to do." Then they bring the plan. What was happening now was the opposite: Treasury and the White House were largely relying on Congress to provide the plan.

"The first thing that struck me as bizarre about this process was they were actually letting Congress make decisions when Congress probably shouldn't be making decisions in that environment," said one senior congressional staffer involved in the negotiations. "The Treasury had no plan. The White House had no plan. And so the congressional committees came up with it. It was weird. Each committee was told, 'Sit down and come up with your ideas.'" The ultimate result of this process was a series of packages that kept on expanding in scope and cost.

Economist Glenn Hubbard had noticed the lack of engaged leadership at the White House in mid-March. Hubbard, who has extensive contacts within the Republican Party, had crunched numbers on a program to replace the revenue of small businesses that might be shuttered by the pandemic. With another conservative economist, the American Enterprise Institute's Michael Strain, they estimated what might be needed to tide companies and their workers through a twelve-week shutdown — a number based on China's three-month lockdown. Replacing 80 percent of lost service-sector revenues for twelve weeks would cost $1.2 trillion, they concluded.

Trump was fixated on the idea of a payroll-tax cut, which most economists, including Hubbard, thought was ridiculous. It would do practically nothing for workers furloughed or fired, and those who weren't losing their jobs didn't need it. Hubbard turned his attention to a pair of Republican senators, Marco Rubio and Susan Collins, whom Mitch McConnell had tasked with developing a small-business relief program.

Some Republicans were choking on the spending estimates that Hubbard and others were throwing around. To Hubbard, aggressive fiscal action now was by far the cheaper option to break what he called "the doom loop"—his worry that a massive supply shock would turn into a demand shock. If trade disruptions or health precautions forced businesses to idle their factories or close stores, more workers would go without paychecks, further sapping demand and forcing businesses to make more drastic layoffs. Missed rent or a wave of bankruptcies would put pressure on landlords—and, in turn, on the banking system. "What could have been a short, sharp downturn turns into a long, protracted downturn, great recession, or even depression," Hubbard later said.[2] "That's what we're trying to prevent."

<hr />

The night of Monday, March 16, McConnell summoned Steven Mnuchin and Larry Kudlow to the ornately decorated Mansfield Room on the Capitol's second level, just off the Senate floor. The venue allowed senators to space out more easily than in McConnell's private conference room. Sitting under the room's giant chandelier, about a dozen GOP senators debriefed Mnuchin and Kudlow on the now $1 trillion-dollar-strong Coronavirus Aid, Relief and Economic Security Act, which bore the acronym CARES. McConnell had taken charge of what was becoming the third virus-driven spending bill after Republicans chafed at being forced to swallow the product Pelosi and Mnuchin had cooked up the prior weekend. Senate Republicans deemed the House bill, which had focused on paid-leave provisions, utterly unsuited to meet the present moment. *What good is paid leave,* the GOP senators groused, *if there are no jobs to take leave from?* Over the weekend, McConnell's focus had switched from amending the House package to starting anew on a third relief bill, and this time he was going to make sure that the GOP—not

Pelosi or Mnuchin — sat in the driver's seat. It helped that the House had adjourned and was not even in town that week.

McConnell was wary of repeating the political disaster that had followed the $700 billion Troubled Asset Relief Plan in 2008. (That bank bailout had quickly turned toxic.) Now, with elections just a few months away, McConnell didn't want lawmakers spending the summer and fall talking about how terrible this latest package was. To avoid a rerun of 2008 and to move quickly, McConnell assigned four different working groups to come up with different components of the bill. Increasing the number of people with their hands on the bill would save time and boost ownership over the final product. That Monday evening, the senators offered an update on their work to head off any unpleasant surprises later. As the meeting wore on, Kudlow looked at McConnell and shook his head. "I think the total necessary is going to run well above a trillion. Well above a trillion."

The room fell silent.

"Two trillion?" someone in the room asked.

"It could well be," Kudlow weakly offered.

That was a staggering sum. Richard Shelby of Alabama couldn't understand why Republicans had embraced the idea of lump-sum payments: *Wouldn't that money be better directed to people who lost their jobs?* Lindsey Graham argued for delaying such payments until the lockdowns lifted. "You can't stimulate something that's padlocked," he told reporters.[3]

Later, Mnuchin thanked Kudlow, who had more credibility with conservatives, for speaking up.

The Paycheck Protection Program

McConnell had charged senators working on the bill to get their best ideas to him by Thursday. Then he said something the senators rarely heard from him: *You're doing this — not your staff.* "This is a member-driven exercise," McConnell instructed. "You have staff to help with details and provide background, but this is not something to be turned over to staff. You personally are here until this is done."

When lawmakers are in Washington, their day is heavily scheduled into five-minute blocks from dawn to dusk. But as lockdowns spread across the country and the Capitol emptied of the trade groups, lawyers, and lobbyists who normally crowd its hallways and cafeterias, everyone's schedules opened up.

Rubio set up shop in the hearing room of the Senate Small Business Committee with a laptop. His staff had been toying with how to use the Small Business Administration's loan-guarantee program to cover companies' payroll costs by doubling the maximum loan amount to $10 million. Collins, meanwhile, had been working on a way to provide loan forgiveness to small businesses. They combined the two ideas and began selling the result to Republicans. Lawmakers were hearing from nervous constituents about the implications of schools and businesses shutting down. The Rubio-Collins hybrid offered a highly scalable way to get money to hair salons, dry cleaners, and bars and restaurants.

Some Democrats preferred providing more aid in the form of unemployment insurance. Another group of Democrats kicked around a separate idea: replace a portion of the incomes for eligible businesses (as Britain, Australia, and most European countries were doing).

Around 11 p.m. on Wednesday, March 18, as staffers huddled to put the final touches on the legislative language for their loan-interruption proposal, Rubio popped into an adviser's office. "Here's what we're going to call it — PPP, the Paycheck Protection Program." They sent it on to McConnell's office.

Measure twice, legislate once

Earlier that day, McConnell had dispatched Senator Pat Toomey of Pennsylvania to frame a separate effort coming out of the Senate Banking Committee to provide around $200 billion for the Treasury to backstop loans to airlines, cargo carriers, and other potentially distressed firms that were about to be walloped by the virus. Unlike the small-business plan, these loans would have to be paid back.

Powell had kept Toomey apprised that week of the Fed's efforts to support funding markets with its "unusual and exigent" lending efforts. But Toomey could see it wasn't enough, and the two men had broached the subject of getting a bigger infusion to the Treasury so the Fed could lend more broadly. Initially Toomey's staffers had figured roughly $50 billion would provide ample reinforcements for the Exchange Stabilization Fund (ESF). Toomey shook his head and said, "It's going to need to be a lot more than that."

Toomey wasn't alone in that view. During a Thursday-night phone call with Congressman Patrick McHenry, the top Republican on the House Financial Services Committee, Mnuchin floated a potential $50 billion infusion for Fed lending programs.

"Why fifty?" McHenry asked. "Is that going to be enough?"

Mnuchin explained the math. Because every $1 in Treasury money made the Fed comfortable enough to lend $10, "That fifty will get us $500 billion in Fed lending," Mnuchin offered. "If it isn't enough," he added, "we can always come back and ask for more money after we pass this thing."

McHenry gulped. "You do *not* want to do that," the Republican urged him. "As soon as we pass this thing, you do not want to come back to Congress. The number of things you'll have to give in order to get another bill through Congress — it's going to be extraordinary."

"OK, fine, we'll do a hundred," Mnuchin said. (Yes, this really is how certain big decisions get made: off the cuff and in a hurry.)

Thanks for moving, thought McHenry, *but all that tells me is you haven't really done the math.*

After hanging up with Mnuchin, McHenry called Paul Ryan, the former House speaker. Ryan had retired from Congress in 2018, but he still had influence and wanted to help. McHenry had been in Washington for just four years when Congress responded to the financial crisis in 2008, making him far too junior to have been involved in any of the big debates. Ryan was well versed in the finer points of the earlier crisis response. As McHenry recounted his call with Mnuchin, Ryan cut in:

"He wants to come back to Congress? You don't wanna come back to Congress! Who's got the pen on this? Who do I need to call?"

The answer: Mike Crapo of Idaho, the chair of the Senate Banking Committee. Crapo would soon press into service Andrew Olmem, a former Republican committee staffer who was Kudlow's deputy on the National Economic Council, to camp out in the banking committee's room and help draft the bill.

That weekend, McConnell and senior staffers also heard directly from Ryan on the need to dramatically boost the Treasury's war chest for Fed lending. The emphasis on getting a bundle of money for the Exchange Stabilization Fund revealed the extent to which Congress was outsourcing much of the heavy lifting for the Fed. McHenry urged his fellow Republican lawmakers to make this their No. 1 priority. "You want a wall of money," McHenry explained to House Minority Leader Kevin McCarthy. "You want to walk around with a wall of money to stop everything."

McHenry made sure Powell knew he had his full support. "I'm a pretty traditional Republican," McHenry later reflected. "I want financial regulation to be boring. I want markets to be boring. I want the Fed to be boring. But in the midst of this thing, I get it. We could all see what was happening to our constituents and in the real world."[4]

Toomey was also hearing from contacts on Wall Street about how the system was gumming up. "There was a unanimity of the view that the best approach here would be to have so much firepower that the market would calm down and return to functioning," he said. "I had become convinced...we should go with a larger number."[5]

By the weekend, Mnuchin's $50 billion had ballooned by a factor of ten. Toomey, McHenry, and other Republicans were talking about a $500 billion infusion to the Treasury, of which $75 billion might be earmarked to make loans to businesses in hard-hit industries. The rest was going to turbocharge the Fed's "unusual and exigent" lending, potentially creating a huge safety net for big US companies and whomever else the central bank decided could benefit from its firepower.

Toomey insisted to Mnuchin, Powell, and his Republican Senate colleagues that these expanded Fed powers be temporary. Amazingly, the first time he pitched his colleagues on the $500 billion figure, there was no pushback.

Legislative prescriptions

In early March, before the NBA canceled its season, Senator Mark Warner had gathered his senior staff and given them a heads-up. "This virus is going to be a real problem. We need to get all these letters out to people," he instructed.

A flurry of activity followed, with staffers firing off letters to regulators and other agency heads asking them what steps they were taking to protect consumers, renters, and borrowers.

Warner also began soliciting ideas from policy advisers who had served in Barack Obama's Treasury Department about how to leverage the Fed's lending powers. Republicans' approach to prop up businesses would leave a potential gap between the companies that were too large to qualify for help under Rubio's Paycheck Protection Program and those that were too small to qualify for whatever direct lending the Treasury might make available with the reinforced Exchange Stabilization Fund. In between were middle-market companies — regional chains of movie theaters, gyms, hotels — that might be left out. Warner workshopped a proposal that would take a slice of funds from the Treasury to backstop a Fed program that would lend directly to these businesses on Main Street.

Powell liked the idea but didn't want the Fed to take responsibility for it. For starters, Warner wanted to find a way that these low-rate loans might one day be forgiven — something the Fed cannot do.

"Mark, this is all great," Powell told Warner, "but Congress should do this. Don't ask us to do this." He explained that the Fed could help companies for a period of time, but it needed to have confidence those firms could pay back their loans at a certain point.

"I understood from an institutional standpoint where Chairman Powell was coming from," Warner said later. "I didn't agree with him."

For Democrats, it was a simple matter of trust. They didn't trust Trump, and they did trust the Fed. Lawmakers had watched Bernanke and Yellen brush aside misplaced inflation hysteria after the 2008 crisis, and later they had seen Powell capably deflect Trump's bluster. Warner personally enjoyed a warm and budding friendship with Mnuchin and thought highly of Justin Muzinich, the investment banker who was the deputy Treasury secretary. Yet the rest of the Democratic caucus had major reservations about handing any money to the Treasury.

"The Fed had more credibility," said Warner. "People were not sure that the Treasury would operate without a lot of political bias. We'd seen from the Trump administration this constant willingness to call out specific companies if they ran afoul of Trump."

The Fed was also seen as more capable than Mnuchin's Treasury Department, which was distressingly thinly staffed at the senior level. The empty offices reflected, at least in part, what associates described as Mnuchin's desire to micromanage. The result was that the Fed had more horsepower — it could turn these programs around faster and better than the Treasury.

Republicans, who had been so unhappy with how the Fed responded during and after the 2008 financial crisis, were now perfectly comfortable with the central bank quarterbacking the crisis response. Because the Fed was already unveiling emergency lending facilities, "It just seemed to me there was a logic to continuing with the process that was already underway," said Toomey.

Powell and his colleagues realized they would have little choice but to run with Warner's idea for a Main Street lending program once it became clear that Congress was going to unload it on the Fed. The financial crisis was more than a decade old, but central-bank staffers who had been there in 2008 needed no reminding about the political hazards of using their crisis-fighting tools to help big banks while doing little to fend off foreclosures on Main Street.

As negotiations progressed, Democrats attached more strings to the loans — terms that only compounded the program's complexity. Firms that took loans would have to rehire at least 90 percent of their workers within four months of the end of the public-health emergency. Recipients could not offshore jobs or alter existing collective-bargaining agreements for two years after the loans were repaid.

As a rule, the Fed loathed the idea of turning Bagehot-style "lender of last resort" backstops into elaborate vehicles to engineer broader labor or social-policy agendas. Yet Fed lawyers generally weren't deeply involved in the legislation. At one point Mark Van Der Weide, the Fed's general counsel, dryly offered a common talking point to Hill staffers: "You know, we at the Fed generally resist legislative prescriptions." Translation: *On lender-of-last-resort actions, micromanaging already-complex technical details is not the key to success.*

Eventually the language was watered down to the point where the legislation instructed the Fed to do nothing specific; it simply offered suggestions that the Fed was free to ignore.

"You can't pass legislation via Zoom"

After Republicans on Thursday presented their opening offer, McConnell turned to his senior staff and said, "Now what?" The ball was in Senate Minority Leader Chuck Schumer's court.

Democrats shot down McConnell's opening offer late that day. "[A]n utter disgrace," declared influential AFL-CIO President Richard Trumka on Twitter. "It gives free money to corporations…and does nothing to keep people working or help the unemployed. The labor movement will oppose this Main St bailout of Wall St with everything we have."

After bipartisan negotiations began on Friday, March 20, the price tag of each component of the bill kept going up. Individuals earning up to $75,000 would receive one-time cash payments of $1,200 and parents could receive $500 per child, which together would cost nearly $300 billion. Over the next two days, Mnuchin secured a little-noticed provision that preemptively authorized the FDIC to revive at any point in 2020 its crisis-era program of backstopping bank-issued debt and non-interest-bearing deposits that exceeded the $250,000 limit.

Democrats secured a significant expansion of federal payments to the unemployed on two fronts. First, a new "pandemic unemployment assistance" program would provide weekly benefits to millions of people who had lost their jobs but would not normally be eligible, including self-employed or "gig" workers. Second, the program temporarily added $600 per week in benefits through July — a huge bump up from the $25 per week that Congress approved after the 2008 crisis. At one point, Sen. Ron Wyden, a Democrat, showed Mnuchin how much a fourth month of unemployment benefits would cost using the calculator feature on his iPhone. Mnuchin acquiesced.[6] Other provisions provided months-long moratoria on foreclosures and evictions, and the ability for the vast majority of mortgage borrowers to seek a payment forbearance of six to twelve months.

Mnuchin camped out in an ornate parlor room around the corner from Schumer's offices in the Senate, where he went through the bill line by line. His makeshift Capitol office became a beehive of activity as staffers from the four different working groups took turns ferrying updates or seeking resolution to various impasses. An ambitious goal to close the deal that Friday came and went when talks broke off around 10:30 p.m. Staff members worked through the night. The principals assembled again the next morning, a Saturday.

Many of the thousands of Hill staffers had stopped working in Capitol offices as a health precaution, leaving a skeletal group of Senate aides putting in even more grueling twenty-hour days. Lawmakers were trying to practice social distancing in the committee rooms, "but it was pretty futile," said one staffer. Another aide periodically came through the hearing room for the Senate Banking Committee with Clorox wipes in an equally hopeless bid to disinfect the wood-paneled chamber.

At one point shortly before midnight on Friday, assistants to Schumer and Warner had found themselves in a room working alongside Mnuchin, who was reviewing and approving specific provisions on his own. Democrats mostly saw Mnuchin as a fair and candid broker, though he sometimes yelled at Senate aides when they dared to explain the finer points of capital-markets mechanics: "I've worked on Wall Street! I know this!" Mnuchin wasn't fazed when a Democratic senator, Ohio's Sherrod Brown, joined the negotiations by speakerphone and launched into a political diatribe about how terrible Trump was — the kind of speech usually reserved for the cameras.

On Saturday, Toomey and Mnuchin struggled to settle a dispute they were having over whether airlines should have to reimburse the government for aid. Toomey had Mnuchin call Trump to intercede, but the president demurred. *Figure it out among yourselves,* he said.

"I can't imagine the pressure that Mnuchin had," said Warner, "because here you had both Democrats and Republicans really looking for something, and you had a boss that was not engaged — a boss who thought the only metric was how the stock market is doing."

"I can't emphasize enough having just [seen the president] impeached, then the White House has to engage with Pelosi and Schumer — Mnuchin was the one kind of credible and neutral voice that there was a trust in," said a senior GOP adviser.

Lawmakers were both impressed — Mnuchin showed up in person and rolled up his sleeves — and dismayed: his reluctance to delegate slowed progress. "This was $2.3 trillion, and I was working on behalf of the president, and I wanted to make sure I knew exactly what was in the deal," said Mnuchin.[7]

There was also a certain X factor to the negotiations: fear that the virus might rip through the Capitol, sidelining so many lawmakers that it became impossible to pass legislation. House members went home to their districts the week before, and the Senate was trying to ensure their measure would have enough bipartisan support that it could pass on a simple voice vote. Otherwise it would require a majority of the chamber — 216 legislators — to return to Washington to cast votes.

McConnell had been explicit that the Senate would stay until the bill was done, which didn't sit well with some Democrats. After all, more than half of the Senate was over the age of sixty-three, leaving a high-risk group vulnerable to contracting the virus. "There was a very palpable fear of how we were going to control this pandemic internally," said one long-time Senate aide. "We needed something that if Congress couldn't reconvene quickly, this could see us through," said a second veteran staffer.

"It felt like a race against time as well as a race against covid," said a third senior staffer. "After the fact, everything seems like it was destiny. But at the time you kept worrying that someone was going to contract covid, and you didn't know who it was going to be, and maybe you weren't going to be able to complete the legislation before that happened. Members of Congress might get sick. The Treasury secretary might get sick. You can't pass legislation via Zoom."

The "Slush Fund"

The bill's price tag was on its way to $2.3 trillion — more than the gross domestic product of Canada. The new bill now included $500 billion for the Treasury, of which $46 billion would ultimately be earmarked for industry-specific bailouts; the other $454 billion would be set aside for Mnuchin to backstop lending by the Fed.

Mnuchin thought a bipartisan deal was within reach on Sunday morning. But when Schumer reviewed the latest version that morning, the $500 billion war chest for the Treasury secretary stopped him in his tracks. It also wasn't clear that Republicans had agreed to Democrats' proposed "Marshall Plan" to surge $150 billion in relief to hospitals and health-care providers. Schumer and Pelosi, who had flown back from San Francisco to join the talks, balked. More money would be needed for unemployment insurance, hospitals, and state and local governments.[8]

At a meeting that morning, Pelosi began with a prayer in which she quoted Pope Francis. "What he did was to pray that those who have responsibility for the care of people would be enlightened to take that responsibility and act upon it," she later recalled.[9]

When she finished, Mnuchin responded, "While you are quoting the pope, I'm going to quote the markets."

McConnell insisted they would proceed with a procedural vote later that day to tee up a final vote on Monday. But by late morning, Democrats came out sharply against the measure and raised especially fierce objections to the $500 billion being funneled into the ESF. Massachusetts Senator Elizabeth Warren, who had dropped out of the race for president earlier that month, unleashed a long Twitter thread. "Trump wants our response to be a half-trillion dollar slush fund to boost favored companies and corporate executives," she objected. "It even sounds like

Trump hotel properties like Mar-a-Largo [sic] could receive huge bags of cash — and then fire their workers — if Steve Mnuchin decides to do a solid for his boss with taxpayer dollars.... If this isn't fixed, all Democrats should all stand together and vote no."[10]

Though this crisis was totally different, the politics felt ominously like a rerun of 2008. Not just progressives objected to the so-called *slush fund*. The lack of oversight for the Treasury money was "the same ol' story from Mitch McConnell," said West Virginia's Joe Manchin, the Senate's most conservative Democrat. "It's throwing caution to the wind for the average person working on Main Street; it's balls to the walls for the people working on Wall Street."[11] The deal appeared to be slipping out of reach, with Pelosi threatening to start from scratch in the House.

Senators received an unsettling reminder of the stakes that afternoon. The office of Rand Paul, a Kentucky Republican who had gone for a swim in the Senate's gym pool that morning, announced at 1:36 p.m. that he had tested positive for Covid-19. The announcement sent shock waves through the Senate GOP ranks. Both of Utah's senators, Mike Lee and Mitt Romney, announced they would quarantine after having been in close contact with Paul, joining two other Republicans who were already quarantining as a precaution. That left a total of five Republican senators unavailable to vote.

McConnell called a vote at 6:03 p.m. to end debate on the bill, which required sixty votes to pass. It fell short. All forty-seven Republicans present voted *yes*, with forty-seven Democrats opposed. Accusing Schumer of blowing up a deal that had looked reachable earlier that day, McConnell departed the Capitol visibly angry.[12]

Equally annoyed was Toomey. Democrats, he believed, had raised no concerns about inadequate oversight until announcing just after noon on Sunday that they would oppose the bill for that reason. Mnuchin met with Schumer for the sixth and last time that day just before midnight, when he left the Capitol.

"We're very close. The teams are going to work through the night," he offered.[13] Mnuchin knew that $500 billion in the ESF was critical because the Fed was about to throw another kitchen sink at the problem.

Dunkirk

Powell spent that weekend at his home overlooking the 10th hole of the exclusive Chevy Chase Club. But though he was physically just a few miles north of Congress and the Treasury Building, Powell spent much of Saturday and Sunday on the phone with Mnuchin. The two men were ironing out term sheets for two forthcoming emergency-lending programs — one to backstop newly issued corporate bonds in the primary market and another for existing securities in the secondary market.

The programs meant the Fed would effectively purchase bonds directly from companies such as Walmart or Comcast in order to ensure that large corporations would be able to maintain employment and normal operations through the pandemic. In exercising this authority, the Fed was once again doing something it never had before.

Powell traded updates he was receiving from lawmakers with Lael Brainard. She had been among the last to work in her office in the Fed, but by week's end Brainard was logging into WebEx and Skype meetings from the upstairs of her home in Northwest Washington. Lehnert called in from a guest bedroom at his Arlington home that he had converted into a makeshift office to discuss the construction of the emergency-lending programs with Van Der Weide, the Fed's general counsel. Conditions all over were far from ideal, but none of them needed to be urged to work around the clock.

For Lehnert's team — tasked with managing worst-case economic scenarios — this was the Super Bowl. In addition to the two corporate-bond programs, Lehnert was making final arrangements to relaunch a crisis-era program to backstop the market for consumer and business loans that were bundled together and sold off as securities — the Term Asset-Backed Securities Loan Facility, or TALF.

Before the crisis, Lehnert often enjoyed unwinding at day's end with a glass of wine, but now he found he couldn't stand a sip of alcohol. He quit drinking as the crisis intensified. To relieve stress, Lehnert went for runs before the sun rose every morning and meditated for 20 minutes using the Headspace app on his iPhone. That summer, he bought a Disney+

subscription so he could watch *Hamilton* with his sons. They viewed it over and over.

Powell was still pushing the Fed to move much faster than its normal deliberate pace. Even if the i's weren't dotted on a program, it was better to announce plans with the available details and fill in the rest later on. "My thought was, I remember this really clearly, 'OK, we have a four- or five-day chance to really get our act together and get ahead of this. We're gonna try to get ahead of this,'" he recalled in an interview. "And we were going to do that by just announcing a ton of stuff on Monday morning."[14]

Right away, Powell got institutional resistance to his hurry-up-and-go approach: *The paperwork couldn't be done in time. The Fed didn't announce things before they were ready.* Powell replied that his colleagues should imagine their monetary efforts were the emergency rescue of British forces from France in World War II: "This is like Dunkirk — get in the boats and go." Assembling a motley fleet of 800 vessels and rescuing over 300,000 Allied soldiers in eight days — that counts as a miraculous story of people rising to meet the moment.

Later on, Powell returned to the metaphor, "It was time to get in the boats and get the people, not to check the inspection records and things like that."[15]

At 12:37 p.m. on Saturday, Powell emailed out a Microsoft Word document titled "Near-term plan March 21" that outlined everything Brainard and Lehnert were working on. "This will be an evolving work in process...Feel free to share with Fed colleagues," he wrote. "Thanks for everyone's amazing work."

At that point, Powell understood that the pending legislation would provide at least $200 billion in funding for these programs. But with Congress unlikely to pass the bill until later in the week, they needed to rely — again — on whatever was left in the ESF. Mnuchin committed to provide $10 billion each to backstop the two corporate-lending safety nets and another $10 billion for the TALF, bringing to $50 billion the amount he had unilaterally committed from the ESF.

Powell and the Fed governors were nervous about the midsize-business lending program. "It's either going to be enormous and we'll be criticized for making a lot of loans that banks would never make," Clarida told Powell, "or it's going to be criticized as being too stingy and too tiny."

Clarida also worried that they would have to face off with defaulted borrowers. What if the Fed made a loan to, say, Ford that the automaker struggled to repay? The Fed would have to get involved in a potentially messy loan workout. "Fed to Ford: Drop Dead," the headlines might read.

For her part, Brainard was consistently more concerned with the damage to the economy and the Fed's standing that would accrue if the central bank was seen as helping the best-off while doing little for everyone else. *If the Fed was going to buy corporate bonds,* she argued, *it needed to do something for municipalities too.* Later, when the Fed decided how much to charge for its corporate-lending backstops, she would ask why they didn't have at least as generous a pricing scheme for the bonds issued by cities and counties.

Brainard was pushing the Fed and the Treasury to accept more risk. If ever there was a time to take losses, she argued, it should be now: *Why be beholden to the standards of 2008 and 2009, when Washington's rescues didn't lose money? Why is that the right standard? It shouldn't be.*

Powell was close behind her. Fed officials had a clear appreciation of income and wealth disparities, and the shock would exacerbate them by falling hardest on low-income service workers — those who couldn't work from home and relied on public transportation. Both Powell and Brainard believed the emergency-loan facilities risked exacerbating those disparities if they didn't take enough risk. Their views weren't uniformly shared inside the Fed, but the consensus was "Let's push as hard as we can."

At the same time, Fed officials realized Congress had required the Fed to get the approval of the Treasury secretary for any emergency lending. At 11:30 a.m. on Sunday, March 22, Powell, Brainard, Clarida, and Quarles reviewed the final term sheets before sending them on to Mnuchin for approval. If everyone approved, they would unveil the latest fireworks on Monday morning.

All roads lead to BlackRock

Meanwhile on Fox, Mnuchin was promising legislation that would have "a significant package working with the Federal Reserve," with "up to $4 trillion of liquidity that we can use." From that Van Der Weide inferred that with an assumed debt-to-equity ratio of 10 to 1, the Treasury would have $400 billion available to invest in Fed lending. He shared a news article on the interview with his colleagues.

Powell also consulted with Mnuchin often that weekend — if not every hour, then every other hour — over how to price and structure the programs. The programs would purchase debts of up to five years for companies with at least an investment-grade rating. Mnuchin didn't have to be briefed on the arcane details: his OneWest Bank had borrowed $34.4 million from the TALF to buy mortgage-related investments in 2009.[16]

Deciding who was going to run the back-office logistics and support for any novel buying of corporate bonds could also lead to criticism. The Fed had relied on outside investment managers — among them Black-Rock, Pimco, and Goldman Sachs — when it decided in 2008 to begin purchasing mortgage-backed securities. The relationship had raised questions about conflicts of interest. Now the Fed was again choosing among the largest asset managers.

That weekend, Powell and Mnuchin quickly but uncomfortably settled on BlackRock. As the world's largest money manager, it had the where-withal to quickly help the New York Fed run the corporate-bond purchase programs. It was a stressful decision because working with BlackRock would be politically fraught. For example, BlackRock happened to be the largest sponsor of vehicles that invested in bonds called exchange-traded funds, or ETFs. And now, the Fed was about to propose buying up ETFs — with BlackRock's help. Critics would reasonably ask: *Why did the Fed keep going to this vendor over and over and over again — and to buy some of its own products?* The Fed didn't feel like it had a better alternative: either go with BlackRock or risk scuttling the economy. *Get in the boats and go.*

Mnuchin's public calendar later revealed sixty calls that Saturday and

Sunday — including nine with Powell and five with Laurence Fink, BlackRock's chief executive. Lawmakers ultimately didn't press Powell or Mnuchin too hard over this, even though the decision was quietly scandalous among BlackRock's competitors on Wall Street. "Somebody with a lot of expertise was going to have to come in and do this, so I accepted that," said Toomey.

Powell had one final piece of business: the Treasury market. The Fed was on pace to blow through its promised $500 billion in purchases later that week. Even though there was technically no set cap on the purchases, the market had forced the Fed to clarify matters. At 2 p.m., Powell gathered the reserve-bank presidents on a conference call to update them on what was happening and secure their formal support to announce unlimited purchases.

James Bullard, president of the St. Louis Fed, had earlier that day warned that the steps being contemplated to stop the virus could send the unemployment rate as high as 30 percent — a clear plea for Congress to step up its fiscal support. "It is totally stupid to lose a major industry because of a virus," Bullard told Bloomberg News. "Why would you want to do that?"[17]

Powell wanted to unveil their latest arsenal before markets opened in the US on Monday morning. With the news that Congress had failed to agree on a relief package that Sunday, after-hours and overseas markets were reeling. Mnuchin, Powell, Kudlow, and Fink held a final call at 7:25 p.m. to review the following morning's announcements.

At the White House, Donald Trump was having second thoughts over the measures being taken to shut down the economy to suppress the virus. "WE CANNOT LET THE CURE BE WORSE THAN THE PROBLEM ITSELF," he tweeted shortly before midnight. He went on to suggest that he might reverse the federal push to practice social distancing for fifteen days.

"Jerome, good job"

The Fed's announcement hit the wires at 8 a.m. on Monday, March 23, with uncharacteristically blunt language: "While great uncertainty remains, it has become clear that our economy will face severe disruptions.

Aggressive efforts must be taken across the public and private sectors to limit the losses to jobs and incomes." With that, it announced its new programs to make loans available to corporations.

"This is the closest you will hear the Fed to publicly exhorting other branches of government," said Michael Feroli, JPMorgan's chief US economist, in a note to clients that afternoon. "In broad terms, the Fed has effectively shifted from lender of last resort for banks to a commercial banker of last resort for the broader economy."[18]

Still, there were real concerns about whether the Fed's actions alone would suffice. True, the central bank was crossing red lines it had never crossed before. But the Fed was near the limit of what it could do on its own, and the Treasury's purse to backstop losses via the Exchange Stabilization Fund was approaching its maximum.

"The ESF isn't that big," cautioned Jan Hatzius, the chief economist at Goldman Sachs, after the Fed's announcements. If more companies were downgraded to junk as they faced big losses in revenues, a market backstop for investment-grade firms might be of limited help.

The ball was now firmly in the court of the White House and Congress. Toomey seized on the Fed's announcement to illustrate why it was important for Congress to turbocharge the ESF, which Democrats continued to assail as a slush fund. "It is true that the Fed theoretically has an infinite balance sheet, but the Fed has constraints in how it can deploy that. The Fed is not allowed to lose money," Toomey said that morning on CNBC. Stock futures briefly ventured into positive territory after the Fed's moves were announced.

A few hours later, Trump called Powell — this time to congratulate him rather than berate him. "Jerome, good job. You really did it," Trump told Powell during a short phone exchange at 11:43 a.m. Powell, who had spent the last eighteen months ignoring all sorts of verbal abuse, was gracious and offered his thanks. "I was proud of him. That took courage," the president told reporters that afternoon. "And I think, ultimately, we will be rewarded because...he's really stepped up over the last week."

Markets went on another roller-coaster ride. The Dow Jones Industrial Average tumbled nearly 1,000 points, recovered most of those losses as hopes rose that Congress would secure a deal, then faltered when the talks again fizzled. It closed down 582 points. The yield on the ten-year Treasury note dropped to 0.763 percent, a sign that the Fed's massive purchases were blessedly beginning to relieve more of the pressure.

Date 2020	Covid-19 Cases	Covid-19 Deaths	Dow Jones Average	VIX Fear Index
Monday, March 23	50,998	582	18,591 (↓ 582)	61.59 (↓ 4.45)

The art of the deal

That night Mnuchin joined Schumer in his Capitol Hill office, where the Democratic leader threw a log on the fire as both men worked into the night to secure a compromise. Mnuchin agreed to boost funding for hospitals. To resolve Democrats' concerns over cronyism, Congress would name five members to an oversight board for the $500 billion that would fund big-business and other emergency-loan programs. The legislation also prohibited businesses controlled by Trump, lawmakers, or Cabinet secretaries from receiving loans or investments from Treasury programs. They signaled a deal was close at hand as talks broke up for the night.

Schumer and Mnuchin's claims of progress produced euphoria on Wall Street. On Tuesday stocks surged nearly 2,113 points, or 11.4 percent, the largest daily point gain. The percentage gain was the greatest since March 15, 1933 — the day after Roosevelt's five-day bank "holiday" came to an end during the depths of the Great Depression — and the fourth-biggest ever.

But the deal was not yet complete.

Date 2020	Covid-19 Cases	Covid-19 Deaths	Dow Jones Average	VIX Fear Index
Tuesday, March 24	61,894	817	20,704 (↑ 2,113)	61.67 (↑ .08)

At 1:37 a.m. on Wednesday morning, Mnuchin and Schumer jointly announced they had reached a deal, even though their work was not

totally finished.[19] Schumer met with McConnell on the Senate floor. The two senators "decided to say we had a deal," Schumer said, "to keep the momentum going and give some relief to the markets."[20]

The Senate passed the CARES Act later that day on a 96-0 vote — a remarkable achievement for a legislative body notorious for moving glacially and that had gone through a divisive impeachment process just one month earlier. Some Republicans would later call the effort McConnell's finest moment. Congress's approval of money for the Fed's newly announced lending programs was an important vote of support, potentially tamping down criticisms of the central bank's having overstepped its authority.

Some former central bankers were aghast at the Fed's decision to purchase newly issued corporate debt, lending directly to companies. It was an "indefensible attempt by the Fed and the administration to sidestep Congress," wrote Narayana Kocherlakota, who had departed as president of the Minneapolis Fed in 2015. The Fed was sacrificing "its independence to do the White House's bidding," he warned.[21]

Stephen Cecchetti, a former research director at the New York Fed, and Kermit Schoenholtz, a former chief economist at Citigroup, warned that "engaging in such decisions will make it far more difficult for the Fed eventually to return to the standard of central-bank independence that it has guarded for decades."[22]

Powell knew there were risks but concluded it would be indefensible to withhold clearly legal uses of the Fed's authorities "because we find it icky," he told his staff. "We've crossed a lot of lines and probably aren't done yet." Figuring out how to exit would be a nice problem to have, because it would mean they had won the fight.

That didn't mean Powell was complacent about the risks. Lawmakers could come to the Fed later and say *Fix climate change* or *Use your digital printing press to finance every highway repair.* "There will come a time when we're saying *no* to people," Powell told his staff.

But in retrospect, the week of March 23 would prove to be the turning point for markets, even as the virus would go on to reach devastating levels of infection and death. It was a stark example of how *promising to* do a lot — "whatever it takes," as Mario Draghi had put it — meant officials might be able to get away with doing less. The Fed had stopped a financial meltdown that could have turned a cataclysmic recession into a full-blown depression. The speed with which markets recovered meant few would ever realize how close the economy had come to a much grimmer fate.

Date 2020	Covid-19 Cases	Covid-19 Deaths	Dow Jones Average	VIX Fear Index
Wednesday, March 25	74,551	1,058	21,200 (↑ 496)	63.95 (↑ 2.28)

Unlimited ammo

Just after 7 a.m. on Thursday, March 26, Powell tried to project a calm posture during a rare, live-broadcast TV interview for NBC's *Today* show. "When it comes to this lending, we're not going to run out of ammunition. That doesn't happen," he told host Savannah Guthrie.

He offered a layman's breakdown of how the Fed was following Bagehot's advice. "What's happened is all over the world investors have pulled back to very less-risky things. That's understandable. But what that's meant is that many places in the capital markets, which support borrowing by households and businesses — I'm talking about mortgages and car loans and things like that...have just stopped working," Powell said. "So we can step in and replace that lending under our emergency-lending powers, and we will do that."

The economy was being placed into the equivalent of a medically induced coma to keep the virus from overwhelming the nation's hospitals and its public-health infrastructure. The goal now was to prevent these hopefully temporary disruptions from leaving lasting scars. Waves of business failures would make it harder for furloughed or laid-off workers to return to jobs once the pandemic subsided. The more that workers could remain attached to their old employers, the less likely they would drop out of the workforce and lose valuable skills. The experiences of the "jobless recovery" that followed the 2001 recession and the Great

Recession of 2007–2009 had starkly illustrated the costs of sustained employment losses.

Every Thursday morning, the Labor Department reports how many applications for unemployment benefits from the week before have been received by all 50 states and the District of Columbia. For most of 2019 through early March of 2020, they ran between 200,000 and 250,000. At 8:30 a.m., about an hour after Powell finished his *Today* show interview, the Labor Department issued its tally for the week of March 16: an estimated 3,283,000 Americans had sought unemployment benefits. Yet even that astronomic total likely *understated* the number of layoffs, given that state systems had been unable to process all the workers seeking benefits. The figure was four times the previous high of 695,000 (in October 1982, at the end of Paul Volcker's campaign to tame inflation).

To illustrate the scale of such losses, a vertical bar chart ran across the bottom of the front page of *The New York Times*, leaving the most recent week's data in its own column, climbing all the way up the right-hand side of the page. Suddenly Mnuchin's prediction of 20 percent unemployment from a week earlier looked not alarmist but reasonable. "It's not like I can go get another job," a laid-off Philadelphia construction worker told *The Wall Street Journal*.[23]

Date 2020	Covid-19 Cases	Covid-19 Deaths	Dow Jones Average	VIX Fear Index
Thursday, March 26	92,143	1,371	22,552 (↑ 1,352)	61.00 (↓ 2.95)

"Three weeks like we've never seen before"

On Friday afternoon, Trump sat in his brown leather chair at the Resolute Desk, his favorite black Sharpie in hand, to sign the CARES Act. The nearly $2 trillion bill had passed the House without an individually recorded vote hours earlier after both parties reached an agreement to avoid requiring all 435 lawmakers to return to Washington to cast their votes. Five lawmakers had tested positive for the virus, and one was on oxygen support in the hospital.

Trump made sure that each $1,200 check to an American taxpayer would bear his distinctively scrawled bold signature. Mnuchin stood with McConnell behind the president's right shoulder, their hands at their waists. "I've never signed anything with a *T* on it," Trump said in a philosophical nod to the bill's nearly $2 trillion size. "I don't know if I can handle this one, Mitch."

The longest job-market expansion on record — 22 million jobs over 113 consecutive months — had come to a screeching halt. But though the news was likely to get much, much worse, the one-two punch of extremely bold Fed action backed up by massive spending in Congress was beginning to work wonders.

The Dow posted its largest weekly gain since 1938, rising 13 percent despite a 915-point sell-off on Friday. Other measures suggested the panic of the prior weeks might be breaking. The VIX ended the week lower after five consecutive weekly increases. And spreads between yields of US government debt and investment-grade bonds had begun to decline after hitting highs not seen since early 2009.

Date 2020	Covid-19 Cases	Covid-19 Deaths	Dow Jones Average	VIX Fear Index
Friday, March 27	111,358	1,782	21,363 (↓ 915)	65.54 (↑ 4.54)

The good news for the country was that Congress had moved with breathtaking speed to reload the Fed's ability to lend. The CARES Act asked the Fed to charge headlong into areas of credit and fiscal policy that the central bank had long avoided. By offloading more of the crisis response to the Fed, politicians were offering a vote of confidence that the technocrats could figure out the details while shielding themselves from blame on the tough choices that loomed.

Powell caught his breath, but not a break. Within days the US death toll would surpass 2,000, and the number of cases nationwide would eclipse the officially reported totals out of China. New York City's hospitals were so badly deluged that the USNS *Comfort*, a 1,000-bed hospital ship, docked in the city's harbor on March 30 to provide more care.

Construction crews erected a sixty-eight-bed emergency field hospital of long white medical tents on Central Park's East Meadow lawn.

Donald Trump, who in mid-March had mused about reopening the country by Easter, now reversed himself. "This could be a hell of a bad two weeks," he said during a March 31 briefing. In his next breath, he upgraded that ominous assessment: "This is going to be three weeks like we've never seen before."

Chapter Thirteen

FATE AND HISTORY

In a matter of days, Congress, the Fed, and the Treasury had applied two hard-learned lessons from the 2008 financial crisis and the grinding recovery that followed. Lesson one: Go big. Lesson two: Go fast.

For Powell and the Fed, the weeks of March and April were a "total blitz" marked by sleepless nights and a workday that sometimes began before 5 a.m. at Powell's home office. "You feel like hell all the time," Powell said. "Dead on your feet, not sleeping well, just an awful feeling — very stressed and consciously aware that your decisions are really going to matter for people. And you know that everything you do in this time is going to be held up under a very bright light and examined, and you better damn well get it right."[1]

Powell left the house only for media appearances, which he recorded from a studio in the Eccles Building. Powell also knew he had to avoid catching the virus. News that the respected head of the central bank wasn't on his feet would only amplify the sense of panic. Normally a security officer ferried him to work in a black SUV. Now, when he did venture to the Fed's headquarters at 20th Street and Constitution Avenue, Powell climbed behind the wheel of his Tesla Model S to make the fifteen-minute drive alone.

There weren't many ways to unwind, other than neighborhood walks with his wife and daughter when possible in the evenings. He had broken his little toe after tripping on a canvas tote bag at home, preventing him from using his stationary exercise bike.

The muni market

The $3.9 trillion market for municipal debt became a top priority after the March 23 announcements. The CARES Act didn't explicitly mandate that the Fed lend to states and municipalities. Instead, it provided a big nudge by directing Steven Mnuchin to "endeavor to seek" that the Fed create such a lending program.

Not that Powell needed prodding. Even before Trump signed the law, Powell had shed any reservations about crossing this line. "We're like in a war here," he said. "Municipalities and state and local governments carry out the basic functions of government — a lot of the health care runs through them. We have this authority and I don't know how I would justify saying that we're not going to use it because we don't like that particular part of the law. If those markets are going to be closed and hospitals are not going to be able to pay those people, it's hard to see how we don't do something."[2]

Like many well-off New Yorkers with second homes outside the city, former Treasury official Kent Hiteshew and his wife, Pat Jenny, had fled Manhattan's covid crisis in mid-March. On Friday, March 20 — the day after they decamped to their summer home in rural northwest Connecticut — Hiteshew received a phone call from Lael Brainard, who peppered him with questions about what was happening in the muni market. The Fed had never before intervened in this market, and Powell and Brainard didn't know much about it. *What's breaking down?* she asked. *And what can we do about it?*

Hiteshew had come highly recommended by former Obama administration colleagues at the Treasury Department. He had been a twenty-four-year veteran of the public-finance desks at Bear Stearns and JPMorgan Chase before being tapped to lead the Treasury's new Office of State and Local Finance. Hiteshew helmed the federal response to the insolvencies plaguing Detroit and, later, Puerto Rico. He was now semi-retired, working part-time as a consultant at Ernst and Young.

The muni market was badly broken, Hiteshew explained, *and that's not a market where you normally see these kinds of stresses.* Retail investors had pulled $45 billion out of municipal-bond funds. New bond issues by school districts were being withdrawn or canceled. That Friday, Mnuchin had made official that the IRS would extend the tax-payment deadline to July 15. The move gave breathing room to households and businesses, but it would create fresh strains for state governments. Treasurers count on an infusion of income-tax revenue every March and April to pay their bills. The delayed deadline was blowing huge holes in state budgets at a time when raising money in debt markets was nearly impossible.

"You have a situation where you clearly have a ninety-day liquidity problem, you have unknown plummeting of sales and income taxes, and issuers couldn't access the market," said Hiteshew.[3]

Still, municipal borrowers' fundamental solvency hadn't changed, so extending bridge financing made sense. Although Hiteshew didn't know much about the legal parameters of the Fed's "unusual and exigent" authorities, he pointed out a few ways Brainard could tweak their new money-market-fund backstop.

On Saturday Brainard called Hiteshew with a different question: *Would you work for the Fed for six months?*

Why not? Hiteshew figured. He had been forced to cancel an upcoming cycling trip in Croatia and a two-week vacation in Scandinavia with Jenny. On Thursday, March 26, a FedEx truck parked by the driveway outside Hiteshew's Connecticut home. The driver dropped off a package that included a Fed-issued iPhone and laptop. *Get in the boats and go.*

Work began immediately with Brainard, Andreas Lehnert's team, and a couple of other advisers that included Matthew Lieber from the New York Fed. The Fed wanted to restore normal market functioning while avoiding the unpalatable task of picking and choosing which individual municipal securities they should buy. Unlike the corporate-bond market, the municipal-debt market is illiquid, opaque, and fragmented. There are thousands of individual issuers, and some of those securities do not trade often. Hiteshew feared that initial proposals to build some index of municipal debt and then purchase securities accordingly would take too long to get off the ground, consuming time they couldn't spare. Lawmakers in Albany were wrestling *now* with how the state of New

York, whose fiscal year ended on March 31, was going to fund itself over the next few months.

The easier route would be for the Fed to become a direct lender. Hiteshew recommended that the central bank offer to buy newly issued municipal debt from a list of eligible issuers at predetermined rates, based on the issuer's credit rating. The rates would be set slightly higher than what a normal, functioning private market might charge. Powell decided the Municipal Liquidity Facility — yet another "unusual and exigent" program — would be run by the New York Fed.

That left the question of which cities and states would be eligible — as politically fraught an issue as any the Fed was facing. Their initial list included every state plus the District of Columbia, all counties of at least two million residents, and all cities of at least one million. They would buy debts of up to two years issued by any of these seventy-six borrowers, in amounts up to 20 percent of their 2017 revenues — a hefty sum. Mnuchin agreed to provide $35 billion to cover losses.

Hiteshew calculated that if every eligible issuer had gone to the Fed and said *Please lend us 20 percent of our annual revenues because we're toast right now,* the result might have been $300 billion in lending. In keeping with its "Go Big, Go Fast" ethos, the Fed decided to announce that the Municipal Liquidity Facility's total capacity would be even larger — $500 billion — as a way to signal an overwhelming commitment to that market. The entire muni market doesn't even borrow $500 billion in one year.

Welcome to the debt carnival!

Exchange-traded funds — bundles of securities that can be bought and sold like any other stock — revolutionized investing after they burst onto the scene in 1993. ETFs, as they are also known, offer investors a way to receive instant cash, much like an ordinary stock investment, even though the underlying bonds or other assets may take longer to sell. For years, central bankers had identified this type of alchemy as a potential risk to stable financial markets. On Monday, March 23, when the Fed agreed to purchase certain ETFs, they knew it would be one of their most controversial decisions. But they believed it gave them the fastest, best way to enter the corporate-bond market while they figured out how to design their broader backstop.

Almost immediately, senior officials at the Securities and Exchange Commission grew highly nervous about the proposition. They pointed a finger at the Bank of Japan, which had been buying ETFs for almost ten years and was on course to overtake a giant government-pension fund as the largest owner of domestic stocks later that year. "How are you going to get out of the ETFs?" one SEC official protested to Lehnert. "You'll be just like the Bank of Japan."

In the days that followed, Powell began toying with an even more provocative question: whether to purchase the debt of companies that weren't rated investment-grade — so-called "high-yield" or "junk" debt. Years of relying on easy credit and low rates — not just in the United States, but across the industrialized world — had encouraged companies to load up on debt. The corporate-bond market grew from $5.5 trillion in 2008 to $8.8 trillion in 2019. That total included $1.2 trillion in junk debt secured by corporate assets known as "leveraged loans," a market that had risen by nearly 50 percent since 2015.

Private-equity firms fueled much of the growth. They borrowed billions to buy big names such as Dell Technologies and Staples Inc. Their companies sometimes ran without enough cash to handle a garden-variety recession, let alone the hard stop now underway. In a May 2019 speech, Powell had acknowledged these risks. In the event of a downturn, policymakers feared over-indebted businesses would appease lenders by firing workers and reducing investment, thus exacerbating existing economic problems.

Powell's predicament partly resulted from the success that the Fed's announcements had achieved in thawing the market for corporate debt after March 23. Over the next two weeks, highly rated companies whose debt might now be eligible to be bought by the Fed — including General Mills, Mastercard, Nike, Oracle, and Pfizer — found they were able to borrow in larger quantities, and at much lower yields, than was imaginable before the Fed's announcement. Even though the Fed had yet to purchase a single corporate security (and even though businesses were facing an unprecedented hit to their bottom lines), investors, their confidence restored, went on an epic buying spree.

No company illustrated the speed with which the Fed's announcement had buoyed investors better than Carnival, the world's largest cruise-line operator. Its business had collapsed as covid halted cruises worldwide. It was bleeding cash. Bankruptcy wasn't out of the question. Yet Carnival had been contemplating borrowing billions in the market at punitive interest rates to tide it over.

In mid-March, with bond markets frozen, Carnival had considered taking a high-interest loan from a group of hedge funds calling themselves "the consortium." They were offering Carnival, which months earlier had used its solid credit rating to borrow at a 1 percent interest rate, a lifeline that would charge a rate of more than 15 *percent* while giving the lenders a possible stake in the company, according to *The Wall Street Journal*.[4]

Within days of the Fed's announcement, however, Carnival was able to borrow $4 billion from large institutional investors at 11.5 percent. "The immediate survival of the company, which employs 150,000 people, is no longer in question," wrote the *Journal's* Matt Wirz. Most striking: Carnival, because it doesn't base its operations in the US, wasn't even eligible for the Fed's corporate-debt backstop.

News of the financial salvation ricocheted through the (virtual) corner offices of corporate America, across (virtual) trading floors on Wall Street, and even along the actual corridors of the West Wing. If the hardest-hit companies like Carnival, with its fleet of 104 ships drydocked indefinitely for months, could raise money in capital markets, who couldn't? It was a turning point — and the Fed was doing all this without spending a dime. The breathing room was helpful to officials at the New York Fed who were still figuring out how, exactly, they were going to get their corporate-bond-purchase program off the floor.

Lorie Logan's team was also regaining control of the Treasury market. They had bought a staggering $75 billion *per day* between March 19 and April 1. As an additional safeguard against foreign central banks' selling of Treasuries, the Fed had unveiled a new program that allowed those banks to temporarily raise dollars by exchanging them for Treasuries maintained in accounts at the New York Fed. By the end of that week, the Fed had loaned nearly $400 billion to foreign central banks through the existing swap lines, ensuring a steady supply of dollars in London, Frankfurt, Tokyo, and Seoul.

The Fed's balance sheet swelled to $6.1 trillion by April 8. It had grown almost $2 trillion in just six weeks.

Date 2020	Covid-19 Cases	Covid-19 Deaths	Dow Jones Average	VIX Fear Index
Wednesday, April 1	223,169	5,337	20,943 (↓ 974)	57.06 (↑ 3.52)

Crossing lines, creating cliffs

"We've made good progress," Boston Fed President Eric Rosengren said on April 1, the day Carnival completed its giant offering. Investment-grade companies "are still accessing the market at a premium, but they are accessing the market." On the other hand, Rosengren noted with concern that markets where the Fed had *not* intervened still faced "very difficult challenges."[5]

Indeed, there was a growing chasm between companies inside the central bank's lending perimeter and those outside, including junk bonds, leveraged loans, and privately issued mortgage securities. Just five companies had issued junk-rated debt since March 4, including Pizza Hut owner Yum! Brands, Inc. The prospect of waves of companies going bankrupt was making investors hesitate to step into a market the Fed was unwilling to enter.

Companies barely rated investment-grade, with some $3.4 trillion outstanding, faced an especially acute risk: the perilous precipice known as the *"triple-B* cliff." If they were downgraded from *BBB status*, they would become junk debt that some large investors, such as insurance companies, cannot touch.

The Fed's successful backstop of the investment-grade market was exacerbating the risks of these "fallen angels" that went over the *triple-B* cliff—falling one notch lower than BBB on the credit rating scale that ranged from *AAA* to C. On March 23, hours after the Fed announced plans to buy investment-grade debt, US automaker Ford Motor Company had its credit rating cut by Standard & Poor's, one of the big ratings agencies. Ford was now the largest fallen angel in the country. Two large retailers — Macy's and Gap — likewise lost their investment-grade ratings a few days later.

What would happen to the economy if more companies that were forced to shut down indefinitely could not borrow? That was the question bedeviling Powell, Brainard, and Lehnert. To avoid a widening rift between the market haves and have-nots, Fed officials recommended that Powell extend the Fed's lending perimeter to include companies that had been rated *triple-B* at the time of the Fed's March 23 announcement. More controversially, they recommended that the Fed purchase ETFs that invest in junk debt because they feared these "high-yield" bonds might buckle, creating a wave of bankruptcies that would cause long-term scarring in the economy. Given the speed with which markets had cracked up in March, Powell decided it was better to err on the side of doing too much than not doing enough.

"*This is not 2008, 2009. That's what we kept telling ourselves,*" said one high-ranking official involved in the decision. "*This is a truly exogenous shock.* We're not going to promote moral hazard because people are going to recognize that this is a hopefully once-in-a-lifetime pandemic. And it's not going to create incentives for unreasonable and excessive risk-taking in future financial and economic cycles because everyone recognizes this as being unique....Sometimes you have to save the undeserving few to protect the deserving many."

The decision would be the most controversial that Powell made. Even though all five governors approved it, not everyone inside the Fed system agreed with it. Robert Kaplan wished they had found a way to stay out of the junk-debt market. It wasn't a perfect compromise. But *perfect* wasn't necessarily the goal in early April. "The objective was to move quickly," said the Dallas Fed chief. "In hindsight, I might quibble with drawing the line here versus there. But I'd say it was 'close enough.'"[6]

It wasn't just the Fed. The same calculus that prioritized speed applied to the Treasury's sprint to get the Paycheck Protection Program up and running. The $350 billion small-business relief program faced a rocky start when it set up shop on Friday, April 3. Several of the country's biggest banks complained to the Treasury that confusing rule changes had left them unready to process applications.

"This is a problem," Congressman Patrick McHenry told Mnuchin during a phone call that weekend.

"Yeah, I know," Mnuchin responded. "And we're going to work around the clock to fix it."

McHenry wasn't sure he was being heard: "This is a big fucking deal! And you guys look like shit on how this is going."

"OK. OK," said Mnuchin calmly.

The challenges of having a thinly staffed department came into sharper relief that week, as it fell to Mnuchin and the few advisers he trusted, including Deputy Secretary Justin Muzinich, to get the money flowing—not only to small businesses, but also for a separate airline-bailout program.

Despite initial hiccups in the rollout, the Paycheck Protection Program proved so popular that weekend that thousands of banks worked overtime uploading applications to the SBA's portal. Within days, the Treasury warned that the initial $350 billion in funding would be gone in two weeks. After a week of partisan bickering, Congress topped up the program with an additional $310 billion in funding.

The initial $350 billion cap, however—and the first-come, first-served basis for doling out the loans—fueled a huge backlash when it emerged that larger, publicly traded companies had legally qualified for PPP cash. The Ruth's Chris Steak House chain and the fast-food eatery Shake Shack were among a handful of companies villainized for taking assistance at a time when many smaller businesses were struggling to get their foot in the door of a bank.

Additionally, some of the hardest-hit firms discovered that the loans weren't as useful as they had hoped. To have the loans forgiven, companies had to spend 75 percent of the funds on eight weeks of payroll. Some restaurants, hair salons, and other small retailers said they were operating with skeletal staffs and lacked enough business to justify bringing back their entire workforce.

Meet the tests

On Thursday, April 9, the Fed unveiled its latest volley of lending programs, sketching out how, exactly, Mnuchin would deploy the money that Congress had given him in the CARES Act. He provided $195 billion for five lending programs, which the Fed estimated could enable $2.3 trillion in new lending. For the first time, the Fed and the Treasury detailed a "Main Street Lending Program" — $600 billion aimed at companies too large to access forgivable small-business loans but too small to borrow in corporate-debt markets. Fed and Treasury lawyers worked overnight exchanging versions of term sheets, and the Fed didn't receive Mnuchin's signed copy of the documents until 7:55 a.m. — five minutes before the central bank sent out an embargoed news release to reporters.[7]

In another reminder of the economic devastation that was unfolding, at 8:30 a.m. the Labor Department reported that another 6.6 million people had applied for unemployment insurance over the prior week, bringing to nearly 17 million the number of applicants since the pandemic hit the US. The deluge was overwhelming creaky state labor-department websites and phone lines. The day before, the United States had recorded 1,973 deaths over the preceding twenty-four-hour period, the deadliest day yet; a total of 18,000 people had now died. The evening news and cable television featured overcrowded hospitals, with nurses wearing garbage bags and other makeshift protective gear. At virus briefings, Trump dispensed cheerful predictions of miracle cures and quarreled with reporters over the benefits of testing.

Powell, by contrast, spoke with measured, solemn language. At 10 a.m. that Thursday morning, Powell delivered an online speech, followed by a moderated Zoom discussion with the Brookings Institution, that offered a few lines framing why the Fed was taking such extreme steps. "None of us has the luxury of choosing our challenges; fate and history provide them for us. Our job is to meet the tests we are presented." His lines were the exact opposite of the normally colorless lexicon of central bankers — more Churchill than Greenspan.

Powell shed his traditional reluctance to tell lawmakers how to do their jobs, and he did so in unusually moral terms. "All of us are affected, but the burdens are falling most heavily on those least able to carry them.... They didn't cause this. Their business isn't closed because of anything they did wrong. This is what the great fiscal power of the United States is for — to protect these people as best we can from the hardships they're facing."

These were extraordinary words from a Fed chair who during earlier hot-button policy debates had promised to "stay in his lane." *The great fiscal power of the United States should be used to make people whole.*

Date 2020	Covid-19 Cases	Covid-19 Deaths	Dow Jones Average	VIX Fear Index
Thursday, April 9	466,736	18,027	23,719 (↑ 286)	41.67 (↓1.68)

"A thank-you letter to the Fed"

Markets were well on their way to a recovery, even as the economy deteriorated further. Just as the March 23 announcements had started to repair the corporate-bond market, the April 9 announcements immediately capped borrowing costs in the municipal-debt market and triggered a sharp revival of debt issuance. On April 17, Ford said it expected to report a $2 billion quarterly loss amid a 21 percent plunge in vehicle sales from a year earlier. A few days after that the carmaker announced that it had raised $8 billion in the junk-bond market — the largest such deal on record.

Two weeks later, on April 30, Boeing raised a stunning $25 billion in a blowout bond offering — the largest-ever bond deal outside an acquisition. The CARES Act had set aside $17 billion for Mnuchin to make direct loans to firms "critical to national security," a provision widely understood as a potential Boeing bailout. Now the Fed's actions were allowing these companies to sidestep the government altogether — and dodge the strings the Treasury could have attached, including potential equity stakes for the American taxpayer. Companies with investment-grade ratings sold $227 billion in bonds in April, shattering the all-time high set a month earlier.

"You saw all kinds of companies grabbing everything," said Warren Buffett at Berkshire Hathaway's shareholder meeting in May. "And every one of those people…ought to send a thank-you letter to the Fed because it would not have happened if they hadn't operated with really unprecedented speed and determination."

Nobody knew exactly what the consequences would be of the Fed pumping so much credit into the system, said Buffett. "But we do know the consequences of doing nothing, and that would've been the tendency of the Fed in many years past — not doing nothing, but doing something inadequate. Mario Draghi brought the *whatever it takes* to Europe and the Fed then…did *whatever it takes, squared,* and we owe them a huge thank-you."

When it came to halting the financial panic, "the announcement of all the facilities was the turning point," said Eric Rosengren, the Boston Fed president. "What was striking to me was that we didn't need the facilities to be operating to get most of the benefits.…You could see it in the spreads immediately."[8]

To describe the cataclysmic meltdown in the Treasury market that had been narrowly avoided in late March, Fed vice chair Randal Quarles would later approvingly quote a phrase the Duke of Wellington had used after defeating Napoleon at Waterloo: "For a while in the spring," said Quarles, "the outcome was 'a damn close-run thing.'"[9]

The announcement of those backstops illustrated an important lesson about crisis management: if you promise to do more upfront, you may not have to do as much as you think. For example, Andreas Lehnert had been pulling together another emergency backstop to bail out mutual funds that had invested in corporate debt, which would have represented yet another bailout of the *shadow financial system* that operated outside the banking sector and was aggravating a broader panic. (The prospect of a rescue of these open-end bond funds hasn't been made public until now.) In late March those funds came under extreme stress, raising serious concerns at the SEC. But the announcements of the other corporate-bond backstops had eased a wave of redemptions hitting the mutual funds. The Fed never had to pull the trigger on a separate mutual-fund bailout.

By April, there was no telling whether subsequent virus waves would force rolling lockdowns and lead to rising corporate defaults and missed mortgage payments. Whereas March 23 proved to be the bottom for the stock market, "we had no idea that that was the bottom," said Lehnert. "We had no idea. We just had this sense that we were one step ahead of a really serious financial-market disruption that would be even worse for the economy than what we were already seeing."[10]

Brainard, who had navigated the messy politics of bailouts after the 2008 crisis, felt confident that the Fed could get financial markets functioning effectively in part because the nature of the current crisis was different. The most complicated part of a policy response typically concerns the morality play that forces policymakers to dance around the following question: *Are you really going to reward these bad actors who have taken these bad bets?* The current crisis felt much more like a war or an act of God. Absent were any qualms about bankers being unjustly rescued after gaming the system to secure *triple-A* ratings for dodgy mortgages.

"Catholicism without hell"

Lawmakers didn't greet the Fed's announcements nearly as favorably as Wall Street. Researchers at the Brookings Institution soon found that by allowing only the largest cities and counties to qualify for the municipal-debt backstop, the Fed had excluded the thirty-five American cities with the largest fraction of Black residents. "We are not suggesting the Fed had racist intentions when setting this limit," they wrote. "To the contrary, everything suggests the Fed was just acting quickly in [an] unprecedented area."[11]

Congress — the Fed's boss — quickly made clear it wasn't thrilled. Maxine Waters, the California Democrat who chaired the House Financial Services Committee, cited the Brookings analysis in a letter asking Powell to revise the thresholds to avoid "exacerbating racial disparities in the federal government's response." That same day, Mike Crapo, Republican chair of the Senate Banking Committee, sent a letter lamenting how none of the municipalities in Idaho — or other rural states — would be able to borrow from the Fed. In response, the Fed lowered the population thresholds near the end of April, increasing the number of potential municipal borrowers to 261. It relaxed those limits again in early June.

Even if officials felt they had no choice, their actions would exacerbate a moral hazard, one that provoked disquiet across the political spectrum. And even if the Fed's actions had politicized the central bank's autonomy, it might well take years before the costs of its decisions became evident.

"There's an old saying — variously attributed — to the effect that 'capitalism without bankruptcy is like Catholicism without hell.' It appeals to me strongly," wrote Howard Marks, co-founder of hedge fund Oaktree Capital Management.[12] Oaktree had been one of the members of "the consortium" that had offered a pricey rescue to Carnival before the Fed's market intervention. His market musings were widely read on Wall Street, and he boldfaced the next two lines for emphasis: "Markets work best when participants have a healthy fear of loss. It shouldn't be the role of the Fed or the government to eradicate it."

Paul Singer, who ran the hedge-fund firm Elliott Management, warned that the Fed was sowing the seeds of a bigger crisis. "Sadly, when people (including those who should know better) do something stupid and reckless and are not punished, it is human nature that, far from thinking that they were lucky to have gotten away with something, they are encouraged to keep doing the stupid thing, keep believing the unbelievable, and keep assuming that they were just plain wrong to be concerned about 'old-fashioned' restraints."[13]

Objections to the Jesuit-trained Powell's *make people whole* mantra weren't limited to the free-market libertarian set. The breathtaking speed with which the Fed moved and with which Wall Street rallied after the Fed's announcements infuriated Dennis Kelleher, a former corporate lawyer and high-ranking Senate aide who runs Better Markets, an advocacy group lobbying for tighter financial regulations. "Literally, not only has no one in finance lost money, but they've all made more money than they could have dreamed," said Kelleher. "It just can't be the case that the only thing the Fed can do is open the fire hydrants wide for everybody. This is a ridiculous discussion no matter how heartfelt Powell is about 'we can't pick winners and losers' — to which my answer is, 'So instead you just make them all winners?'"[14]

Powell later defended, with only a touch of hesitation, his decision to purchase ETFs that had invested in junk debt. "We wanted to find a surgical way to get in and support that market because it's a huge market, and it's a lot of people's jobs.... What were we supposed to do? Just let them die and lose all those jobs? Some of these people, I'm really glad they weren't sitting around the table. I really am.

"In hindsight, was it worth it? I don't know. I have to say, if that's the big indictment of our policy — buying high-yield ETFs — then I think we did pretty well. If that's the biggest mistake we made, stipulating it as a mistake, I'm fine with that. It wasn't time to be making finely crafted judgments."

Powell hesitated again before concluding. "Do I regret it? I don't — not really."[15]

Chapter Fourteen

UNCLE SAM'S CLUB

During the panicked days of March 2020, Powell had relied on the metaphor of the Dunkirk evacuation: *Get in the boats and go.* After the race to get back to England in late spring of 1940 was over, the victory wasn't quite as clear. Aftermaths are usually a lot messier.

Powell and the Fed had also thrown together a forceful response to a crisis in record time, especially by the standards of a central bank. By the end of March, the markets were beginning to function normally and the Dow was on a steady upward trend. But once people had a chance to breathe, there were new questions, more pushback, and a lot of work still left to do.

With a virtual workforce, the Fed's crisis-management operations relied on a hub-and-spoke approach. Jay Powell sat at the center of the senior-most hub, receiving reports on the banking system from Randal Quarles, on the lending programs from Lael Brainard and Andreas Lehnert, on market functioning issues from John Williams and Lorie Logan, and on longer-run monetary-policy issues from Richard Clarida and Williams. From the end of March through the first week of July, it was a daily sprint to get the novel market backstop programs up and running.

Outrage and workarounds

The CARES Act provided a huge pile of cash for the new lending programs, but it also created a batch of new complications. The law said Fed lending programs could extend credit only to a business "created or orga-nized" in the US or under its laws, with "significant operations in and a majority of its employees based in the United States." After April 9, when Steven Mnuchin specified how much money from the CARES Act would fund each lending operation, the Fed either had to abide by these stric-tures or find a creative workaround.

Some lawmakers wanted to handcuff the loans to prevent companies from laying off their workforce or buying back stock and paying lavish dividends to shareholders and large compensation packages to chief exec-utives. The Fed shared the same job-preserving aims, but its lawyers and economists were generally nervous about limiting the programs in ways that discouraged or stigmatized the companies that used them, some-thing that might neuter Bagehot's dictum on dousing panics. Just as the Fed resisted being told what to do by Congress, it also resisted micro-managing corporate-survival strategies during a pandemic.

It was clear that, following a sharp, immediate, and potentially sus-tained drop in business, some companies just weren't going to be able to keep all their workers. If the choice was between a company liquidating altogether or surviving by taking on debt and cutting some workers, the latter option wasn't the worst one. From the Fed's perspective, it simply didn't make sense to tell companies to borrow money only if they kept employees they didn't need for an indefinite period.

Fed lawyers found a few ways to slip loose from some of the congres-sional strings. Congress had restricted companies from distributing money to shareholders if they took a "direct loan" backed by any of the Treasury's war chest. But these limits on share buybacks and dividends didn't apply to cases where the Fed or the Treasury engaged in "securities transactions," and Fed lawyers concluded that the corporate-debt back-stops fit the latter definition, meaning the curbs wouldn't apply.

That rationale sparked a populist uproar. "The U.S. plans to give $500 billion to large companies. It won't require them to preserve jobs or limit executive pay," declared an April 28 *Washington Post* headline describing the Fed's program for new corporate-loan issuance, which had yet to extend any loans. Ultimately, the mere announcement of the Fed's backstops proved so successful that the program was never used. But no one knew that at the time, and the story drew thousands of responses on social media. "This is bullshit," wrote Ilhan Omar, the Minnesota Democratic congresswoman.[1]

The CARES Act was proving especially unpopular with progressive Democrats, who were upset that the Senate had unanimously approved the measure. "The almost pervasive refusal to hold either Bernie Sanders or Elizabeth Warren accountable for supporting the worst bill in 25 years is a great example of what is broken on the American left," wrote one prominent progressive commentator on Twitter.[2]

After the CARES Act passed, Warren asked Mnuchin and Powell to tie strings to the programs. Her requests went far beyond what Congress had required and included maintaining 95 percent of a firm's pre-pandemic workforce, providing a $15 minimum wage, and giving a seat on the board of directors to workers.

Several Democratic advisers urged lawmakers to consider a wage-subsidy program. The United Kingdom, for example, was offering to pay workers directly — up to 80 percent of salaries, with a limit of £2,500 per month (around $3,200). Canada provided 75 percent of an employee's pre-crisis wages up to the first $58,700 (around $47,700 US) for qualified businesses, which supplemented an existing unemployment-insurance program. Wealthy nations across northern Europe and the Pacific Rim were concocting similar schemes that nationalized private payrolls.

By contrast, the US was relying on a combination of Fed lending, the PPP grants, increased unemployment benefits, and direct stimulus checks. The hope was that businesses would receive enough aid to keep people employed, but there were no specific requirements that they do so. The European-style approach enjoyed support from a handful of Democrats and Republicans, who favored the idea of preserving employer-employee relationships. It would cost more money, but it might reach workers at companies that lacked the strong banking relationships that were often necessary to secure PPP funds.

The idea foundered in part because other Democrats feared it would represent too large a giveaway to businesses or because they were concerned it would siphon away political capital they needed to secure an extension of the more-generous unemployment benefits when those lapsed at the end of July. Ultimately, employment excluding food, accommodation, and retail exceeded its pre-pandemic level in Canada by March 2021, while in the US it remained 5 percent below its pre-pandemic peak.[3] But only time would tell which strategy had fostered a stronger outcome. Ending wage subsidies too soon could send unemployment higher but continuing them for too long could subsidize businesses that, in a post-pandemic economy, might not be viable or require the same amount of labor.

"The worst of all policies"

Walter Bagehot's axioms about financial panics in *Lombard Street* could be boiled down to one overarching recommendation: "To lend a great deal and yet not give the public confidence that you will lend sufficiently and effectually is the worst of all policies," he wrote. In early April, the Fed faced a version of that threat: a stumbling block that threatened to undermine the potency of the backstops it had announced to great fanfare.

The restriction in the CARES Act that limited help to companies with a majority-US workforce was threatening to hobble the lending effort before it could begin. Because of globalization and the act's specific language, many companies generally considered large US manufacturers didn't technically meet the requirement. Household names such as Ford, General Electric, U.S. Steel, Honeywell, Mattel, Johnson & Johnson, United Technologies, 3M, and Caterpillar might not have met the US-employment threshold. The reverse was also true: Because of how the corporate entities were structured, US-based subsidiaries of foreign companies like Toyota and Volkswagen might be eligible.

The situation hardly seemed like what Congress had intended, and it threatened to strangle the Fed's ability to follow through on its March 23 announcements unlocking private markets. What if investors realized the fine print of CARES meant the Fed's safety blanket didn't allow the central bank to do what its leaders had promised?

In the weeks after beating back the initial financial panic, untying this Gordian knot proved to be one of the thorniest challenges facing Powell, Brainard, Lehnert, Daleep Singh, and their teams in Washington and New York, along with BlackRock. Some investment executives were antsy that the Fed wouldn't be able to purchase any bonds at all. Fed lawyers might be able to find some wiggle room, but Mnuchin emphatically insisted that the Fed not cut any corners.

Singh's fears that the program would be permanently hobbled became increasingly intense. *We may not feel comfortable launching this*, he thought. *We're going to make mistakes. There could be lawsuits.*

The strings that lawmakers had attached to the Treasury's war chest had a buried escape clause: The restrictions didn't apply to "securities that are based on an index or that are based on a diversified pool of securities." This workaround had been necessary to allow the Fed to purchase exchange-traded funds. Now Singh and Lehnert used that to deliver a compromise allowing them to honor the agreement. What if the Fed reverse-engineered its own index of securities that fit the parameters of the previously announced corporate-debt buying program? They could comb through the bonds in the $9.3 trillion corporate market to find companies that satisfied the lending program's criterion: nonbank corporate debt for firms rated investment-grade as of March 22 for securities of no more than five years in duration.

Working with BlackRock, Singh's team devised this bespoke "broad market index," composed of nearly 800 companies including Apple, Verizon, AT&T, and Toyota. They could toggle their purchases up or down depending on various measures of market functioning. If those measures indicated sustained improvement to levels that had prevailed before the pandemic shock in March, the New York Fed could pause the purchases entirely. If market functioning deteriorated anew, on the other hand, the Fed could ramp up its corporate-bond buying once more.

It took the Fed weeks to finish all this work. The market-index solution was not announced until June 15.

While many lawmakers grew unhappy that the Fed was taking so long to get its programs going, others thought it was overkill. *Given the record amounts of corporate-bond issuance,* Senator Pat Toomey asked the Fed chair at a hearing a few days later, *why did the Fed need to buy any bonds at all?*

The Fed needed to show it could honor its promises, Powell answered. The Fed didn't want to "run through the bond market like an elephant, snuffing out price signals and things like that," he said.

In private, Powell told Toomey that the central bank's credibility was at stake. "You have to honor your commitments," he said during one phone call. Powell thought this related to everything the Fed did: *If you said you were going to do something, you needed to* follow through. Toomey wasn't entirely convinced but didn't press the point too strongly.

Loans or grants

The speedy revival of the corporate-debt market and the bumpy but fast launch of the Paycheck Protection Program threw into sharper relief the gap for companies that couldn't benefit from either or didn't receive enough support from the PPP. Congress kicked this can to the Fed in the form of the Main Street Lending Program. It was a program few at the Fed had campaigned for, and it was shaping up as one of the hardest things officials there had ever done. Lend freely, and the Fed might own many more defaulted loans down the road. Don't lend enough, and the Fed would stand accused, again, of enriching Wall Street while letting Main Street go down the tubes.

The Main Street program asked banks to make loans to companies that would have had a reasonable chance of paying them back had a virus not destroyed their business. Then they would sell 95 percent of the loan to the Fed, keeping a 5 percent piece to ensure the program didn't become a dumping ground for shaky debts. Banks could also earn fees for managing payments for the entire loan.

To get the job done, the Fed's lawyers were very busy looking at what they could do, what they couldn't do, and what were just suggestions. Unlike with the corporate backstops, the Fed's lawyers concluded that the central bank's purchases of business loans arranged by banks constituted "direct loans," meaning the Fed would require companies to refrain from distributing cash to shareholders and to ensure that executive compensation did not exceed certain limits specified in the CARES Act.

But the Fed and the Treasury opted to largely ignore other suggestions outlined by Congress. The goal of the program wasn't to employ a fixed amount of the workforce, but rather to vouchsafe that viable companies had a lifeline so they could employ more workers once the pandemic passed and demand recovered. Fed officials believed the requirements that Mark Warner, Warren, and other senators were asking to impose would render totally unworkable an already difficult-to-scale program.

———

By the end of March, Mnuchin and Powell had initiated a standing daily conference call every afternoon. Powell was often joined on these calls by Williams in New York and Brainard and Lehnert from Washington. Rosengren, whose bank would be administering the Main Street loans, sometimes participated, though Mnuchin was fastidious about not allowing too many people to join the calls. They would sometimes begin with Mnuchin and Powell employing a good-humored formality, with Mnuchin addressing Powell as "Mr. Chairman."

From the outset, Mnuchin had different ideas from the Fed about Main Street, and he struck colleagues at both the Fed and the Treasury as particularly unenthusiastic compared to the PPP or the corporate bond-buying backstops. One result was that even though Powell, Brainard, and the other governors might have disagreed among themselves over how aggressive their lending backstops should be, they never had to resolve those disagreements because they almost always found themselves pushing for easier terms than Mnuchin would accept.

Mnuchin liked to cite the example of how former Treasury chiefs Hank Paulson and Tim Geithner hadn't lost money on the Troubled

Asset Relief Program — indeed, that 2008–2009 crisis-era lending had turned a surprising profit. The secretary made clear that he wanted to be able to look back and claim he had been an equally responsible steward of the taxpayers' money. "If Congress wanted me to lose all the money, that money would have been designed as subsidies and grants," Mnuchin told reporters during a Zoom briefing on April 29.[4] Over time, the Fed governors thought Mnuchin was acting more like an investor who wanted to get the best deal possible and protect himself against any losses, leading to program terms and features that struck Brainard as miserly.

The Fed and many economists thought this was the wrong way to frame what they were doing. The 2020 shock wasn't a banking crisis that required recapitalizing a handful of financial institutions. It was an economy-wide crisis.

Fed presidents heard the same thing over and over from businesses in their districts about the Main Street loans: *This doesn't help us. Our business is shuttered. We don't need more debt.*

Glenn Hubbard, the well-connected Republican economist, told officials he was worried the program was too conservative. The initial loan floor of $1 million was too large for smaller businesses. Hubbard fretted it left companies inadequately addressed by the CARES Act completely exposed. "If the Fed doesn't lose money," Hubbard said, "that says they weren't lending to borrowers who needed the money."[5]

The new money test

There was an inherent tension in the program design: banks that thought they were making a good loan to a solid borrower would want to keep the whole thing, not sell 95 percent of it to the Fed. Banks that thought they were making a risky loan, by contrast, would not want to keep even 5 percent of it, let alone sell the rest to their regulator.

According to one Fed official, policymakers knew from the beginning that there would be a problem at the intersection between the people who can get loans but don't need them and the people who need loans but can't get them. "People said, 'What's the matter with you people? Are you that stupid?' No, we're not that stupid. We knew the intersection was going to be a problem, but we didn't have a brilliant idea unless the Treasury was willing to ease the credit terms for those borrowers who couldn't get loans otherwise."

Though the Fed could not forgive debt outright, some at the Fed thought they could have designed features that would have provided more subsidies to borrowers, including by allowing banks to refinance existing debt into a lower-rate, longer-maturity loan. In the corporate-debt back-stops, Mnuchin had signed off on allowing companies to use new debts to roll over existing ones. But he refused to permit rollovers in the Main Street program.

"It's a big deal if you can refinance your liability side of your balance sheet at very low interest rates," said Rosengren, who thought the Trea-sury erred by making the terms insufficiently generous. "Why should the largest companies in the country be able to refinance the liability side of their balance sheet, but not medium-sized firms, and then small firms be able to take it as a grant? Midsize firms were treated disproportionately poorly relative to small firms and large firms, and they employ an awful lot of people."[6]

One banker warned Adam Lerrick, an adviser to Mnuchin, about the hazards of allowing banks and borrowers to use the program to roll over existing debts. "Tomorrow, if you do that, you will own every single oil-and-gas, hotel, and restaurant loan in our portfolio. And cruise lines? You'll own those in minutes."

The Treasury came up with what it referred to as the "new money" test. The goal of the program wasn't to shuttle existing loans from banks to the Boston Fed, but rather to make sure borrowers received new money, on net, to get to the other side of the pandemic. Bankers argued that the Fed and the Treasury could help extend that bridge by turning a loan that was coming due in nine months into a loan that lasted for several more years. But the Treasury remained unswayed.

"If you have a loan that matures in nine months," Lerrick told the banker, "it's your job to restructure that loan to get the borrower to the other side. It's not our job to pay you off at one hundred cents on the dollar."

Mnuchin put his foot down on allowing the Main Street program to let companies roll over their existing debt. According to Rosengren, he was "quite concerned that we not do a 'backdoor bailout' of banks and that we not take substantial losses on the program."

Mnuchin often defended his choices by reminding colleagues that he was the one who would have to sit before congressional committees to defend bailing out the banking system or losing a bundle of taxpayer money.

By contrast, Powell made clear to his staff that he didn't want them to worry about any political fire. "His attitude was, 'Whatever we do, I'm going to own it. You guys just row on the fucking oar. I will take the arrows,'" said one senior staffer. Powell could be impatient and demanding, but staffers said they rarely saw him lose his temper.

Sometimes after their daily 5 p.m. conference call with Mnuchin, Powell would follow up with a few Fed staffers to rally the troops. "I think I heard some good news," Powell would say, even if Mnuchin had nixed a Fed proposal or ordered up more painstaking analysis. At other times, when Mnuchin truly dug in his heels, Powell simply acknowledged the obvious without any bitterness: "Well, the secretary is going in a different direction here."

Secretary Minutiae

Part of the problem was that Congress had been vague about its intentions for the $454 billion it was giving Mnuchin for the lending programs. Did lawmakers expect the Treasury to be conservative and turn a profit? Or were they comfortable with the Treasury making riskier loans that might result in some taxpayer losses? Congress never answered this question clearly. One academic later described the end result as a compromise that was "like trying to administer mouth-to-mouth resuscitation through a cocktail straw."[7]

Mnuchin viewed the Main Street program as something designed to solve a problem that went away almost immediately. In mid-March, as companies drew down their preexisting credit lines, concerns mounted that the banking system might not be able to quickly provide new credit. The one-two punch of the PPP and the corporate-debt announcement took care of that problem.

The disagreements between the Fed and the Treasury, which for the most part stayed hidden from public view, were surprising because the Trump administration wanted *less* stimulus — the opposite of the dynamic that had played out the year before, when the president was badgering Powell for the type of policy normally reserved for periods of weak growth or recession. The holdups over the program's initial design slowed its entire launch, upsetting many in Congress.

Mnuchin's zeal for delving into the most intricate lending details earned him the moniker "Secretary Minutiae" among some Fed and Treasury staffers. He was also reluctant to delegate, with the exception perhaps of Muzinich. White House staffers were routinely bemused at sending something to a Mnuchin deputy only to receive a call from the secretary himself, offering his input. Fed officials concluded they were able to pull Mnuchin their way more often simply because their teams of dozens of analysts could outwork him. "The guy was really smart, really hardworking, had a mind like a steel trap," said a Fed official. "But he's just one man."

The Fed produced an initial term sheet as part of the April 9 announcements but continued to work furiously behind the scenes to persuade Mnuchin to widen the program's aperture. Lehnert later reflected on his deep dive into the plumbing of commercial-banking agreements as he worked to structure the $600 billion lending effort. "This is not what you think about when you're in grad school. Never in a million years did I imagine I would be doing this," he said. "None of us signed up to *run* a bank."[8]

Shutting down Milk Street

The persistence of the virus meant businesses in certain hard-hit sectors were going to need more money to survive. Marc Epstein shuttered his Milk Street Café in downtown Boston after the pandemic sent workers scattering from the adjacent office towers in March. His business, which he opened in 1981, relies heavily on corporate catering — the kinds of in-person meetings or special events that were unlikely to resume until people felt comfortable enough to board a plane, meet in groups, and eat food together.

Epstein furloughed most of his seventy-two employees. He reopened for six weeks in the fall of 2020 and brought some of the workers back to meet the requirement that most of his $694,000 PPP loan be used for payroll so it could be forgiven. Then, after the money ran out, he closed Milk Street again on October 25.

Staying open wasn't worth the cost. Daily sales were a measly 2 to 3 percent of what they had been before the pandemic. With his son-in-law and chief operating officer, Mitchell Baratz, Epstein resolved to keep the restaurant closed until the neighborhood's office workers returned — whenever that might be. It would almost certainly require a vaccine. "It was just clear staying open puts us out of business very quickly, whereas hibernating gives us a chance," said Baratz. In October 2020 the pair applied for and received a $1.5 million Main Street loan, which they planned to use to help defray reopening costs.

Lose-lose

In April the oil-and-gas industry had launched an all-out push for new federal relief from the White House. There was no way Congress was likely to approve dedicated relief for the energy sector, but GOP senators from oil states pressed Mnuchin to offer a lifeline. In response to the pressure, the Treasury asked the Fed about creating a "distressed energy liquidity facility." *No way*, said the Fed, shutting the idea down. Lehnert's one-pager on the proposal pointed out the Fed could not help individual industries. "This is a terrible idea," he concluded.

When the terms of the Main Street program were subsequently relaxed on April 30, Republican senators from oil states and Energy Secretary Dan Brouillette claimed that the adjustments had been made at the behest of the oil-and-gas industry — it isn't clear whether this was performative pandering or because they had actually prevailed on Mnuchin to expand the program. Fed officials never discussed making changes to the program for the benefit of any industry, and loans remained unattractive for most energy companies, who were too indebted to qualify. Still, the public pressure on Mnuchin from oil-drilling companies — on top of statements from Trump, Brouillette, and GOP lawmakers that exaggerated the changes as a major lifeline — gave oxygen to a narrative that the Fed itself was intentionally engaging in a stealth bailout of the energy sector.

The whole kerfuffle was a lose-lose for the Fed. Not only were the program's terms *still* tighter than it preferred, but its efforts to pry the Treasury from its more-conservative position were now being weaponized as a publicity campaign by environmental groups, which wanted the Fed to use its regulatory prowess to address climate change.

As the brouhaha over the "oil-and-gas bailout" illustrated, the Fed was quickly coming under political pressure from all sides. Lawmakers reasonably demanded to know, by mid-June, why the program wasn't ready. Powell was inundated with letters from legislators pleading for help. Republican senators from Kansas asked for a lending program to help movie theaters. Democratic congressmen asked for $5 billion in help to the ailing passenger-bus industry.

Date 2020	Covid-19 Cases	Covid-19 Deaths	Dow Jones Average	VIX Fear Index
Thursday, April 30	1,073,244	59,646	24,345 (↓ 288)	34.15 (↑2.92)

V, U, or *K*?

Normally, recessions occur because of some imbalance in the economy. Inflation gets too high and the Fed has to raise rates to a level that tips the economy into recession, or asset and debt bubbles burst, leading businesses and consumers to retrench. This recession was different. Instead of studying railcar loadings and cargo shipments, forecasters had to model infection rates and virus transmissibility. By the end of April, public restiveness over stay-at-home orders was rising, though many consumers were staying away out of their own precaution.

Private-sector economists were debating what kind of downturn the nation faced. Larry Kudlow thought it might be a recovery that, when drawn on a chart, looked like the letter *V*. This sharp plunge and rapid sharp snapback would require the nation to get a better grip on the virus. By contrast, a *U*-shaped recovery had a longer trough and a more protracted recovery. The worst-case scenario, an *L*, meant a Depression-like permanent decline in the nation's economic well-being.

On Friday, May 8, the Labor Department reported that 20.5 million workers had lost their jobs in the prior month. It was a mind-boggling tally — an entire decade's worth of job gains obliterated in a single month. The unemployment rate, at 3.5 percent in February, shot to 14.7 percent in April. If the figures had been adjusted for workers who improperly classified themselves as employed while they were furloughed, the unemployment rate would have reached nearly 20 percent. A special Fed survey in April underscored just how much the downturn was hitting the worst-off: 2 of every 5 people working in February with a household income of less than $40,000 a year had experienced a job loss in March.[9]

That spring, the discussion about which letter of the alphabet best approximated the likely recovery turned to something different: a *K*. One leg of the economy — composed of white-collar workers in service jobs who could work from home and sectors like technology that didn't require frequent human-to-human contact — might see a mild downturn followed by a brisk recovery, or even no downturn at all. The other leg of the *K* would continue to see a gruesome decline in income or spending, including restaurants, hotels, entertainment, and any other activities organized around bringing groups of people together — with equally dire consequences for the millions of people employed in those industries. The long lines of cars snaking for miles outside food banks told the story of millions of Americans who were without work or money as a result of the Pandemic Crisis.

Still, there were hopeful signs. The seven-day average of new covid cases hit a high on April 10 before leveling off. A few days later,

Goldman's Jan Hatzius wrote a piece entitled "Thinking About the Restart." Even though the headline unemployment report was likely to set records, noted Hatzius, "the silver lining is that most job losses are coming in the form of temporary layoffs." The majority of workers eligible for traditional unemployment benefits were receiving more money than their lost wages, if and when they were able to secure benefits. Whereas economists would normally worry that such generous wage-replacement rates would discourage workers from seeking jobs, that was less of an issue when people were being directed to stay at home. "It was actually a very easy way of getting a lot of money out there and helping the people that most needed it. So it was really stunningly successful," said Hatzius. "The extra $600-per-week unemployment benefit was very powerful and it wasn't obvious that we paid a price for it."

Aggressive relief measures were also delaying potential loan losses, an additional cushion to the banking system. By the middle of May, nearly 4.2 million homeowners, or more than 1 in 12 eligible borrowers, had been able to delay mortgage payments. "Default rates were much more muted than what we'd expected," said Andrew Olmem, Kudlow's deputy on the National Economic Council. "The assistance we provided to folks who are unemployed and also the recovery rebates made sure that Americans were able to pay their financial obligations despite having record unemployment. That in turn meant the healthy banking system stayed healthy. We didn't have that problem of cascading defaults that we had a decade ago."[10]

The Fed's response had played a critical role in rehabilitating markets. "It was a remarkable show of strength and willingness to confront depression dynamics when it really mattered," said Hatzius. "I was very, very impressed with how the system came together despite the political divisions, which were enormous. I would not have predicted that in a presidential election year with Donald Trump in the White House."[11]

By late May, Powell allowed himself to feel more hopeful about the economy, even though the official data was gut-wrenchingly awful. He read a May 27 interview with Paul Krugman, the liberal economist, who said the covid slump looked more like the severe-but-short-lived recessions of the early 1980s than the 2008 crisis: "Right now, I don't see the case for a multiyear depression. People expecting this slump to look like the last one seem to me to be fighting the last war."[12]

A crucial question, of course, was *How many of these job losses will be permanent?* One widely circulated paper estimated that 42 percent of the 22.5 million job losses since February would be permanent, implying that 9 to 10 million people would still be out of work once the economy reopened. If this assessment was roughly accurate, that would be on par with the employment losses of the 2007–2009 recession. It had taken the US economy five years to recover those jobs.

Powell began to worry more in public about what would happen if fiscal lifelines were exhausted that summer. "We're doing a fair job of getting through these first few months — more than a fair job," Powell said at a virtual news conference on June 10.

"The question, though, is that group of people who won't be able to go back to work quickly — what about them?"

Chapter Fifteen

TWIST OF "FAIT"

A statement attributed to Vladimir Lenin aptly described the state of affairs in the United States over the summer of 2020: *There are decades where nothing happens, and there are weeks when decades happen.* As the summer wore on, rifts in Washington grew wider and division in the country exploded.

As the most acute financial portions of the Pandemic Crisis receded into the background, the White House behaved like the public-health emergency was on its way out. Trump, who had largely placed the onus for managing the national response on governors, was urging the nation to reopen for commerce.

The president was also dismissive of wearing masks, something the CDC had been recommending since April 3 as a simple intervention that could slow the spread of the virus without lockdowns. Mnuchin, on the other hand, had been among the first to speak up about the need to follow health precautions at crowded meetings inside the Situation Room. "Look, are we going to live by the guidelines we're putting out?" They needed either to spread out or to wear masks, he said. In a meeting in a dining room behind the Oval Office in July, Kudlow tried to convince Trump that his mask-related culture war was damaging medically and politically.

"It's becoming way too political, and it shouldn't be," Kudlow said. "I'm not the political genius, but I don't think it's helping you for the campaign." Trump just glared at him in response.

The three were more aligned when it came to whether a fourth package of government spending would be necessary. Kudlow insisted the economy would recover quickly from the pandemic, a view that synced with Trump's insistence that life would soon be back to normal. "We're not going to spend our way out of that," Kudlow told Fox Business on May 15.[1]

For millions of Americans, however, the pandemic was very much not over, even if markets had moved on. When the Black unemployment rate in 2019 fell to its lowest level since records began in 1972, the economic situation of African Americans remained fragile relative to that of Whites. Their unemployment rate remained roughly double the White rate; they had a lower percentage of homeownership; and they had less job security. During the pandemic, relatively more Blacks and Latinos lost their jobs than did White workers. They were also twice as likely to die from covid as Whites. The pandemic was hitting lower-income Americans and minorities much harder than the population as a whole, reflecting disparities in the nation's health care system, disproportionate rates of households living in densely populated housing, and overrepresentation in front-line occupations.

"I keep hearing the same refrain: *Not since the Depression Era, Not since the 1930s*," said Amanda Cage, chief executive of the National Fund for Workforce Solutions, on a webinar that included Jay Powell, Richard Clarida, and Lael Brainard on May 21. "But we have a modern-day image of what 20 percent unemployment looks like. It looks like Englewood on the South Side of Chicago."

It was in this context that a third crisis boiled over: broad social unrest broke out after a white Minneapolis police officer was videoed pressing his knee on the neck of George Floyd, a Black man who pled for his life before dying. Floyd's May 25 death, which a jury would rule a murder the next year, led to protests across the country. Some turned violent.

————

The wrenching divisiveness of 2020 overshadowed a surprisingly good jobs report that came out on Friday, June 5. Employers had added a record

2.5 million jobs, defying economists' predictions of 8 million additional job losses. The report offered a strong indication that the worst of the downturn might have passed. Yet although the official jobless rate fell to 13.3 percent (from 14.7 percent in April), the unemployment rate for Blacks actually ticked higher, to 16.8 percent (from 16.7 percent). For Asians it climbed to 15 percent (from 14.5 percent).[2] These figures excluded the many Americans idled from their jobs but misclassified as employed, or who had stopped looking for work and thus were not counted as unemployed.

Trump was exultant over the numbers as he gathered in the Oval Office with Pence, Mnuchin, and Kudlow. The unexpectedly early turnaround in hiring was the shot in the arm his reelection bid desperately needed. After the meeting broke up, the advisers joined Trump under the hot sun at a Rose Garden ceremony lasting nearly an hour, where the president addressed the myriad crises facing the country. At one point, he bizarrely invoked the deceased George Floyd.

"Hopefully, George is looking down right now and saying, *This is a great thing that's happening for our country. This is a great day for him,*" said Trump. "It's a great day for everybody. This is a great, great day in terms of equality."

Date 2020	Covid-19 Cases	Covid-19 Deaths	Dow Jones Average	VIX Fear Index
Friday, June 5	1,895,109	105,128	27,111 (↑ 829)	24.52 (↓1.29)

Back to the boardroom

Four days later, on June 9, Powell sat down at the end of the massive table inside the Fed's boardroom to open a two-day meeting of the Federal Open Market Committee. It was an event that perfectly captured the moment. On one hand, the Fed was getting back to its rhythm of eight FOMC meetings a year. This was not an emergency meeting or a midnight email, but a return to the deliberative process. On the other hand, Powell presided over a deserted room, peering at an oversize monitor displaying the rest of the committee, who joined via WebEx.

Powell opened the meeting with a rare statement to acknowledge "the tragic events" in Minneapolis "that have again put a spotlight on the pain of racial injustice in this country. The Federal Reserve serves the entire nation.... Everyone deserves the opportunity to participate fully in our society and in our economy.... We will take this opportunity to renew our steadfast commitment to these principles, making sure that we are playing our part."

In fact, a reckoning over racial disparities had slowly been bubbling to the top of the Fed's agenda for years. The central bank had long taken a color-blind approach to economic outcomes by focusing on broad aggregates. For example, the transcripts of Fed policy meetings in 2015 show race was mentioned only twice.

The Fed had historically steered clear of issues of inequality and race on the grounds that the central bank's tools, and its statute, enabled it to address only inflation and overall employment. If it sought to target the distribution of income or the relative employment of people by race, it might fail, causing inflation to rise. Under their emerging rethink, Fed officials were still committed to keeping inflation low. But they had a newfound view that, after years in which inflation hadn't responded to lower and lower levels of unemployment, they could exploit this dynamic and positively address narrower outcomes without paying any price in higher inflation.

Such a transformation could help Powell achieve the economic outcomes he sincerely believed were essential by making it harder for the Fed to justify raising interest rates based on a forecast that lower unemployment would undesirably accelerate inflation. But it could also expose the Fed to greater criticism from elected leaders on both sides of the aisle — from Republicans who worried that the Fed was politicizing its mandate or from Democrats who, if and when the Fed concluded it was time to raise rates, attacked the central bank as racially insensitive.

A new framework

By the time of the June meeting, the economy looked like it might no longer be getting worse, and Powell began to focus on a different worry: that the central bank would face a rerun of what had occurred after the 2007–2009 downturn. The Fed would exhaust its firepower by keeping interest rates pinned near zero and buying massive amounts of government debt, forcing any meaningful stimulus to come from Congress — whereupon Congress would declare, "We're done spending more money!" Powell continued to make an unwavering plea to Congress: *We can't do this alone. We need your help.*

By July 2020, interest rates were held near zero and the Fed was purchasing significant quantities of bonds. Further meaningful monetary stimulus would require offering more specifics around how long the central bank's spigots would stay open. Powell concluded that they should disseminate these specifics when the FOMC finished the work it had begun the year before to revamp its inflation-targeting framework.

Powell and Clarida had initially tried to lower expectations about the changes, calling them "evolutionary rather than revolutionary." They were wary of overly rigid or mechanical strategies, and the reserve-bank presidents were similarly reluctant to tie the hands of future FOMC members.

Powell launched the framework review after concerns within the economics profession had percolated for years over what many saw as an existential challenge facing central banks around the world during the last decade. Over long periods of time, high inflation and high interest rates went hand in hand, as did low inflation and low rates. If, in normal times, interest rates were low, then when recession loomed, the central bank had less room to cut them. Rates could get stuck at zero without reviving the economy. Inflation could then be pushed even lower. That would cause the public to *expect* low inflation, and its behavior would make that expectation a self-fulfilling prophecy.

First Japan and now the Eurozone had fallen into just such a trap. Before the pandemic, there were troubling signs that the same thing was happening in the United States: the Fed had been unable to consistently hit the 2 percent target set in 2012, in part because it lacked sufficient interest-rate ammo. Taking a cue from research conducted by academic luminaries that included Ben Bernanke, Powell decided the Fed needed to redesign its approach to targeting inflation to steer away from any monetary black holes.

With Clarida, he had been driving the committee to a shift that sounded subtle but could in fact be quite radical. If inflation had run below 2 percent, the Fed would seek to push inflation temporarily above its 2 percent target in order to 1) persuade the public to expect inflation to average 2 percent and 2) set prices and wages accordingly.

Powell was moving the Fed toward a new regime, dubbed "flexible average inflation targeting," or FAIT, that would allow for periods in which the committee, instead of aiming for 2 percent no matter what, would deliberately nudge inflation somewhat above 2 percent in some circumstances.

This would radically change interest-rate setting. Instead of preemptively lifting interest rates to head off higher inflation — a practice the Fed had followed since the Volcker years — the central bank would wait until actual inflation had risen. By themselves, the changes might matter little. But if Congress delivered a bolder relief package and inflation began to accelerate, the Fed was saying it would sit on its hands longer than it had in the past — including, for example, when Trump's tax cuts had sparked concern about "overheating" the economy in 2017.

Powell proposed one other important change. In the past, the Fed would raise rates when unemployment fell below its "natural rate," on the theory that such a move would keep inflation from rising. For the two years of Powell's chairmanship until the pandemic hit, unemployment had been below — sometimes significantly — the Fed staff's estimate of its natural rate. But inflation hadn't risen. The new policy formulation would no longer raise interest rates simply because unemployment was low, so long as inflation didn't rise too far above 2 percent for too long.

The Fed's leadership had begun to circulate internal drafts of their revised policy framework at the end of 2019, and they shared it with the full committee in January 2020. After Powell returned from Riyadh in February of 2020, they thought they might be able to conclude their review and announce their changes in April. The pandemic forced them to table those discussions. But by June of that year, they were thinking about how to finish the work.

Powell and Clarida spoke together with each reserve-bank president to try to forge a unanimous vote on the new policy. They went into their policy meeting at the end of July 2020 believing that three or four reserve-bank presidents — Esther George of Kansas City, Raphael Bostic of Atlanta, Robert Kaplan of Dallas, and Loretta Mester of Cleveland — might not support the new statement. The pair had been willing to push forward without unanimity but knew it would make a much bolder splash if everyone agreed. At the July 28–29 meeting, George listed a series of concerns she had with the new policy before explaining why she would nevertheless approve the changes. Whatever doubts others had, they too fell in line. The policy shift delinking interest-rate increases from the unemployment rate was approved unanimously.

Powell formally unveiled the changes during his keynote speech on August 27 at a virtual conference that replaced the annual confab normally staged in Jackson Hole, Wyoming. Powell invoked the bank's June 2019 "Fed Listens" conference in Chicago, which had featured panelists speaking about the benefits unfolding in low- and moderate-income communities as employers began competing for workers.

"It was just riveting," Powell said. "To hear them talk about what a tight labor market means in their communities was something that none of us will forget. We knew it intellectually, but hearing it and hearing it a lot over the course of 'Fed Listens'" had made a strong impression.

Date 2020	Covid-19 Cases	Covid-19 Deaths	Dow Jones Average	VIX Fear Index
Thursday, August 27	5,819,843	172,857	28,492 (↑ 160)	24.47 (↑1.20)

The new strategy raised some unanswered questions. If the Phillips curve is set aside, what would guide the Fed's inflation forecasts? Fed officials and academic economists were especially attuned to the role of expectations, though most conceded they didn't fully understand what drove those expectations.

Powell's outreach with lawmakers also led to few if any complaints from Capitol Hill. Democrat Denny Heck, who since becoming a Washington State representative in 2013 had pressed every Fed chair to place more attention on the employment side of the dual mandate, was ecstatic. "It's the most significant economic policy advance in forty years," said Congressman Heck. "There's no close second."

The Fed was subtly shifting its focus from fighting inflation toward promoting employment. For the plodding central bank, it was a transformation potentially as radical — if not as sudden — as Volcker's October 1979 declaration of war on inflation.

Some economists voiced skepticism over how useful the changes would be. In August 2019, one year before the Fed announced its policy changes, Larry Summers had warned that the Fed was at risk of following in the feeble footsteps of Europe and Japan.

"Simply put, tweaking inflation targets, communications strategies, or even balance sheets is not an adequate response to the challenges now confronting the major economies," he wrote.[3] What was needed, Summers argued, was for central banks to admit they were out of bullets in order to spur fiscal authorities to promote demand by spending more money.

Charles Plosser, a former president of the Philadelphia Fed and a frequent critic of Bernanke and Yellen's policies, articulated a different critique — that the previous decade of monetary policy hadn't managed to push inflation to the Fed's 2 percent goal. "[H]ow do they anticipate fine-tuning expectations and inflation outcomes as they suggest to achieve this new goal?" he wrote in an email to former colleagues. "Why have they not been able to get inflation to 2 percent despite their efforts? What will change that will enable them to now succeed in overshooting by just the right amount?"

Powell was unfazed. "I'm not at all concerned that people are saying, 'Oh, it's not credible,'" Powell said two months after the announcement. "It'll be credible when we get inflation meaningfully above 2 percent for an extended period and we don't react to it. We'll just say, *Look at that.* That's the only thing that can build your credibility after a decade of running below 2 percent inflation."[4]

When the Federal Open Market Committee met again on September 15 and 16, it laid out a three-part test to fulfill its new framework: To raise interest rates from near zero, inflation needed to reach 2 percent; officials needed to be convinced that inflation would run moderately above 2 percent for some time; and evidence had to suggest that labor markets had reached "levels consistent with...maximum employment." Powell would be leaving the punch bowl out for longer than his predecessors.

"This makes us look terrible!"

Congress adjourned in August for its summer recess without making much progress on another round of virus relief. By August 9, the United States had reached five million confirmed virus cases and 163,000 deaths. After the $600-per-week in additional jobless benefits expired at the end of July, Trump proposed a short-term top-up of $300 per week by executive order, along with an extension of rental-eviction protections.

Democratic nominee Joe Biden, who had been unusually tight-lipped about who was advising him on the economy, hosted his first briefing with his running mate, California Senator Kamala Harris. Joining them were two campaign advisers, Jared Bernstein and Heather Boushey, along with Janet Yellen and two other outside economic experts. Notably absent was Larry Summers, the former Treasury secretary for Bill Clinton and economic adviser to Barack Obama. Biden liked him, but Summers was so unpopular with the party's left wing that he had become a political liability.

Yellen's views did not differ substantially from those of Summers, yet she remained in much better political standing with the party's progressives and centrists. She worried that Congress risked repeating the mistakes of a decade earlier: "You had an economy that still had high unemployment," said Yellen. "Like then, the Fed is at the zero bound and clearly struggling to get the economy moving and back on track. This is not a good time to have fiscal policy switch from being accommodative to creating a drag."[5]

The Fed's lending backstops, meanwhile, remained lightly used even though they had provided an important security blanket to investors. Of the potential $2.3 trillion in lending, the Fed had purchased just $15 billion in assets. It was an extraordinary statistic. The mere announcement of the new programs had sufficed to calm the markets, spurring private lenders to rush back in. Mnuchin and the Fed agreed to extend the September 30 deadline for the lending backstops until at least the end of the year. The Main Street Lending Program finally opened for business in July, but as loans slowly trickled out, lawmakers in both parties urged Powell and Mnuchin to ease the program's terms. Through July, no companies had asked the Fed to help underwrite the issuance of new corporate debt, because private markets were booming. The Fed's program for existing corporate debt had bought only $12 billion in securities or exchange-traded funds.

The backstop for the municipal-debt market was proving more controversial. By the time the Fed bought its first loan — a $1.2 billion instrument issued by the state of Illinois — interest rates for most state and local borrowers had fallen well below the Fed's penalty rates. Kent Hiteshew, the Fed's recently hired muni-market guru, never received phone calls from state and local finance executives, debt issuers, or budget directors complaining about the pricing or terms. But the Fed was getting pounded from the left for making the terms too stringent and the pricing too expensive, and for allowing too few issuers. (One of those critics, Massachusetts Senator Elizabeth Warren, had been part of a group in 2014 that urged then-Chair Janet Yellen to ensure that such emergency borrowing carried a penalty rate. The Fed subsequently modified its rules accordingly.)

By August, Powell had heard from members of Congress that the Fed was charging too much for these loans now that interest rates had settled lower. The board sought Mnuchin's approval to lower the rates it would charge. Mnuchin wasn't as focused on the particular details as he had been during earlier negotiations and, despite some hesitation, approved the Fed's request.

Mnuchin struck Fed officials as unusually ill-tempered after he saw that New York's financially beleaguered Metropolitan Transportation Authority had, one week later, sold $450.7 million in debt to the Fed at a rate of around 1.9 percent — less than the 2.8 percent on offer from Wall Street banks. The MTA had been able to exploit a quirk in its credit ratings, which together with the Fed's recent rate reduction for its lending program enabled the transit system to finagle better terms from the Fed than from private banks.

"This is so ridiculous! This makes us look terrible!" Mnuchin told the Fed during a conference call. Expressing concerns he'd been snookered, Mnuchin demanded the Fed adjust its pricing matrix so the same thing never happened again. "Let's fix this," he insisted.

The MTA had the capacity to borrow several billion more dollars from the Fed, and Mnuchin worried that other issuers would see what had happened. Powell was sympathetic to Mnuchin's concerns, but the latter's rebuke discouraged Fed staffers. Brainard thought the program was doing exactly what had been intended: allowing a critical public-transit authority that had been walloped by covid to maintain its fiscal health. She didn't think the Fed or the Treasury was taking on any inappropriate risks.

"Don't let [covid] dominate your lives"

After setting a record on July 19, the seven-day average of new covid cases drifted lower through mid-September, falling by almost half, while the US death toll surpassed 200,000 later that month. Yet cases soon began climbing again in a third wave, particularly in states that had reopened soonest and most fully. Infections nearly doubled to a new high by the end of October.

Donald Trump was among the fresh cases. He announced testing positive for covid around 1 a.m. on Friday, October 2, days after he had mocked Biden on stage at their first presidential debate for wearing a big mask. Trump was admitted to Walter Reed National Military Center that Friday, where he received the steroid dexamethasone and an experimental antibody cocktail. After being discharged three days later, on

Monday, October 5, he taped a perversely counterfactual message from the White House: "Don't let [covid] dominate your lives."

Even though the pandemic was raging, the economy was recovering faster than the Fed and many professional forecasters had expected. The economy had shrunk by 9 percent during the April-to-June quarter compared with the previous quarter — the steepest decline in more than seventy years of record-keeping. But it bounced back at a record 7 percent pace during the July-to-September quarter. The labor market too was recovering, recouping by the end of September around half of the twenty-two million jobs lost in March and April. The pace then slowed. The unemployment rate fell to 7.9 percent — though by counting people who had stopped looking for work, it would have been somewhere between 9 and 10 percent.

Members of both parties continued to sound out Powell for his views on additional spending. While shying away from specific numbers, he urged lawmakers to do more for the unemployed, for small and medium businesses, and for cities and states. He sounded like a broken record during public appearances in August, September, and October. "There's still a healthy economy under here, except for this area that's been directly affected by covid," Powell said during a question-and-answer session after he unfurled the policy shift on August 27. Millions of people were out of work in segments of the economy devoted to getting people together, feeding them, flying them, or having them sleep in hotels. "We need to stay with those people," Powell said.

On Tuesday, October 6, Powell added a tinge of desperation in an online speech to private-sector forecasters. He worried that Americans might not take appropriate care to keep virus cases from climbing to levels that would force new curbs on activity and more layoffs. This, in turn, could slow the recovery in a way that triggered "typical recessionary dynamics, as weakness feeds on weakness," exacerbating long-standing inequality in the economy. "That would be tragic," he said, again using unusually emotional language.

"The recovery will be stronger and move faster," predicted Powell, "if monetary policy and fiscal policy continue to work side by side to provide support to the economy until it is clearly out of the woods."

Date 2020	Covid-19 Cases	Covid-19 Deaths	Dow Jones Average	VIX Fear Index
Tuesday, October 6	7,433,886	202,846	27,773 (↓ 376)	29.48 (↑1.52)

Election endgame

Mnuchin had spent weeks trying to broker talks with Nancy Pelosi, but despite his efforts, Republicans worried he might give away the store. For this round of talks, Mnuchin had been paired with Mark Meadows, the White House chief of staff. As a congressman, Meadows had developed a reputation as someone who excelled at blowing up deals rather than making them. Senate Republicans were divided over the benefits of another spending package. Trump couldn't make up his mind about what he wanted. While hospitalized at Walter Reed, he had fired off an all-caps tweet calling on lawmakers to "WORK TOGETHER AND GET IT DONE."

A few hours after Powell's online speech, McConnell told Trump that any deal between Pelosi and Mnuchin would only further divide the Senate GOP, prompting the president to announce that he was shutting down talks on a spending agreement until after the election.

But Trump appeared to have second thoughts, or rather third, later that very evening. He called on Congress to pass smaller relief bills, including one that would send checks directly to Americans. He also retweeted a CNBC article that read, "Fed Chair Powell calls for more help from Congress, says there's a low risk of 'overdoing it.'" Trump appended his own commentary: "True!"

Four weeks later, in an election that set turnout records, voters denied Donald Trump a second term.

Chapter Sixteen

PERIL AND POSSIBILITY

Donald Trump's election defeat deprived him of the chance to remake the Federal Reserve. Trump had appointed three Supreme Court Justices, but his attempts to install loyalists on the Fed's board in 2019 had run into opposition from Senate Republicans, forcing his picks — Herman Cain and Stephen Moore — to withdraw. Now his last-ditch attempt to confirm another loyalist to the board — Judy Shelton, a supporter of the gold standard — failed after former Fed officials, including Alan Greenspan, lobbied Senate Republicans to oppose her. Powell had largely protected his institution from presidential broadsides. (Trump's other nominee, St. Louis Fed research director Christopher Waller, was confirmed on a party-line vote.) But Powell faced different political and economic concerns in the final weeks of the Trump administration.

Between September and the end of October 2020, US covid cases doubled to 80,000 per day. By Thanksgiving they had more than doubled again, to 180,000, as more Americans appeared to forgo social distancing as the holidays approached. Economists at JPMorgan Chase projected a slight *contraction* in the US economy during the first quarter as more Americans retreated from public life to shelter from the virus. "This winter will be grim," the economists wrote.[1]

This time, Powell would have to navigate economic uncertainty with familiar problems — a Congress stalemated on another relief bill — but without the support of former allies.

Whither emergency lending?

Steven Mnuchin had banded with Powell to stabilize financial markets earlier that year. In the fall, that success gave way to a surprising skirmish over whether the emergency lending programs were still needed. Senator Pat Toomey had been pressing Mnuchin to shut them down at the end of the year. Toomey had always been wary of handing such power to the Fed and never intended for the programs to continue beyond December.

Adding to Toomey's concern was how a group of House Democrats were pushing Powell to drop the rate charged on its loans to cities and states to near zero, while extending the repayment periods to at least five years. "That was exactly the kind of activity that I wanted to make sure did not happen," Toomey later said. Since the summer, Toomey had been telling his colleagues that "by far the highest priority" for Republicans should be "the complete and unambiguous termination of these facilities and removal of the cash."

Democrats, who had initially decried the lending programs as a "slush fund" for Mnuchin, were now eyeing some of those same programs as a way to provide more stimulus if a Republican-controlled Senate proved an obstacle to the new Biden administration. Senate control for the coming two years was still undecided and would hinge on the outcome of two Georgia special elections in January.

Although the lending backstops were barely being used, Powell deemed it reckless to shut them down at year's end. Given the hazards as the virus raged that winter, the programs represented an inexpensive insurance policy. Powell had been telling Mnuchin and Toomey that a three-month extension would be a reasonable precaution. "When the right time comes, and I don't think that time is yet or very soon, we will put those tools away," Powell said during a webinar on November 17.

Powell, a lawyer, had also studied the CARES Act. Even if Mnuchin refused to authorize a short-term extension of the facilities, the Treasury had already transferred more than $100 billion out of the $454 billion to the legal entities that the Boston Fed and the New York Fed were using to run their respective lending programs. That money belonged to the Fed no matter what Mnuchin decided. The Fed could continue to make loans out of these facilities with plenty of cash in reserve — if a future Treasury secretary agreed to reopen the lending programs. But there was a catch: if Mnuchin not only refused to give the programs a longer lease on life but also asked the Fed to *refund* its initial investment, Powell wouldn't be able to thread this needle and the programs would end for good.

On Thursday, November 19, Mnuchin called Powell to tell him the Treasury secretary didn't have the legal authority to extend the lending backstops beyond December 31. A letter released publicly that afternoon upped the ante by asking Powell to return most of around $100 billion in funds. With Mnuchin having delayed the decision until the election result was clear — Biden had been declared president only on November 7 — the whole kerfuffle struck senior Fed officials as the kind of partisan political move the Treasury just didn't engage in — certainly not during a crisis.

It left Powell in a tough spot. Some Fed officials argued that there was no clause in their contractual agreements that provided for the Fed to give money back to the Treasury early. Yet Powell immediately decided there was nothing to be gained by picking a fight with Mnuchin, Toomey, and any other Republicans over this. Instead, Powell gave Mnuchin a heads-up on the terse statement he planned to issue in response, and Mnuchin initially signaled no objection. "The Federal Reserve would prefer that the full suite of emergency facilities established during the coronavirus pandemic continue to serve their important role as a backstop for our still-strained and vulnerable economy," it read.

The Fed and the Treasury rarely quarreled in public. Such fights didn't inspire confidence in global markets. But Powell didn't want anyone to mistake Mnuchin's decision as a signal that the Fed thought the economy was out of the woods or that it might soon pull back its other stimulus.

Date 2020	Covid-19 Cases	Covid-19 Deaths	Dow Jones Average	VIX Fear Index
Thursday, November 19	11,726,284	244,180	29,483 (↑ 45)	23.11 (↓0.73)

Democrats called on Powell to stiff Mnuchin's request for returning the unspent funds, which Powell rejected out of hand. On Friday, Powell sent Mnuchin a letter agreeing to his wish. Powell wasn't spoiling for a row with Mnuchin.

The Zoom where it happens

While Powell navigated the politics of a lame-duck administration, the incoming president needed to make a decision that would set a tone for Fed-Treasury cooperation in the coming years. Joe Biden's choice of Treasury secretary was an early test of his ability to bridge the dueling wings of the Democratic Party. Progressives wanted Biden to make a clean break from centrist Democrats in the mold of Robert Rubin, Larry Summers, and Tim Geithner.

But would the pragmatic Biden accept a fire-breathing crusader like Elizabeth Warren, who might spook Wall Street or require a messy Senate confirmation fight? Warren had made no secret of her desire to be considered. With Biden unlikely to pick Warren, his advisers asked her whom she would support. Warren's answer was unequivocal: *Janet Yellen.*[2]

Yellen was a shrewd choice. She wasn't close to Biden, and his economic team hadn't included her in its policy discussions. But Biden greatly respected her experience. With impeccable credentials, she would reassure Wall Street and win support from at least some Senate Republicans. Yellen was unapologetically liberal in her views but intellectually curious, pragmatic, and nonideological. The left regarded her as a hero for her push at the Fed to pay more attention to the social benefits that accrued from tighter labor markets.

In 2013, Warren and other Senate Democrats had blocked Obama from tapping Larry Summers to succeed Ben Bernanke as Fed chair when they threatened to derail his nomination. It forced Obama to break an earlier promise he had made to Summers and paved the way for Yellen to move from vice chair to first female chair of the Fed. Now Biden had the chance to make history by naming her the first female Treasury secretary — after seventy-seven male predecessors. As Biden's team considered its agenda, it became clear just how helpful it would be to have someone with Yellen's gravitas in the job. And her reputation had been sterling when she departed the Fed. At her sendoff in 2018, Powell and others popped their collars to mimic the brightly colored Nina McLemore power-suit jackets that Yellen often sported.

After Biden's victory, Jeffrey Zients — who knew Yellen from his days as National Economic Council director in Obama's second term and was now advising Biden on the presidential transition — called Yellen to see if she was interested in serving as Treasury secretary. Yellen told Zients she wasn't looking for a job — and besides, there were plenty of exceptional candidates out there.

Zients saw that she hadn't exactly closed the door. He called back a few days later. "We really would like you to do this," he said. Yellen agreed to go through the vetting process. The prospect of serving the country again during especially trying circumstances proved impossible to refuse.

On Thursday, November 19, Biden teased to reporters that he had settled on his pick. "You'll find it is someone who I think will be accepted by all elements of the Democratic Party," he said.[3] On Friday afternoon Yellen met the incoming president by Zoom for a short conversation, where Biden formally offered the job, and Yellen accepted.

Substantial further progress

Not only did Yellen prove to be acceptable to most Democrats and many Republicans, but along with newly promising developments on a bipartisan spending bill, her nomination as Treasury secretary reassured investors. Moreover, by December 1 lawmakers had coalesced around an approximately $900 billion relief bill. Mitch McConnell promised Republicans David Perdue and Kelly Loeffler, whose January 5 runoff elections in Georgia would decide Senate control, that Congress would not leave Washington without a deal.

Another milestone in efforts to fight the pandemic arrived in late

November: partnered drugmakers Pfizer and BioNTech announced that a new, RNA-based vaccine had proven to be 95 percent effective against Covid-19. A second drugmaker, Moderna, announced similarly remarkable results for its vaccine candidate a few days later.

But even if vaccinations might allow greater easing of public-health restrictions imposed to curb the virus, it hardly felt that way at the time. The seven-day average for US deaths from the virus in December surpassed the April peak of around 2,200 per day. By year's end, the United States was reporting more than 3,000 deaths per day on a regular basis. Claims for unemployment benefits had begun rising, and the unemployment rate had fallen in November for the wrong reason: more workers had stopped seeking jobs.

At the Fed's final meeting of the year, on December 16, officials reinforced their earlier pledge not to raise interest rates anytime soon and clarified that they would continue to buy $80 billion in Treasuries and $40 billion in mortgage securities per month. In its heavily scrutinized policy statement, the FOMC said those purchases would prevail until officials decided they had made "substantial further progress" toward their job-growth and inflation goals. Projections released at the meeting showed officials expected not to meet those goals for at least another three years. Powell said the Fed anticipated seeing some one-time increases in prices due to a potential reopening boom in the spring, but these were unlikely to create sustained higher inflation. "It's not going to be easy to have inflation move up," he said. "It will take some time, because that's what we believe the underlying inflation dynamics are in our economy."

By December, the Fed's easy-money policies were strongly supporting sectors unhampered by the pandemic. Interest-rate-sensitive goods such as homes and cars were booming. After the pandemic had struck in early April 2020, national real-estate brokerage Redfin had furloughed one-third of its staff and laid off another 7 percent. But by July, the company was hiring. Automated real-estate appraisals and online-video home tours had enabled more transactions to occur, even with social-distancing measures in place. Home-buying demand quickly returned to pre-pandemic levels, fueled by work-from-home policies, the desire for more space, and falling mortgage rates.

Homes were in such short supply that single-family home prices jumped 10 percent in December from a year earlier, a growth rate not seen since the housing bubble of 2004–2006. "This is the housing market that people have been expecting since, you know, 2010," Powell said at his December 16 news conference. "Not many [people], when the pandemic hit, thought, *Oh, this is what will produce that housing market.* But it has."

Finishing the job

But Powell focused more on the fact that Congress, not the Fed, had the tools to finish the job. "In the near term, the help that people need isn't just from low interest rates," he said. Powell returned to the idea of a bridge across the "economic chasm" created by the pandemic. "For many Americans, that bridge is there and they're across it. But there's a group for which they don't have a bridge yet, and that's who we're talking about here....It would be bad to see people losing their business, their life's work in many cases, or even generations' worth of work, because they couldn't last another few months, which is what it amounts to."

Stock markets had recouped their losses from the spring, returning to new records, even though eleven million fewer Americans were working than in February. This troubling disparity made the Fed extremely vulnerable, again, to the critique that had haunted the Eccles Building after the 2008 financial crisis — that it cared only about helping Wall Street, not Main Street. (Because the Fed's tools operate through financial markets, they were much better suited to making it cheaper to borrow than to providing relief to unemployed households or businesses disrupted by the pandemic. That explained why Powell kept encouraging Congress to spend more money.)

A few hours after the news conference, congressional leaders announced they were nearing agreement on a $900 billion spending package. It would offer $300 per week in extra unemployment benefits through mid-March, replacing the CARES Act's $600 weekly payments, which had expired in July. The package also allowed certain small business to obtain a second PPP loan, and it provided more generous tax credits for hard-hit businesses that retained workers.

But that Friday, the deal faced a holdup: Toomey had introduced language that would not only nail closed the doors for the Fed's emergency lending facilities but also might limit the Fed's ability to use those tools in a future crisis. Toomey had insisted on the language after the Democrats' furor over Mnuchin's initial decision had led them to circulate plans to relaunch the facilities once Biden took office. "That scared the hell out of me," said Toomey.

The battle over the Fed's arcane emergency-loan powers threatened to scuttle the bill. From retirement, Bernanke issued a rare public statement, asking Congress to "ensure, at least, that the Federal Reserve's emergency lending authorities...remain fully intact." Representative Patrick McHenry asked Powell at one point if Powell needed his help: "Do I need to lie down on the tracks to stop this?"

Powell demurred. McConnell and Toomey had made clear to Powell that this was a dealbreaker.

Meantime, some Democrats warned Powell that he was torching his own credibility by refusing to protest loudly and publicly. Senate Minority Leader Chuck Schumer, for example, exhorted Powell to pound the table and exclaim, "We need these!"

Another Democratic senator asked Powell to make a more desperate appeal. "Tell them the economy's going to die if you don't do this."

"I'm not gonna do that," Powell responded.

Getting in the middle of a fight between the leaders of both parties in Congress was the last place on Earth that the Fed chair wanted to be. But Powell was stuck: Say nothing, and Democrats would resent the Fed for failing to defend tools that the new administration might prefer to use. Get loud, and Republicans would begrudge the Fed for sticking its nose even deeper into politics — all to defend lending programs that weren't being heavily used.

Ultimately, a group of Democrats worked with Toomey on compromise language that restricted the Treasury's ability to launch clones of the Municipal Liquidity Facility, the Main Street Lending Program, and the corporate-debt backstops but stopped short of explicitly curbing the Fed's emergency-lending powers.

The end of "unusual and exigent"

In the end, the closure of the emergency programs proved inconsequential: they had already accomplished their mission, and now vaccines and extra federal spending would do the rest. The Fed never purchased a single newly issued bond through its Primary Market Corporate Credit Facility, which had been authorized to lend up to $500 billion. The Fed bought just four bonds through its backstop for municipal-debt markets, including one more each from the state of Illinois and New York's MTA, bringing its total holdings to $6 billion. It had purchased $14 billion in existing corporate bonds and ETFs. In July and August 2021 it would gradually sell those holdings to private investors, avoiding the ETF-handcuffs fate of the Bank of Japan that had alarmed other financial regulators.

The announcement that the Fed's Main Street Lending Program would go away spurred a last-minute crush of applications. The program extended 1,830 loans, with more than half of those completed in December. The largest loan the Fed purchased was for $300 million, to the company that owned the LA Fitness chain of health clubs. (The smallest was a $100,000 loan to a family restaurant in Ridgefield, Connecticut.) The program loaned $50 million to a chain of movie theaters in San Antonio, Texas; $16 million to the owner of a minor-league affiliate of the Houston Astros baseball team in Round Rock, Texas; and $4.4 million to a Division I college athletic league, the Sun Belt Conference. The $17 billion in total lending was a fraction of the $600 billion authorized and the $525 billion administered through the first rounds of the Paycheck Protection Program.

Nonetheless, the crisis showed that the government lacked a well-geared system to deliver relief to businesses — other than those big enough to tap bond markets. "There is a cost if, whenever we have [financial panics], we do programs that only help large institutions, because in the long run that makes it much riskier to be a small or medium-sized firm," said Eric Rosengren, whose team at the Boston Fed worked around the clock over the holidays to process loan purchases.[4]

A PPP loan of nearly $925,000 had given a lifeline to Tina and Glenn Beattie's company, which owned and operated thirty-six Denny's restaurants in five states across the Midwest. "For a brand like Denny's, you don't think takeout," said Tina, who started in the restaurant business as a hostess at a Denny's franchise in Mesa, Arizona, in 1993. "Throwing tables in the parking lot was not going to increase the number of guests we had." By the end of the summer, business had rebounded so that sales were down by around 40 percent — better than the 60 percent decline that had occurred after their restaurants were allowed to reopen.

Beattie said applying for the PPP money felt like a race against time before the program ran out of money. Ultimately, she said, the loan saved the company: "It was manna from heaven." She and Glenn were able to keep paying workers while preserving their relationships with vendors and landlords. But the PPP money could go only so far, so Tina began looking for a Main Street loan later that year. The couple asked twenty different banks and found no takers.

By the fall she had located a potential lender — and spent $30,000 to prepare her audited financials to process the loan. "That was money we took out of working capital at a tenuous time — that's how much we thought the program would be of value," said Tina. "It would have given us some breathing room."[5] While Mnuchin's announcement on November 19 had ignited a last-minute surge for those who had already started the lending process, it marked the end of the road for the Beatties' application.

They decided in early 2021 to permanently close two of their thirty-six establishments, in Evansville, Indiana and Effingham, Illinois. In March 2021 the Beatties received another $1.3 million from the PPP, made possible by the $900 billion spending bill.

"A disgrace"

Congress passed the $900 billion package on Monday, December 21, sending it to the White House for signature. "This overall bill, I think, is fabulous," Mnuchin told CNBC that morning. The Treasury Department issued a statement on Tuesday thanking President Trump for his leadership on the legislation.

But that evening Trump knocked over the apple cart again. He released a video on Twitter with an extraordinary message: the bipartisan measure "really is a disgrace," he said. The "ridiculously low" $600 checks needed to be bigger — $2,000 per person, by his thinking. Trump had mostly ignored the negotiations surrounding the bill, stewing instead over his thus-far-futile attempts to overturn the election result. Democrats immediately seized on Trump's call for larger, $2,000 stimulus payments. "Let's do it!" Pelosi tweeted.

Mnuchin was aghast, according to people who spoke with him at the time. He explained to another White House official that he didn't see how the politics of what Trump was doing made any sense. The looming Georgia runoff election was everything, and Trump's call for checks immediately put Senators Loeffler and Perdue, who had voted for the bill, on their back feet. Painted into a corner, they later endorsed Trump's call for larger checks.

Trump had stopped speaking to McConnell after the Senate leader acknowledged Joe Biden in mid-December as the winner of the November 3 election. Instead, McConnell and his advisers would speak to Trump through Mnuchin. They dispatched Perdue and Lindsey Graham to Mar-a-Lago to coax Trump into signing the bill. On Christmas Eve, McConnell's office had to find Senate clerks willing to work overtime to get the 5,000-page bill formally printed, signed by presiding officers, and physically shipped to Andrews Air Force Base before a 4 p.m. flight so that Trump could sign it. The president backed down and signed the package five days after his blustering video.

But the damage was done. The Georgia special elections closed with both Democratic challengers vowing $2,000 checks if Democrats won the Senate, using the issue as a cudgel to attempt unseating Loeffler and Perdue. Biden initially wavered before rallying around Trump's call for the larger payments.

White House officials believed the whole debacle had cost Republicans control of the Senate when the two Democrats won both Georgia seats in the January 5 vote.

The following day, January 6, 2021, will live in infamy. The violent insurrection at the Capitol, when a joint session convened to certify the Electoral College result, had been stoked and provoked by Trump's rhetoric, both in the days beforehand and at a rally that morning outside the White House. Several Cabinet officials resigned in protest, including Education Secretary Betsy DeVos, Transportation Secretary Elaine Chao, and Acting Secretary of Homeland Security Chad Wolf.

Mnuchin, who was on a trip through Israel and the Middle East at the time, briefly considered resigning, but refrained, according to people who spoke with him. (Mnuchin denied this. "Never in my four years did I consider resigning from the job," he said.)[6] "We were all pissed off," said one senior administration official. "We hated what happened on January 6, but we agreed that we needed to stick around. It was silly to resign to make some statement, and [Trump] needed some adult supervision. He had two weeks to go." (After leaving office, Mnuchin would launch a multibillion-dollar private equity fund, called Liberty Strategic Capital, focused on technology and financial services investments.)[7]

Biden and Yellen faced an increasingly grim economic and public-health situation as Trump's term came to this pitiful end. The Labor Department had reported on January 8 that the economy had lost jobs in December, driven by big declines in hospitality and education. Virus deaths were setting records, spurred by increased socializing over the holidays. Hospitalizations, which had never surpassed 60,000 during the prior peaks in April and July, jumped to *130,000* by early January.

Thousands of National Guard troops poured into Washington for Biden's swearing-in on January 20, the largest military presence in the city since the Civil War.[8] The National Mall, a two-mile expanse from the Lincoln Memorial to the US Capitol, was closed to the public for the socially distanced ceremony. Yellen sat under a blue blanket wearing a white disposable mask, and Powell accompanied his wife, both in cloth masks, to the inauguration behind fences ringed with razor wire on the West Front of the Capitol grounds. It was a stark visual symbol of both the pandemic and the riot. After taking the oath of office, the new president asked the country to join him in a silent prayer to remember those who died.

"We will press forward with speed and urgency," Biden promised, "for we have much to do in this winter of peril and possibility."

Date 2021	Covid-19 Cases	Covid-19 Deaths	Dow Jones Average	VIX Fear Index
Wednesday, January 20	24,251,909	396,387	31,188 (↑ 258)	21.58 (↓1.66)

Chapter Seventeen

THE INFLATION SURPRISE

In 2018, a few weeks after Powell succeeded Yellen as Fed chair, he had hosted a farewell dinner for her at his home. Now, in January 2021, he was handing a baton of sorts back to her. Little of what Powell had done to avoid a recession in 2019 or a depression in 2020 was going to matter if the recovery petered out.

Powell had already committed to not repeat the mistakes of the past decade. The Fed would wait longer to withdraw stimulus and would telegraph its moves carefully. Biden, Yellen, and Democratic leaders in Congress were about to make a similar pledge.

Lessons learned

Biden and his senior staff, many of them veterans of the Obama administration, had been scarred by how their $831 billion economic-stimulus package in 2009 did not yield its promised benefits of a faster recovery. The lessons were straightforward: *Spend aggressively and do it lastingly. The amount of water you need to refill the glass is probably more than you think.* There were important political lessons, too: *Make any economic help obvious. Make sure people know where that check in their mailbox came from. Targeting aid can be useful, but don't tie yourself in a pretzel trying to hit a bull's-eye. Complexity is the enemy of successful implementation.*

In 2009, a centerpiece of Obama's stimulus had included a payroll-tax cut that offered roughly $1,000 to individuals. But it showed up in tiny, $40 increments in biweekly paychecks. Voters could be forgiven for hardly noticing.

Democrats believed these initial errors had been compounded when, on the defensive over the Tea Party push for budget austerity, Democrats too readily agreed to curb federal spending in 2011 and 2012. Better to ask for more and let the political process slim it down, they concluded.

Republicans hadn't paid much worry to debt during the Trump years, and Democrats were in no mood to fret about red ink now. The publicly held debt had swelled by $7 trillion, to $21.7 trillion under Donald Trump — equal to the total output of the US economy for the first time since World War II. "Did you hear them complain when they passed close to a $2 trillion Trump tax cut?" Biden asked reporters at a March news conference.

Biden's answer to the lessons of the recent past was a massive $1.9 trillion spending package dubbed the American Rescue Plan, which he unveiled just weeks after Congress had approved the earlier $900 billion deal. Together this spending amounted to nearly 14 percent of gross domestic product — a staggering outlay. Biden's plan would provide another $300 per week in extra unemployment benefits through the first week of September 2021, $350 billion for state and local governments, plus more money for schools to reopen and to speed vaccinations and other virus-mitigation efforts. To cut child poverty, it also included a new child-care tax credit that would automatically deposit $300 every month into the bank accounts of many parents of a young child.

Ironically, the most talked-about provision was a direct result of Trump and his December tantrum calling for $2,000 checks. That forced Biden's team at the last second to add $1,400 checks — the difference between Trump's vaunted $2,000 and the $600 that had actually been included in the December deal — as a concession to political reality: Democrats had won the Senate races in Georgia partly on the promise of the larger checks. The upshot is that the Rescue Plan, which had started at $1.1 trillion, ended up providing *substantially* more stimulus than Yellen and the economic team had ever envisioned.

This spending push would relieve the burden from the Fed, which had been the only game in town after the turn to austerity in 2011. Although the recovery that followed the Great Recession would set records for its length, the Fed's bond-buying remained controversial; yes, it had strengthened the economy, employment, and wages, but the channel through which it worked — boosting the prices of stocks, bonds, and real estate — disproportionately benefited the holders of those assets, who tended to be wealthy. Biden's fiscal push didn't have that patrician side effect. "The Fed always sings with an upper-class accent," said Sherrod Brown, the Democratic Ohio senator who became chair of the Senate Banking Committee in January. "And so those of us that don't think Congress should sing with an upper-class accent as often as it does, we knew . . . we had to get Congress to focus on the right things."[1]

Most economists had frowned on such expansive borrowing in the past out of concern that the resulting debt would drive up interest rates, saddling taxpayers with ever more onerous interest payments. But in recent years economists had come to believe that the United States could in fact borrow far more than it had in the past. Yellen had cautiously added her voice to this new consensus. "Right now, with interest rates at historic lows, the smartest thing we can do is act big," she said, appearing at her January 19 confirmation hearing via video conference from the spare bedroom that served as her home office.[2]

Yellen's authority helped sell the bill, yet major components of it, such as the $1,400 checks, had resulted from negotiations among Nancy Pelosi, Chuck Schumer, and Biden, based on a number that Donald Trump had pulled out of thin air — as opposed to some finely tuned macroeconomic analysis.

The package was oriented toward seizing what many Democrats saw as a once-in-a-generation opportunity to address worsening inequality. The spending was skewed toward lower earners, who were more likely to spend than save any federal payments. Against that backdrop, Yellen, Jared Bernstein, and other White House economic authorities argued that overheating was a risk worth taking, particularly given inflation's weak response to sinking unemployment rates in recent years.

Message discipline

While Biden's team raced to enact its relief package, Powell focused on avoiding two perceived mistakes of the previous cycle — the "taper tantrum" in 2013 and the interest-rate increase years later based on a model that, in hindsight, underestimated the labor market's ability to accommodate more workers and, as a result, overestimated inflationary pressures. The new policy framework was built on an approach for delaying rate rises that Yellen, as vice chair of the board, had articulated in an important speech back in 2012 — but from which she had somewhat backed away when the Fed raised rates in 2015.

To avoid those errors, the Fed committed in September 2020 that it wouldn't raise rates until specific economic conditions were met. But reporters regularly pressed reserve-bank presidents to cite a timetable for when those outcomes might be reached. In early January 2021, just weeks after the Fed said it would continue to purchase $120 billion in bonds every month until making "further substantial progress" toward its goals, Dallas Fed President Robert Kaplan — who worried that the central bank's promises of seemingly endless easy money was fueling bubbles — said he hoped the Fed could "at least be having an earnest discussion about when it's appropriate" to reduce bond buying later in the year.[3] Atlanta Fed President Raphael Bostic told Reuters he was "hopeful that in fairly short order we can start to recalibrate" the purchases.[4]

All this stray talk grated on an annoyed Powell. He had pledged to give ample advance notice before reducing the purchases, or tapering, but now some of his colleagues were giving the impression they were ready to start, which risked the opposite effect in financial markets of the easy-money promises they had made. In his discussions with members of the Federal Open Market Committee before their January meeting and in a blast email, he asked for better message discipline. Talking about tapering *was* tapering, he said. At the meeting, Powell asked for greater deference: *We all agreed to this new, more patient policy stance, so do us all a favor and don't talk about tapering until we're much closer to having that debate.*

A few days after the meeting, Kaplan said the Fed was "not anywhere close" to a decision on when to taper its asset purchases.[5] And the next week, Bostic said he made a mistake with his loose talk; the Fed, he said, didn't want to give the impression it was eager to pull back. "We're not locked into anything," said Bostic. "Our new long-run framework explicitly says we're going to be willing to let the economy run hot."[6]

Powell spoke frequently over the next few weeks about demonstrating the commitment to the Fed's new framework by not overreacting to a mild rise in inflation. For years after the 2008 crisis, "Many of us, and that includes me, were [forecasting] a return to 2 percent inflation, and maybe a mild overshoot, year after year after year," Powell said during a talk at the Economic Club of New York on February 10. "And year after year after year, inflation fell short of that. So we have tied ourselves to realizing actual inflation." He downplayed worries about a 1970s-style scenario of runaway price increases; globalization and technology, said Powell, had weakened businesses' ability to raise prices and eroded workers' bargaining power. "It's just a different economy," he said.[7]

When asked during an April 2021 roundtable what kept him up at night, Powell returned to the subject of joblessness by pointing to an encampment of homeless people a few blocks from the Eccles Building. "We just need to keep reminding ourselves that even though some parts of the economy are just doing great here, there's a very large group of people who are not. I really want to finish the job."[8]

This stripe of retail politicking made Powell politically popular. "The Fed had forgotten about workers, and Janet Yellen was the first one to turn that around, and to his credit, Chair Powell followed that," said AFL-CIO president Richard Trumka. "[The Fed] is becoming far more responsive to Main Street and less knee-jerk towards Wall Street."[9]

A grand experiment

Congress approved the entire $1.9 trillion package with only a handful of modifications, and Biden signed it into law on March 11. The result was a grand economic experiment. The vaccination program was already unleashing pent-up demand for travel, vacations, concerts, and dining out. On top of this was fiscal stimulus unlike any since World War II, at a time when the Fed was running maximally accommodative monetary policy. Yellen predicted the package would return the economy to full employment by 2022.

In April, economists at the IMF projected the US would be the only large economy to surpass the level of GDP in 2022 that had been forecast before the pandemic hit. US allies breathed relief at the end of Trump's impulsive diplomacy. During a closed-door session at the G-7 meeting in London, Canadian Finance Minister Chrystia Freeland exclaimed, "Janet Yellen is making America great again."

As vaccination rates rose in the spring of 2021 and state and local governments began lifting restrictions, price surges and bottlenecks rippled through the economy. Semiconductor shortages curbed the production of new cars. Rental-car companies, which had liquidated their idle fleets to pay debts during the lockdowns, suddenly needed more vehicles, sending used-car prices skyrocketing. Cargo ships idled outside ports, with containers piling up on the docks or in warehouses. Lumber prices spiked. It was a sign of the global supply chain in disarray. These and other commodities caused measures of inflation to jump, generating rumblings of discontent against the Fed and the administration's stimulus policies.

Powell sought to preempt worries about higher inflation and described them as *transitory*. First, prices had plunged early in the pandemic, so as those declines dropped out of the twelve-month rates of change, the year-over-year comparisons would jump, exaggerating actual pressures. Second, the bottlenecks were not expected to last forever.

For any comparisons to the elevated inflation of the late 1960s be valid, several things needed to go wrong. First, higher prices would need to be more than temporary, altering the market's overall inflation expectations. Second, the Fed would need to sit on its hands while this cost increase unfolded. And third, politicians would need to stymie the Fed if officials wanted to raise rates. The lesson of the 1960s and 1970s was that inflation was not just some impersonal force. It had also been a choice: The Fed had screwed up, year after year — often with lawmakers or the White House urging it not to tighten the money supply. "At the Fed, we are well aware of the history and how it happened, and we're not going to allow it to happen again," Powell said.[10]

If the experiment went well, the economy might avoid the "jobless recoveries" of recent expansions. Perhaps it might generate the broad-based prosperity that had been taking hold before the pandemic and during the late 1990s. But the experiment might equally well lead to colossal mistakes and dangers for the Fed. Reopening the economy was difficult enough. Layering more spending on top of an economy already struggling to rebuild its capacity to deliver goods and services might further aggravate price pressures. Even if the Fed avoided a 1960s or 1970s scenario and raised interest rates to cool down the economy, record amounts of debt sloshing across the globe could make even a slight jump in interest rates a major hurdle for the economy.

The Fed's new framework, adopted in August 2020, also effectively committed officials to react too late. No one at the time had envisioned a supply or demand shock of the magnitude the economy now faced. The framework assumed inflation would eventually rise over a period of years because of escalating demand, not in a matter of months because of constricted supply. Powell had played up the clear benefits of the Fed's new framework — more employment, plus inflation meeting rather than falling short of its target. But Powell hadn't discussed what might happen if inflation accelerated quickly and forced the Fed to raise rates — perhaps by a lot.

During the past two economic expansions, the Fed had raised interest rates gradually, like a driver who takes their foot off the gas well in advance of gently tapping the brakes. But what if the Fed were forced to *stomp* on the brakes? Given record levels of corporate and government borrowing, sharply higher rates could wreak havoc on global financial markets. Emerging markets in particular might have to raise rates as well, though many lagged behind the US on vaccinations.

Of meme stocks and stimmies

Before the Georgia elections at the start of 2021, few economists inside or outside the Fed predicted that, by spring, the economy would be pulsating with $2.8 trillion in new spending. It made some at the Fed uneasy. "In some ways, you might say there's too much spending there, I think," said James Bullard, president of the St. Louis Fed.[11] Policymakers had committed not to make the same mistakes from the past. Were they about to make new ones?

One obvious source of concern was all the easy money sloshing around in markets. When Biden's stimulus was approved, the S&P 500 had risen about 75 percent from its pandemic low on March 23, 2020. The price of Bitcoin, the speculative cryptocurrency, was a staggering ten times higher than just a year earlier. Home prices were booming. Investors were pouring cash into newfangled investments, including something called special-purpose acquisition companies — essentially big pools of cash listed on an exchange, prowling for private companies to buy and take public. In March 2021, an artist sold a "non-fungible token" — a unique electronic file of digital art — for $69 million at Christie's.

That same month, hedge fund Archegos Capital Management ran into trouble. Archegos had made huge, concentrated bets in the stocks of individual companies, including media properties ViacomCBS Inc. and Discovery, using lots of money borrowed from Wall Street's biggest banks. When the stocks began to decline — for example, when Viacom-CBS found tepid demand for an offering of new shares — Archegos was forced to liquidate its holdings, triggering some of the biggest and most sudden trading losses in the history of Wall Street. Japanese investment bank Nomura took a hit of $2.85 billion, while Credit Suisse recorded a staggering $5.5 billion write-down.[12]

The debacle followed an earlier frenzy in a handful of "meme" stocks promoted on social-media platforms by retail investors. In the last week of January, the shares of GameStop soared 400 percent, while those of movie-theater chain AMC jumped 278 percent — moves that appeared completely divorced from the companies' less-than-stellar financial performance. Some investment advisers attributed the burst of trading to the "stimmies"—stimulus checks—newly filling traders' accounts. Deutsche Bank analysts estimated that as much as $170 billion from the last round of stimulus payments had flown into stock markets.[13]

Kaplan, the Dallas Fed president, thought his colleagues needed to show a little more concern about overdoing it. At the very minimum, he said, they should stop informally predicting that rates would not need to rise for another three years (as a majority of FOMC officials had done at their meeting on March 16 and 17). Kaplan worried that the Fed had been forced to intervene so aggressively in markets one year earlier partly because those markets had gotten carried away by the Fed's low-rate pledges. He also expressed alarm that they were so explicit to call inflation *transitory*. "We do have the tools to deal with high inflation—but if you use them late, you may" cause a recession.[14]

"Drunk people staggering around"

The loudest criticism of the Fed and Biden came, surprisingly, from someone who had until recently been on their side—and, in Biden's case, on his team: Larry Summers. Just a few years earlier, Summers had warned that the United States had become mired in a prolonged period of low growth, low inflation, and low interest rates that he called *secular stagnation*. The way out of it, he argued, was more fiscal expansion. Now, Summers was saying that the stimulus, on top of the Fed's policies, was too much, too fast. If he was right, inflation would now menace the economy not just for a year or slightly more, but potentially year after year until the Fed hit the monetary brakes.

Summers, with his characteristic smartest-guy-at-the-economics-seminar swagger, turned up the volume through the spring. He savaged White House and Fed policy as the "least responsible macroeconomic policy we've had in the last forty years" during a March 19, 2021, television interview.[15] Normally the Fed and the Treasury adjust economic policy to counteract destabilizing forces in the economy. But now, Summers warned, policymakers themselves were becoming the agents of that disequilibrium. He compared economic policy to the hospital that inadvertently sickens a patient with an infection while treating them for an unrelated illness.

During a webinar in April, Summers claimed that Powell intended to leave the interest-rate punch bowl out "until we see a bunch of drunk people staggering around." In case he wasn't clear, he heaped on further disparagement: "I hear echoes of the G. William Miller Fed and I hear echoes of the Carter administration economic team."[16]

Rising inflation posed significant political risks for Biden and the Fed, and some Republicans voiced alarm over Powell's new framework. "The very nature of insisting that a problem is transitory, you only know you're wrong after it hasn't gone away," said Patrick Toomey. "They've positioned themselves in such a way that if it is a problem, they're going to be slow to react to it."[17]

"A very unpleasant surprise"

Powell and Yellen had been looking for a string of breakout job reports from government statistical agencies. What they got instead was a string of sizzling monthly inflation reports. On May 12 the Labor Department reported that the consumer price index had posted a 4.2 percent year-over-year gain in April — its largest since 2008. The number was "a very unpleasant surprise," said Richard Clarida in an interview two weeks later.[18]

In May, inflation climbed to 5 percent. *Core inflation*, which strips out volatile food and energy items, was up 4.2 percent, the most since 1992. Both measures would run at those lofty levels through at least the rest of the year. The increases were concentrated in sectors disrupted by the pandemic, and thus presumed by the Fed and many forecasters to be transitory. But there were more and more of these one-off increases, and they were larger than anticipated. Used-vehicle prices rose 10 percent in April, another 7.3 percent in May, and yet another 10.5 percent in June. Car-rental prices soared 53 percent between February and June, prompting some desperate drivers to rent U-Haul trucks instead. Semiconductor-chip shortages were holding back new-car production, which had yet to catch up from the covid-induced factory shutdowns of 2020.

And inflation might gather speed where it had been muted. Rising rents and housing costs hadn't yet showed up in consumer price indexes. If they accelerated, inflation could prove slower to drop back to the Fed's target. Ample savings might lead consumer demand to exceed supply for longer. Suddenly, what had looked like a few months of higher inflation loomed as twelve months — or more. Market- and survey-based measures of inflation expectations began to creep higher, creating growing nervousness inside the Fed about what might happen if the trend continued. For fifteen years in a row, economists and market professionals had underestimated inflation, then overestimated both inflation and interest rates for the next twenty-five years after that. Had the pandemic created a new equilibrium prone to lowball miscalculations?

"We are seeing very substantial inflation," Warren Buffett told shareholders at Berkshire's annual meeting in May 2021, in remarks typical of business leaders throughout the country. "We are raising prices. People are raising prices to us, and it's being accepted."

The inflation numbers weren't the only economic surprise that spring. Job gains had been strong, but not as strong as economists had expected, leaving Yellen, Bernstein, and the Fed puzzled why workers weren't returning to jobs when openings were abundant: *Maybe more workers were staying home because they were still worried about the virus? Lacked childcare? Retired early?* The jobless rate fell steadily, to 4.6% in October, but the share of Americans between ages 25 and 54 who were working or seeking jobs was below levels seen in 2018 and 2019.

At a virtual conference hosted by the Atlanta Fed on May 18, Summers delivered a scorching critique, accusing the Fed of being overly "serene" about inflation and fostering a "dangerous complacency." Powell's new framework had been an appropriate response to secular stagnation, but Summers now believed it was no longer tenable for the Fed to focus on a shortfall of jobs. "Walk outside. Labor shortage is the pervasive phenomenon, and the failure to recognize that and begin an adjustment to that reality, [risks] the kinds of mistakes that we have not seen made in the United States for a long time," he said.

Yellen remained far less convinced. "I still think the medium- to long-run problem is inflation too low rather than inflation too high," she said in a June 2021 interview. "I don't believe secular stagnation is going away, and so most likely, we remain in a world of chronically low interest rates, and there will be more concern in the years ahead about inflation too low than too high. I know it's really easy to forget all of that when you've had such high monthly rates of inflation.... But we've never undergone a shock like this before, and we have to have some humility about how it's going to play out."[19]

For his part, Biden insisted that the shortages now preoccupying employers and the Fed were just what was needed. "When it comes to the economy we're building, rising wages aren't a bug; they're a feature," Biden said during a visit to Cuyahoga Community College on May 27.

Jean-Claude Powell?

When the Federal Open Market Committee met on June 15 and 16, its fourth meeting in Biden's term, it contemplated a far different picture of the economy than it had just six months earlier. Fiscal policy had revved up. So had inflation. Five days before the meeting, Powell got his first look at projections showing a majority of FOMC participants now expected that if the economy performed as they anticipated, they would raise rates at least twice in 2023, versus projections in March showing that most expected to hang tight. Those five days leading up to the meeting were stressful for Powell and Clarida. Even though the projections — arrayed in a matrix chart dubbed the *dot plot* that depicts the path each policy-maker individually expects for the federal funds rate over the next few years — aren't the product of any formal committee agreement, investors often treat them as such. Some reserve-bank presidents worried that such a hawkish messaging shift would turn Powell's post-meeting press conference into a reprise of the market rout unleashed after the Fed's rate increase in December 2018.

Afterward, the shift led one Goldman Sachs strategist to anoint the Fed chair "Jean-Claude Powell," a derisive reference to then–ECB President Jean-Claude Trichet, who had overreacted to inflation fears in 2008 and 2011, driven by high oil prices, with ill-timed rate increases. Powell strongly rejected the premise that the Fed was somehow abandoning its new framework — and its tolerance for higher inflation to secure lower unemployment. The Fed had promised not to raise rates if unemployment fell to low levels so long as inflation remained mild.

But it confronted a completely different scenario now. "We have many millions of people who are unemployed, and we have inflation running well above our target," Powell said. "It's a very difficult version of a standard central banking question."[20] Powell needed to navigate between two different policy errors: tightening too much into a supply shock that could cool the economy around the time that bottlenecks abated, as the Goldman strategist feared, or tightening too little into a demand shock that kicked off a more traditional inflationary cycle, the concern that preoccupied Summers. Indeed, Powell's legacy now rested on watching inflation subside of its own volition or having the Fed engineer the elusive *soft landing*, where the central bank raises interest rates without causing a recession.

If Powell's initial story was right, and inflation organically began to fall as bottlenecks loosened and more people began to look for jobs, maybe he could stick the landing. "I think this is the right thing to do, but even if it's wrong, this is the gamble worth taking, to avoid repeating the mistakes of the past and to get us out of secular stagnation," said Adam Posen, who had confronted a similar question about how to respond to a surge in inflation as a member of the Bank of England's policy committee from 2009 to 2012. Posen had argued against raising rates, correctly predicting the shock would be temporary. "But the Fed is taking more of a gamble now than we did then."[21]

By the fall, inflation pressures were broadening, weakening some conviction at the Fed about how soon prices might decelerate. In November, Powell led his colleagues to start shrinking their $120-billion-a-month bond purchase program so that the stimulus would phase out by early 2022, setting the table for possible rate increases.

Only in the coming years will we learn if the White House, Congress, and the Fed can correctly avoid the mistakes of the recent past, providing support that lifts those on Main Street, not just Wall Street. Or will those entities, abetted by a freak event that disrupted established patterns of global commerce, instead unleash an inflation-fueling money bomb just as vaccines propelled their own economic boom? The risks that the Fed and the White House were wrong about inflation — and that critics like Larry Summers might be right — loomed larger than had been the case in 2009 or 2011.

If inflation stays too high for too long (or if longer-term inflation *expectations* move up too much), the Fed may be forced to make a politically unsavory decision: raise rates, potentially in the absence of the broad job-market recovery Jay Powell laid out as the Fed's goal. The political hazards loom large in part because Powell placed such emphasis on promoting more inclusive growth. Going forward, the Fed may be exposed to critiques of racial insensitivity for raising rates.

Near the end of 2021, one worry was that officials had misjudged how demand, not just supply, was fueling higher prices. If that was the case, a traditional wage-price inflation cycle might accelerate, forcing the Fed to slam on the brakes. A related concern was that persistent supply disruptions — the pandemic had shifted spending towards goods and away from services — could lead to more enduring inflation, especially if the pandemic continued for longer and postponed an anticipated shift back to spending on services.

The particular tradeoffs and judgment calls facing Powell were as difficult as any the Fed's leaders had confronted in many years.

Epilogue

TRIAGE AND ITS AFTEREFFECTS

On November 4, 2021 — a sunny but chilly autumn afternoon — Powell arrived at the White House to meet with the president. Biden had to decide whether to nominate the Fed leader for another four-year term when Powell's first ended in February 2022 or whether to select someone else to lead the central bank.

As previous presidents — including Donald Trump — had discovered, it was one of the weightiest decisions of any administration. The decision had spawned a messy intraparty spat at a time when Biden was most focused on getting his signature domestic spending bills through narrow congressional majorities.

There were good reasons for Biden to reappoint, and Janet Yellen had privately made many of them. Powell had been the architect of a bold rethinking of monetary policy. Powell's unruffled response to Trump's rants and his sound leadership during the pandemic had earned him the trust of markets, lawmakers, and his colleagues on the Federal Open Market Committee. Reappointment would promote continuity, in the mold of Bill Clinton's reappointment of Alan Greenspan and Barack Obama's decision to renew Ben Bernanke's term. This was particularly true given the potential inflection point staring down the Fed as it wrestled with maintaining its inflation-fighting credibility and its fidelity to the new framework.

But sticking with Powell carried political risks for a president viewed warily by progressives in his own party. Some Democratic partisans saw reappointing a Republican white man as a missed opportunity for an administration that prized diversity; several women and minorities now had credentials at least as strong as those Powell had brought to the job four years earlier. And progressives wanted someone tougher on regulation and climate change. Senator Elizabeth Warren, at a September hearing, said she would vote against his potential reappointment before Biden had made his decision. Powell's record to loosen financial regulations imposed after the 2008 crisis "makes you a dangerous man to head up the Fed," she told him.

Biden interviewed one other candidate, Lael Brainard, before choosing to reappoint Powell. The president asked Brainard to serve as vice chair once Richard Clarida's term expired in 2022. At a White House ceremony on November 22, Biden extolled Powell's leadership under fire and his bipartisan support: "At this moment...of enormous uncertainty for our economy, we need stability and independence at the Federal Reserve."

In September 2021, with Biden's decision still months away, the Fed faced a severe reputational crisis after *The Wall Street Journal* reported that Dallas Fed President Robert Kaplan had traded throughout 2020 more than two dozen individual stocks, funds, or alternative asset holdings, with most of those transactions valued at over $1 million, according to financial disclosures released by the bank.[1] Chevron, Delta Airlines, Marathon Petroleum, and Johnson & Johnson were among those stocks Kaplan was trading during a year in which the Fed took extraordinary actions to backstop markets. It reflected colossally poor judgment, even though the bank said the trades somehow satisfied their own rules. Separate disclosures by Boston Fed President Eric Rosengren showed he had made more than three dozen trades, albeit in much smaller sums than Kaplan, in stocks of four mortgage REITs, whose values can be heavily influenced by the Fed's purchases of mortgage bonds.

Even in the most generous interpretation, both instances revealed a naïve blind spot in the Fed's own guidelines, because they fueled the appearance of conflicts of interest.

On September 27, Rosengren announced he had qualified for a kidney transplant in June 2020 and said he would resign from the bank at the end of September, moving forward his planned retirement by nine months. Later that day, Kaplan said he, too, would walk the plank, offering his resignation in a bid to quiet the furor over the investment controversy. Powell quickly promised to modify the Fed's code of conduct and acknowledged that whatever rules had been in place hadn't been sufficient.

The trading revelations complicated Biden's Fed chair decision and tarnished the Fed's aggressive response in 2020. In October, Warren asked the Securities and Exchange Commission to investigate this trading conduct, including investments by Clarida, who had moved between $1 million and $5 million out of one bond mutual fund and into two other stock funds on February 27, 2020, the day before Powell's statement signaling a potential rate cut to quell worries over the oncoming pandemic. Clarida said those trades had been part of a previously arranged rebalancing of his portfolios and denied any wrongdoing. But the timing nonetheless looked *terrible*.

The pandemic struck the most severe blow to the US economy since the Great Depression. Economists, financial-market professionals, and historians are only beginning to wrestle with the implications of the aggressive response by fiscal and monetary policymakers. Altogether, Congress approved nearly $5.9 trillion in spending in 2020 and 2021. Adjusted for inflation, that compares with approximately $1.8 trillion in 2008 and 2009, and around $788 billion during the New Deal. "Fiscal policy came in and made the difference in this cycle," said Powell. "This was a situation where thirty million households are suddenly without an income, and Congress had to replace that. That isn't a matter for monetary policy."[2]

Nonetheless, the Fed's monetary response — its unprecedented emergency-lending programs and massive purchases of government debt — went beyond anything that institution had ever pursued. By November 2021, the Fed's asset holdings had nearly doubled from their prepandemic level to $8.6 trillion.

So what did Powell and his colleagues get right? And what did they get wrong?

Any analysis has to account for another unique factor that clearly hobbled the Fed's economic response: public-health authorities' missteps dealing with the fog of the virus. Testing delays handcuffed the economic reopening, as did Trump's decision to politicize mask wearing. Only the rapid development, distribution, and take-up of effective vaccines could put the pandemic in retreat, promising a swifter return to normal life.

Many private-sector forecasters and economists at the Fed misjudged both the speed of the recovery and the willingness of American society to tolerate much more severe health outcomes. During an interview with *60 Minutes* in April 2021, Powell conceded that the economy had performed substantially better than he had expected: "The other side of that, though, is if you told me at this time last year that 550,000 plus people and counting would die of Covid-19, I would have been shocked."[3]

As the country emerged from the pandemic, critics worried that policymakers were failing to recognize that even though the 2020 shock had been severe, the recovery was likely to unfold far differently from 2008. In avoiding a repeat of the mistakes made back then, policymakers might stumble into making new ones that could prove equally costly. The cure for the economy — the trillions of dollars of triage — carried potentially harmful side effects that may not be clear for months or years. The use of rock-bottom rates had encouraged both the federal government and corporations to take on unprecedented levels of debt. Corporate debt, high before the pandemic, was even higher by the end of 2021. The federal debt rose by $5 trillion between February 2020 and June 2021, to $22.2 trillion, and the Fed's holdings of that public debt rose by more than $2.5 trillion. The Congressional Budget Office forecasted in December 2020 that if rates rose by just 0.1 percentage point more than projected in each year of the decade, debt-service costs in 2030 would rise by $235 billion — more than the Pentagon had requested to spend in 2022 on the Navy.[4]

With so much debt sloshing around the globe, any unexpected monetary tightening risks far greater damage than in the past, both to markets and to the nation's fiscal health. This is one reason why the stakes were so high, at the end of 2021, over how the Fed judged the nature of the inflation surge.

Markets are as focused as ever on the utterances of the Fed chair, which can matter as much as economic data points or corporate earnings. A whole generation of traders has been trained to be "Fed put" traders, operating from the widespread belief that the central bank will always step in to rescue the economy and financial markets. When Powell went to Princeton, most Americans didn't spend time thinking about the Fed. Today, cabdrivers and barbers have a point of view about what the Fed chair is doing. As someone who is often introduced as *The Wall Street Journal's* chief economics correspondent, I can vouch for this personally.

The Fed's low-rate policies have coincided with — and contributed to — a longer-running widening of wealth inequality. Trillions of dollars in triage can save the financial system, but the Fed's economic-stabilization tools are blunt. In 2008, household wealth fell by $8 trillion. It *rose* by $13.5 trillion in 2020, spotlighting the unequal distribution of wealth-building assets such as houses and stocks.[5] The wealthiest 1 percent of US households were $5 trillion richer at the end of 2020 — a nearly 15 percent gain in their net worth. The bottom 50 percent, by contrast, saw their net worth rise just $367 billion — a better percentage gain (18 percent) but still a scandalous wealth disparity.

In many areas the government's response fell short, highlighting glaring weaknesses in the delivery mechanism for household and business relief. Too many workers slipped through the cracks of a creaky unemployment-insurance safety net. Businesses with strong banking relationships were able to get all the aid they needed (and possibly more that they didn't), yet many others missed out entirely. Reports of fraud are likely to increase in the coming months and years.

Jay Powell was able to extricate the Fed from its most controversial lending programs relatively quickly, uncrossing the proverbial red lines. But the uproar over the Fed's loans to small businesses versus big businesses, lawmakers' desire to micromanage emergency lending, and political sniping over MTA or oil-and-gas "bailouts" all highlight the main danger of such extraordinary intervention: that lending will be politi-cized. The risk for the Fed is that its success at shuttering these programs in 2020 provides little guarantee that politicians in future crises won't demand bolder policy actions to advance narrow political priorities.

The imbroglio over Fed officials' trading conduct was especially trou-bling because, if left unaddressed, such stains on the central bank's integ-rity undercut its credibility in markets and with the public. Congress has extended enormous power to the Fed, and to effectively do its job, the Fed needs all the political support it can get. The controversy also breathed new life into suspicions that the Fed is too close to Wall Street. Warren, seeking to deny Powell a second term at the Fed, cited it as evidence of a "culture of corruption."

Trump posed a particular type of political threat to the Fed. Yet other, less-obvious hazards lurk. What happens to the Fed's autonomy if Congress realizes that it can remake the central bank into a government lender? The stimulus payments during the 2020 crisis could be ground-breaking. The advent of digital currencies could make it harder for the Fed to explain why its policies put trillions of dollars to work on Wall Street when millions of Americans are losing their jobs — and why it can't do the same for households.

The justification for Fed independence rests on a simple consensus: the White House and Congress won't interfere with how the Fed chooses to control inflation, and in return the Fed does precisely that. But if the Fed's job expands to include financial stability, climate change, income inequality, and any other number of well-intentioned policy imperatives, it's very difficult to say that democratically elected leaders should have no say in how those policies are carried out. The case for Fed independence quickly disappears as these mandates grow.

The danger for the Fed of being seen as an economic oracle or market magician is that the public demands unelected technocrats solve prob-lems their tools can't readily address. If central banks are given more responsibilities, they will fall short of them more often. Alan Greenspan cultivated an aura of omniscience around the Fed that kept politicians away during good times. But the Fed will in fact be better off if the public recognizes that its leaders are regular people who will err — and that society cannot count on them to correct politicians' mistakes or broader social ills.[6]

The Fed's actions almost certainly exacerbated a moral hazard that could lead investors to take more risks in the future, particularly if glaring fragilities in financial markets are not addressed. If moral hazard does indeed inculcate riskier behavior, it may not be evident for a long time.

The 2020 panic exposed semi-predictable deficiencies in the *shadow banking system* — a catchall term that describes asset managers, hedge funds, and other institutions that provide bank-like services. Money-market mutual funds required their second bailout in twelve years. Corporate-bond funds fared poorly under stress. And the US government's reliance on hedge funds and others to finance rising budget deficits revealed vulnerabilities in the Treasury market.

To smother an incipient financial crisis, the Fed had to quickly purchase $2 trillion of Treasury debt in a matter of weeks. Depending on a few people at the Fed to intervene like this every time there's a shock to the system is a recipe for eventual disaster. After the 2008 crisis, Congress had charged a new entity — the Financial Stability Oversight Council, chaired by the Treasury secretary — with addressing these kinds of weaknesses. But those authorities had hardly been used through 2020, and it remained an open question how far any Treasury secretary could force independent regulators to put the broader system on a stronger footing.

The financial system that the Fed had been created to regulate — one dominated by banks — has migrated outside the banking system. With more capital formation in private credit and equity markets, it was perhaps inevitable that the 2020 panic would require Powell's market-rescuing aerobics. Going forward, regulators will have to examine how to restructure their tools for the financial system of the 21st century, which is far different from the one for which the Fed was designed to be the reserve lender.

Based upon the 2020 experience, it would be hard to declare the much stronger bank-regulatory regime that followed the 2008 crisis an unqualified success. In the latter calamity, Congress and the Fed showered money on the economy — mortgage forbearance, unemployment relief, small-business grants, Fed backstops. Those huge sums crushed the panic before its heat reached the banking sector.

If elevated inflation pressures persist through 2022 and beyond, and the Fed turns out to have misdiagnosed how the economy had shifted, officials could face a painful series of tradeoffs. And even if inflation eventually returns to lower levels, financial-stability worries may keep complicating rate-setting deliberations. Back when recessions occurred because an overheating economy led to higher inflation, the proper level of interest rates could satisfy the Fed's dual mandate of low, stable inflation and sustainably low unemployment, which economists dubbed the "divine coincidence." But as Powell was fond of reminding listeners, the divine coincidence doesn't say that the same interest rate will achieve all this *plus* a third goal: a stable financial system.

Moreover, if policymakers don't want to use interest-rate policy to tamp down financial excesses, they'll need to craft new tools. The US lacks any authority whose main job is to look out for the safety of the financial system as a whole; instead it relies on a fragmented and overlapping structure of financial regulators.

Of course, there was no risk-free option for policymakers in 2020, and the right questions must consider whether the risks that Powell and his colleagues took were sensible given the most likely alternatives. Many of the risks were almost certainly worth taking. *Do less because otherwise the market will expect you to do more next time* was how the Fed thought in 1929. In March 2020, few realized the pandemic would imperil commerce for longer than twelve weeks, let alone twelve months. The ability of large companies outside the Fed's safety net — like Carnival Cruise Lines — to load up on debt and buy time (even as Carnival's fleet sat empty) was a big reason the economy succeeded in recovering as quickly as it did. The supply-chain bottlenecks of 2021 almost certainly would have been worse if businesses had been starved of such lifelines.

Panics are the wrong time to withhold support to prevent a few bad actors from allowing dysfunctional markets to wreck innocent bystanders. But failing to address the shortcomings that forced a more intrusive Fed response would be just as negligent. It's unreasonable to be mad at the fire department for getting the furniture wet when they saved your house from burning down, but it's perfectly justified to blame authorities for failing to work on fire prevention during good times.

Without the experience of the 2008 financial crisis, the Fed might have floundered initially just like the nation's public-health agencies. But it didn't. Quick action stopped a financial panic and averted a potential depression in March 2020. The tense, exhausting days of March, when momentous decisions happened daily, have little precedent in American history. The speed of the Fed's response was shocking — and essential. "It takes more time usually," said former New York Fed President William Dudley. "[The Federal Reserve is] a deliberative body. And I give Jay Powell the credit for that, because moving very, very quickly like that doesn't happen unless the chair wants it to happen."[7]

Powell later confessed that during the darkest weeks of the crisis, the Fed had discussed a "mini-depression scenario" — one in which the virus kept society closed indefinitely. "We didn't know there was a vaccine coming. The pandemic is just raging, and we don't have a plan, nobody in the world has a plan, and in hindsight the worry was *What if we can't really fully open the economy for a long time because the pandemic is just out there killing people?*" Even if that wasn't the most likely outcome, Powell said after the flames subsided, "it was around the edges of the conversation, and we were very eager to do everything we could do to avoid that outcome."[8]

No matter how history judges the spending bills passed by Congress, the Fed's actions in March 2020 were decisive — and, in the judgment of many, courageous. Republican Congressman Patrick McHenry, for one, gave Powell an "A-plus for 2020. On a 1-to-10 scale? It was an 11. He gets the highest, highest marks, and deserves them. The Fed as an institution deserves them."[9] Powell displayed speed and decisiveness at a time when much of the country was struggling with a bottomless pandemic and a president who refused to acknowledge reality.

There are many reasons to be concerned about policies that operate by encouraging people to borrow to boost asset prices. It's a terrible look for a country to seemingly mint billionaires every time a recession hits, and it poses a hell of a dilemma for the Fed. Relying on lower interest rates to spur the economy fuels predictable but sometimes misdirected anger at the Fed. In an era of lower interest rates across the globe, blaming the central bank primarily or exclusively for the widening gap between rich and poor gives a pass to every other actor in economic policy — excusing important but difficult decisions of taxation, regulation, and federal spending that aren't handled by a small group of cloistered technocrats. And whereas growing *wealth* inequality can corrode politics, so too can high joblessness and *income* inequality.

Critics who lay the blame for rising inequality solely at the feet of the central bank must confront the counterfactual scenario in which the Fed *raises* rates to prevent inequality, at the expense of growth and hiring. Would the economy be better off if the Fed resisted using its tools to spur a faster recovery? Would that leave workers, particularly those at the bottom of the wage spectrum, better off? Or would it simply raise the risks of more extreme measures being introduced later? Consider how central banks in Europe and Japan have been forced into ever-more accommodative monetary policy as a result of too-little, too-late blunders. The real problem is that the Fed lacks the tools to deal simultaneously with unemployment *and* inequality.

The fiscal innovations undertaken, often with Powell's support, could reverse the historic pattern in which the poorest and most vulnerable suffer the most in a recession. Could a high-pressure economy force companies to compete for workers, reversing the recent four-decade decline in the share of income that goes to employees? Decisions by Congress to provide more generous income-replacement schemes, coupled with mortgage forbearance and rental-eviction moratoria, may have helped poorer households stave off financial disasters. By October 2020, for example, household checking-account balances for the bottom quartile of income earners were nearly 50 percent higher than the year before, according to the JPMorgan Chase Institute.[10]

Tina Beattie, who with her husband had closed two of their thirty-six Denny's locations, would need the summer season to bring in hefty sales in order to recoup a fraction of the $20 million to $30 million in sales lost during the pandemic. Though Beattie had raised entry-level wages and was offering retention bonuses for servers and busboys, she was finding it harder than she'd expected to compete for workers: some of them could make more in unemployment benefits, while others resisted returning to the workplace because of lingering virus fears.

Tina believes her business wouldn't have survived the pandemic without the PPP and other federal-government efforts to funnel cash to businesses and displaced workers. "Our vendors, they have employees too, and landlords have bills to pay," she said. "To keep the whole ecosystem current not only kept us in business, but it preserved our relationships."

Marc Epstein's Milk Street Café in downtown Boston likewise illustrated the promise — and peril — of the one-two punch from the Fed and the Biden administration. More than anything, his business needed a widespread and successful vaccination effort to bring neighboring office workers back.

By June, Epstein felt optimistic that New England's recent high vaccination rate, combined with school reopenings in the fall, would lead workers to resume their pre-pandemic daily routines. But uncertainty prevailed about whether people would be willing to have catered holiday parties and conference meals — the very activities that drove his sales. That was especially true as the more contagious Delta variant sent cases rising through the late summer. Epstein needed business workers not only to return to their cubicles but to feel comfortable enough to get on planes, travel to meetings, and eat and drink together. The company also faced new hiring challenges. Unable to pay its workers except for the few months during which it used up its PPP money, the café had lost several top staff, including its director of human resources and its executive chef.

Food prices had surged. The restaurant was discussing not printing its menu so it could have more flexibility to raise prices or kill menu items once it reopened in August. "These kinds of inflationary challenges are going to be a big, big challenge," said Epstein. "It is going to be a much lower level of sales with much higher cost."

Despite the logistical nightmares and the potential for higher prices, Epstein praised the Fed's response and Jay Powell's leadership: "I feel it now, more than ever, that Jerome Powell is the single greatest patriot," he said in June 2021.

At a central banking forum in September 2021, someone posed a simple question to Powell: Was the Fed "overdoing it" with its stimulus policies? "The historical record is thick with examples of underdoing it," Powell volunteered. "And pretty much in every cycle, we just tend to underestimate the damage and underestimate the need for a response. I think we've avoided that this time."

The truth is that we may not know for years whether the Fed overdid it. Powell's legacy will ultimately rest on what happens to inflation and employment not in 2021, but in the years to come.

Regardless of what happens from late 2021 onward, what Powell did in 2020 — directly and through his advocacy to Congress — prevented a financial disaster from making a medical and economic disaster magnitudes worse.

The Fed had been lucky during the 2008 financial crisis to have Ben Bernanke, a student of the Great Depression, in charge to avoid the mistakes the central bank had made in the 1930s. The Fed was fortunate again in 2020 to have a serious corporate-finance professional at the helm who had been around Washington long enough to understand what Bernanke and his colleagues had done in 2008.

Jay Powell redefined the Fed. He did this in big ways — deploying the Fed's balance sheet to do things it hadn't ever done, and adapting its framework for a world in which inflation had been inching lower and lower. He did this in small ways, too — speaking like a small-*p* politician rather than in the deliberately obtuse language of Greenspan or the academic lexicon of Bernanke and Yellen. The position still demands the intellectual acuity that his predecessors had brought to the job, and it clearly benefited from the political glad-handing at which Greenspan and Powell excelled.

No central bank is above politics. A central bank is the creation of a political system, and political limits do circumscribe its freedom to operate. Powell recognized this, as well as his own strength as a listener in a town where most get ahead by talking.

For the Fed, getting the policy right isn't worth much if the public and its elected representatives don't understand what the Fed is doing or why. Powell's regular consultations with lawmakers weren't just about protecting his flank when a president threatened to shatter the institution. They were about making sure he knew where lawmakers stood so he could manage the institution's political risk.

"A lot of what explains Jay is this deeply rooted self-confidence," said Marsh Marshall, who has been friends with Powell since the seventh grade at Georgetown Prep in 1965. "There is no insecurity with this guy." When Trump attacked, "He suffered in silence. Jay was convinced he was doing the right thing."[11]

Powell summoned the same inner certainty during the depths of the crisis. In May 2020, just two months after some of the darkest weeks in the country's history, Powell sounded more like a therapist than a lawyer-turned-banker: "We've got to help each other through this. And that's what we're going to do."[12]

Pressed in March 2021 to name the lessons of the crisis, Jay Powell returned to this all-for-one theme. Going big and going fast was important. But so was never losing faith. "Even in terrible times, try to take counsel from your hopes as well as your fears," Powell offered. "We should never sell ourselves short."[13]

ACKNOWLEDGMENTS

This book would not have been possible without the time spent by many sources who helped me better understand the events and decisions that animated the economic-policy response to the pandemic crisis. Because many of them would not be well served professionally by being publicly acknowledged, I will not thank them by name. I am appreciative of their patience and whatever trust they placed in me to tell this story as honestly and accurately as possible.

My agent, Raphael Sagalyn, offered wise counsel, constructive enthusiasm, and no small degree of hand-holding from inception to completion. This book found a champion in Bruce Nichols, and I am thankful for his insights and perseverance in schlepping through rough drafts as this manuscript took shape, as well as the entire team at Little, Brown in bringing forth these pages. Nathan Means delivered an expert's hand in reworking and sharpening the narrative. Allan Fallow provided meticulous copyediting. Carolyn Levin dispensed helpful counsel. I am enormously indebted to Greg Ip, Josh Zumbrun, and David Wessel for reading early drafts and providing valuable suggestions.

This work has only been possible because of the exceptional support provided by the newsroom of *The Wall Street Journal*, which has provided an unrivaled professional home for these last fifteen years and counting. I am particularly grateful to Matt Murray and Paul Beckett for their backing of this project. I would be fortunate to have any one of Nell Henderson, Jon Hilsenrath, Greg Ip, and David Wessel as sources to turn to for insight or advice; it has been an embarrassment of riches to be able to rely at various times on them all.

The foundation of this book came from my reporting on the Federal Reserve and the US economy for the *Journal*. I am indebted to many colleagues who have been terrific teammates. While there are too many to list for any proper accounting, I would especially like to thank the economics team, including Paul Kiernan, Michael Derby, Kate Davidson, Andrew Ackerman, Richard Rubin, David Harrison, Harriet Torry, Amara Omeokwe, Eric Morath, Sarah Chaney Cambon, Gwynn Guilford, Mark Anderson, Josh Mitchell, and Jeffrey Sparshott. I would also like to thank colleagues in New York and Washington, including Jeanne Cummings, Jay Sapsford, Jude Marfil, Bob Davis, Kristina Peterson, Michael Bender, Alex Leary, Ken Thomas, Andrew Restuccia, Peter Nicholas, Vivian Salama, Julia Verlaine, Matt Wirz, Colin Barr, Phil Izzo, Jennifer Forsyth, Neil King, and Jerry Seib. It has been a special reward to spend the last eight years in the newsroom with Josh Zumbrun, who helped me discover my initial zeal for the news through many sleepless nights in the newsroom of *The Hoya*.

Above all, I would like to thank my family: my parents, Carol and Vicente, and brother, Alex, for their unflinching encouragement, love, and support; and for my equally nurturing in-laws, Rosalyn and Tony Smith, and my brother-in-law, Elliott Smith. Book-writing is a taxing enterprise, especially while raising young children during a pandemic. My wife, Mallie, the love of my life, has been as supportive as always, with generous reservoirs of patience for many evenings where I might have been unnecessarily preoccupied with tedious details or omnipresent deadlines. I am endlessly grateful. To Cora and Eliza, you made life during quasi-lockdown ceaselessly entertaining — the best possible recentering during the chaos of these past two years.

NOTE ON SOURCES

This portrait draws on more than one hundred interviews conducted in late 2020 and the first half of 2021 from individuals who shared their time, experiences, materials, and knowledge of the relevant events. In order to secure the most candid accounts from sources whose professional standing could be jeopardized by cooperating for this book, the vast majority were interviewed on the journalistic condition of "deep background." This means that the information was fair game to be included in these pages on the condition that I would not identify the source. Material in this book that appears without attribution in the source notes that follow is largely based on those interviews. The reporting in these pages also builds upon hundreds of interviews conducted over the prior three years with current and former Fed officials, government officials, and those in the private sector or academia who follow their work closely. The book is additionally drawn from hours of congressional testimony, public interviews, and oral histories, as well as email correspondence. I also relied on the public calendars of Jay Powell, Steven Mnuchin, Richard Clarida, Randal Quarles, Lael Brainard, and John Williams.

Throughout the narrative, I have taken care to reconstruct certain scenes and dialogue. Specific conversations or thoughts attributed to individuals in this book were shared by people with firsthand knowledge. The reader should not assume that the information in any particular scene was necessarily provided by one of the participants, as these reconstructions may have come from a colleague with direct knowledge or others who participated in a conference call or Zoom call. The book's endnotes detail some information drawn from portions of interviews with policymakers that were conducted on the record.

I have striven to follow the *no surprises* brand of journalism that is practiced daily by *Wall Street Journal* reporters, which means that key individuals in the book have been made aware of the revelations shared here and have had opportunities to provide their own response. I have done my best to reconcile conflicting accounts and differing recollections or vantage points for these events to present the most honest accounting available.

US economic data in this book is largely drawn from the database of statistics maintained by the Federal Reserve Bank of St. Louis known as FRED. Financial market data in the daily dashboards was sourced from Dow Jones, and the public-health figures are from The Covid Tracking Project (https://covidtracking.com/data/national/). Because Donald Trump's Twitter account was suspended, I have not included links to his tweets in the endnotes. All of his tweets included in this book are publicly available and searchable at thetrumparchive.com.

I have relied on the outstanding work of many of my journalistic peers, including from the Associated Press, Axios, Bloomberg, CBS's *60 Minutes*, CNBC, CNN Business, the *Financial Times*, Fox Business, *MarketWatch*, the *New York Times*, Reuters, the *Washington Post*, and Yahoo! Finance. I have tried where possible to credit these sources, though it is likely I have unintentionally overlooked some news stories that broke important story fragments or details.

SELECTED BIBLIOGRAPHY

The following books provided useful information, in addition to contemporaneous accounts in newspapers, news wire services, magazines, academic papers, and oral histories.

Ahamed, Liaquat. *Lords of Finance: The Bankers Who Broke the World*, New York: Penguin Press, 2009.

Bagehot, Walter. *Lombard Street: A Description of the Money Market*, New York: Armstrong & Co., 1873.

Bernanke, Ben S. *The Courage to Act: A Memoir of a Crisis and Its Aftermath*, New York: W.W. Norton & Co., 2015.

Bremner, Robert P. *Chairman of the Fed: William McChesney Martin, Jr., and the Creation of the Modern Federal Reserve System*, New Haven, Conn.: Yale University Press, 2004.

Binder, Sarah, and Mark Spindel. *The Myth of Independence: How Congress Governs the Federal Reserve*, Princeton, N.J.: Princeton University Press, 2017.

Blinder, Alan S. *Central Banking in Theory and Practice*, Cambridge, Mass.: MIT Press, 1998.

Califano, Joseph. *The Triumph and Tragedy of Lyndon Johnson: The White House Years*, New York: Simon & Schuster, 1991.

Davis, Bob, and Lingling Wei. *Superpower Showdown*, New York: HarperCollins, 2020.

Donovan, Robert J. *Tumultuous Years: The Presidency of Harry S Truman, 1949–1953*, New York: W.W. Norton & Co., 1982.

Eccles, Marriner S. *Beckoning Frontiers, Public and Personal Recollections*, New York: Alfred A. Knopf, 1951.

Ehrlichman, John. *Witness to Power: The Nixon Years*, New York: Simon and Schuster, 1982.

Ferrell, Robert H., editor. *Inside the Nixon Administration: The Secret Diary of Arthur Burns, 1969–1974*, Lawrence, Kan.: University Press of Kansas, 2010.

Friedman, Milton, and Anna Jacobson Schwartz. *A Monetary History of the United States, 1867–1960*, Princeton, N.J.: Princeton University Press, 1963.

Geithner, Timothy F. *Stress Test: Reflections on Financial Crises*, New York: Broadway Books, 2014.

Greenspan, Alan. *The Age of Turbulence: Adventure in a New World*, New York: Penguin Press, 2007.

Greider, William. *Secrets of the Temple*, New York: Simon & Schuster, 1987.

Hackley, Howard H. *Lending Functions of the Federal Reserve Banks: A History*, Washington, DC: Federal Reserve Board of Governors, 1973.

Irwin, Neil. *The Alchemists: Three Central Bankers and a World on Fire*, New York: Penguin Press, 2013.

Lowenstein, Roger. *The End of Wall Street*, New York: Penguin Press, 2010.

Mallaby, Sebastian. *The Man Who Knew: The Life and Times of Alan Greenspan*, New York: Penguin Press, 2016.

Meltzer, Allan H. *A History of the Federal Reserve, Volume 1: 1913–1951*, Chicago: University of Chicago Press, 2003.

Meltzer, Allan H. *A History of the Federal Reserve, Volume 2, Book 1, 1951–1969*, Chicago: University of Chicago Press, 2009.

Meyer, Laurence H. *A Term at the Fed: An Insider's View*, New York: HarperCollins Publishers, 2004.

Nixon, Richard. *Six Crises*, New York: Doubleday, 1962.

Safire, William. *Before the Fall: An Inside View of the Pre-Watergate White House*, New York: Doubleday, 1975.

Schroeder, Alice. *The Snowball: Warren Buffett and the Business of Life*, New York: Bantam Books, 2008.

Taylor, John B. *Getting Off Track*, Stanford, Calif.: Hoover Institution Press, 2009.

Treaster, Joseph B. *Paul Volcker: The Making of a Financial Legend*, Hoboken, N.J.: Wiley, 2004.

Volcker, Paul A. *Keeping at It: The Quest for Sound Money and Good Government*, New York: PublicAffairs, 2018.

Wessel, David. *In Fed We Trust: Ben Bernanke's War on the Great Panic*, New York: Crown Business, 2009.

Woodward, Bob. *Fear: Trump in the White House*, New York: Simon & Schuster, 2018.

Woodward, Bob. *Maestro: Greenspan's Fed and the American Boom*, New York: Simon & Schuster, 2000.

NOTES

Introduction

1. Chloe Taylor, "Economic impact of coronavirus will be clearer in 'three or four weeks,' Mnuchin says," CNBC, February 23, 2020. https://www.cnbc.com/2020/02/23/coronavirus-mnuchin-says-economic-impact-will-be-clearer-within-weeks.html

2. Rob Stein, Laurel Wamsley, "Health Officials Warn Americans to Plan for the Spread of Coronavirus in US," NPR, February 25, 2020 https://www.npr.org/sections/health-shots/2020/02/25/809318447/health-officials-warn-americans-to-start-planning-for-spread-of-coronavirus-in-us

3. Fred Imbert, "Larry Kudlow says US has contained the coronavirus and the economy is holding up nicely," CNBC, February 25, 2020. https://www.cnbc.com/2020/02/25/larry-kudlow-says-us-has-contained-the-coronavirus-and-the-economy-is-holding-up-nicely.html

Chapter 1

1. Jerome H. Powell, "Ending 'Too Big to Fail,'" speech at the Institute of International Bankers 2013 Washington Conference, Washington, DC, March 4, 2013. https://www.federalreserve.gov/newsevents/speech/powell20130304a.htm

2. Gutfreund later settled civil charges that he failed to supervise the firm's top government-bond trader and paid a $100,000 fine. He agreed not to head a securities firm again without prior approval from the Securities and Exchange Commission.

3. Alice Schroeder, *The Snowball: Warren Buffett and the Business of Life* (New York: Bantam Books, 2008), 499.

4. Ibid., 497.

5. Written correspondence to the author from Buffett, May 13, 2021.

6. Ibid., 500.

7. Powell, March 4, 2013 speech.

8. The entire exchange is viewable via C-SPAN: https://www.c-span.org/video/?c4952813/user-clip-salomon-hearing

9. Author's interview.

10. Nick Timiraos and David Harrison, "Mr. Ordinary: Who Is Jerome Powell, Trump's Federal Reserve Pick?" *The Wall Street Journal*, November 2, 2017. https://www.wsj.com/articles/mr-under-the-radar-jerome-powell-trumps-federal -reserve-pick-signals-continuity-1509643306
11. James Freeman, "What If the U.S. Treasury Defaults?", *The Wall Street Journal*, May 14, 2011. https://www.wsj.com/articles/SB10001424052748703864204576 317612323790964
12. Jerome H. Powell, "More on Stanley Druckenmiller and the Risk of Default," *The Wall Street Journal*, May 25, 2011. https://www.wsj.com/articles/SB10001424052 7487048166045763333772282586068

Chapter 2

1. Michael C. Jensen, "Marriner S. Eccles Is Dead at 87; Headed Reserve Board 12 Years," *The New York Times*, December 20, 1977. https://www.nytimes.com/1977 /12/20/archives/marriner-seccles-is-dead-at-87-headed-reserve-board-12-years .html
2. Allan Meltzer, *A History of the Federal Reserve*, Volume 1: 1913 -1951 (Chicago: University of Chicago Press, 2004)., 468.
3. Ibid., 478.
4. Ibid., 574.
5. Radha Chaurushiya and Ken Kuttner, "Targeting the Yield Curve: The Experience of the Federal Reserve, 1942–51," Federal Open Market Committee memo, June 18, 2003, 3.
6. Ibid., 7.
7. "Truman Discerns Peril to Economy in Rising Interest," *The New York Times*, August 29, 1966. https://www.nytimes.com/1966/08/29/archives/truman-discerns -peril-to-economy-in-rising-interest-declares.html
8. Robert P. Bremner, *Chairman of the Fed: William McChesney Martin, Jr., and the Creation of the Modern Federal Reserve System* (New Haven, Conn.: Yale University Press, 2004), 73.
9. Before Donald Trump selected Jay Powell in 2017, Janet Yellen mulled the circumstances under which she would follow Eccles's example and stay on the board after her term as chair ended.
10. Bremner, 73.
11. Chaurushiya and Kuttner, 10.
12. FOMC Minutes, August 18, 1950, 12.
13. Chaurushiya and Kuttner, 10.
14. Robert L. Hetzel and Ralph Leach, "The Treasury-Fed Accord: A New Narrative Account," *FRB Richmond Economic Quarlery*, 87, 1 (Winter 2001): 39.
15. Ibid., 40.
16. FOMC Minutes, January 31, 1951, 9.

17. "Economic Report of the President," U.S. Congress, Joint Committee on the Economic Report, January 1951 (Hearings, 82nd Congress, 1 Sess, January 25, 1951), 158.

18. Hetzel and Leach, 45.

19. Ibid., 45.

20. Ibid., 46.

21. Marriner S. Eccles, *Beckoning Frontiers: Public and Personal Recollections* (New York: Alfred A. Knopf, 1951), 496.

22. Bremner, 76.

23. Robert J. Donovan, *Tumultuous Years: The Presidency of Harry S Truman, 1949–1953* (New York, W. W. Norton & Co., 1982), 358.

24. Hetzel and Leach, 51; Bremner, 80.

25. William McChesney Martin Jr., "Reminiscences and Reflections: Remarks before The Business Council, Hot Springs, Virginia," October 17, 1969. https://fraser .stlouisfed.org/title/statements-speeches-william-mcchesney-martin-jr-448 /reminiscences-reflections-7946

26. Hetzel and Leach, 52.

27. Bremner, 91.

28. Ibid., 160.

29. Wright Patman, "The Federal Reserve System: A Study Prepared for the Use of the Joint Economic Committee," Congress of the United States (U.S. Government Printing Office, 1976, 139).

30. Bremner, 205.

31. Paul A. Volcker, *Keeping At It: The Quest for Sound Money and Good Government* (New York: PublicAffairs, 2018), 55.

32. Kevin Granville, "A President at War With the Fed, 5 Decades Back," *The New York Times*, June 15, 2017. https://www.nytimes.com/2017/06/13/business /economy/a-president-at-war-with-his-fed-chief-5-decades-before-trump.html

33. Ibid.

34. Ibid.; Bremner, 207.

35. Bremner, 203.

36. Ibid., 209.

37. Richard T. McCormack, *A Conversation with Ambassador Richard T. McCormack* (United Kingdom: Xlibris US, 2004), 57.

38. Bremner, 210.

39. "The President's News Conference at the LBJ Ranch," December 6, 1965. https:// www.presidency.ucsb.edu/documents/the-presidents-news-conference-the-lbj -ranch-5

40. Bremner, 211.

41. Months later, on August 28, 1966, former President Truman issued a rare statement warning that higher rates could lead to a serious depression: "Of course, no

one wants runaway inflation," he said. "But I think it is fair to say that kind of inflation is no longer possible in the United States."

42. Richard Nixon, *Six Crises* (New York: Doubleday, 1962), 310.

43. Paul A. Volcker, "Federal Reserve Board Oral History Project," January 28, 2008, 59. https://www.federalreserve.gov/aboutthefed/files/paul-a-volcker-interview -20080225.pdf

44. Bremner, 264.

45. Ibid., 276.

46. Ibid., 277.

47. McCormack, 57.

48. William Safire, *Before the Fall: An Inside View of the Pre-Watergate White House* (New York: Doubleday, 1975), 492.

49. John Ehrlichman, *Witness to Power: The Nixon Years* (New York: Simon & Schuster, 1982), 248.

50. Ibid., 255.

51. "The 1971 Midyear Review of the Economy," U.S. Congress, Joint Economic Committee (Hearings, 92nd Congress, 1 Sess, July 23, 1971), 253.

52. Sebastian Mallaby, *The Man Who Knew: The Life and Times of Alan Greenspan* (New York: Penguin Press, 2016), 140; Safire, 496.

53. Safire, 493.

54. Greenspan has denied that he made the call, including in an interview with the author. Greenspan said he told Colson, "Chuck, I understand there is a telephone on the desk of the President and one on the desk of Arthur Burns. I would suggest they might talk to each other." Alan Greenspan, "Federal Reserve Board Oral History Project," June 9, 2009. https://www.federalreserve.gov/aboutthefed/files /alan-greenspan-interview-20090331.pdf

55. Mallaby, 142.

56. Ibid., 142.

57. Ibid., 143.

58. "The President's News Conference," August 4, 1971. https://www.presidency .ucsb.edu/documents/the-presidents-news-conference-137

59. Safire, 495.

60. Paul A. Volcker, *Keeping At It: The Quest for Sound Money and Good Government* (New York: PublicAffairs, 2018), 106.

61. J. Dewey Daane, "Federal Reserve Board Oral History Project," June 1, 2006, 25. https://www.federalreserve.gov/aboutthefed/files/j-dewey-daane-interview -20060601.pdf

62. Arthur F. Burns, "The Anguish of Central Banking," September 30, 1979. http:// www.perjacobsson.org/lectures/1979.pdf

63. William Greider, *Secrets of the Temple: How the Federal Reserve Runs the Country* (New York: Simon & Schuster, 1987), 66.

64. Binyamin Appelbaum and Robert D. Hershey Jr., "Paul A. Volcker, Fed Chairman Who Waged War on Inflation, Is Dead at 92," *The New York Times*, December 9, 2019. https://www.nytimes.com/2019/12/09/business/paul-a-volcker-dead.html

65. Volcker, 103.

66. "Volcker, Leading Inflation War, Seen Tightening Credit Further," *The Wall Street Journal*, September 12, 1979.

67. Volcker, 105.

68. Joseph R. Coyne, "Reflection on the FOMC Meeting of October 6, 1979," *Federal Reserve Bank of St. Louis Review* 87, 2 (March/April 2005): 313.

69. Joseph B. Treaster, *Paul Volcker: The Making of a Financial Legend* (Hoboken, N.J.: Wiley, 2004), 159.

70. Volcker, 109; Coyne, 314.

71. Author's interview, June 6, 2017.

72. Volcker interview, June 6, 2017.

73. Volcker, 112.

74. Clayton Fritchey (*Newsday*), "Fed comes under pressure," in *Tampa Bay Times*, May 22, 1982.

75. FOMC Transcripts, October 5–6, 1981, 25.

76. FOMC Transcripts, October 5, 1982, 50.

77. Volcker, 141.

78. Sarah Binder and Mark Spindel, *The Myth of Independence: How Congress Governs the Federal Reserve* (Princeton, N.J.: Princeton University Press, 2017), 192.

79. "Bush Pins the Blame for '92 Election Loss on Alan Greenspan," *The Wall Street Journal*, August 25, 1998.

80. Author's interview, May 14, 2017.

81. Author's interview, November 21, 2018.

Chapter 3

1. "…Closing Quote," *The Los Angeles Times*, September 27, 1987, section 4, 3.

2. FOMC transcript, September 15, 2003. https://www.federalreserve.gov/monetary policy/files/FOMC20030915meeting.pdf

3. FOMC transcript, June 24–25, 2003, 132. https://www.federalreserve.gov/monetary policy/files/FOMC20030625meeting.pdf

4. "Open Letter to Ben Bernanke," *The Wall Street Journal*, November 15, 2010. https://blogs.wsj.com/economics/2010/11/15/open-letter-to-ben-bernanke/

5. The Fed doesn't physically print money when it buys bonds — that's the Treasury's purview. But the Fed does have the power to electronically credit money to bank accounts of the primary dealers that sell Treasury and mortgage securities.

6. Peter Wallsten and Sudeep Reddy, "Fresh Attack on Fed Move," *The Wall Street Journal*, November 15, 2010. https://www.wsj.com/articles/SB100014240527487 04327704575614853274246916

7. Philip Rucker, "Perry Takes Aim at Bernanke," *The Washington Post*, August 15, 2011. https://www.washingtonpost.com/blogs/political-economy/post/perry-takes -aim-at-bernanke/2011/08/15/gIQAXwqIIJ_blog.html

8. FOMC Transcripts, September 12–13, 2012, 213. https://www.federalreserve .gov/monetarypolicy/files/FOMC20120913meeting.pdf

9. FOMC Transcripts, September 12–13, 2012, 194. https://www.federalreserve .gov/monetarypolicy/files/FOMC20120913meeting.pdf

10. Janet L. Yellen interview, "Federal Reserve Board Oral History Project," January 3, 2012. https://www.federalreserve.gov/aboutthefed/files/janet-l-yellen-interview -20120103.pdf, 2.

11. Jon Hilsenrath, "Janet Yellen, a Top Contender at the Fed, Faces Test Over Easy Money," *The Wall Street Journal*, May 12, 2013. https://www.wsj.com/articles/SB1 0001424127887323551004578441331455504010

12. Yellen interview, 16.

13. FOMC Transcripts, December 11–12, 2012, 185. https://www.federalreserve .gov/monetarypolicy/files/FOMC20121212meeting.pdf

14. Josh Boak and Christopher Rugaber, "What Powell brings to Fed post: A gift for forging consensus," Associated Press, November 2, 2017. https://apnews.com/article /61d87dfd0d4142febc6c77d8f0ba5263

15. Author's interview.

16. Ben Bernanke, *The Courage to Act: A Memoir of a Crisis and Its Aftermath* (New York: W. W. Norton & Co., 2015), 542.

17. FOMC Transcripts, October 23–24, 2012, 192. https://www.federalreserve.gov /monetarypolicy/files/FOMC20121024meeting.pdf

18. FOMC Transcripts, January 29–30, 2013, 102. https://www.federalreserve.gov /monetarypolicy/files/FOMC20130130meeting.pdf

19. FOMC Transcripts, April 30–May 1, 2013, 149. https://www.federalreserve.gov /monetarypolicy/files/FOMC20130501meeting.pdf

20. Jerome H. Powell, "'Audit the Fed' and Other Proposals," speech at the Catholic University of America, Washington, DC, February 9, 2015. https://www.federal reserve.gov/newsevents/speech/powell20150209a.htm

21. Janet L. Yellen, "Federal Reserve Board Oral History Project," Federal Reserve Board, 19. https://www.federalreserve.gov/aboutthefed/files/janet-l-yellen-interview -20120103.pdf

22. Greg Ip, "The Navigator — Fed Chief's Style: Devour the Data, Beware of Dogma," *The Wall Street Journal*, November 18, 2004.

23. FOMC Transcripts, December 11–12, 2012, 184.

24. Binyamin Appelbaum, "House Republicans Intensify Attacks on Federal Reserve," *The New York Times*, February 26, 2015.

25. FOMC transcript, March 17–18, 2015, 143. https://www.federalreserve.gov /monetarypolicy/files/FOMC20150318meeting.pdf

26. FOMC Transcript, December 15–16, 2015, 100. https://www.federalreserve.gov /monetarypolicy/files/FOMC20151216meeting.pdf

Chapter 4

1. Kate Davidson, "Donald Trump's Comments on the Fed, Interest Rate Policy and Janet Yellen," *The Wall Street Journal*, November 9, 2016. https://www.wsj.com /articles/donald-trumps-comments-on-the-fed-interest-rate-policy-and-janet -yellen-1478724767

2. Nick Timiraos, Michael C. Bender, and Damian Paletta, "Gary Cohn Has Emerged as an Economic-Policy Powerhouse in Trump Administration," *The Wall Street Journal*, February 11, 2017; for a more detailed account, see Bob Woodward, *Fear: Trump in the White House* (New York: Simon & Schuster, 2018).

3. Demetri Sevastopulo and Gillian Tett, "Gary Cohn urges Trump team to do more to condemn neo-Nazis," *Financial Times*, August 25, 2017. https://www.ft.com /content/b85beea2-8924-11e7-bf50-e1c239b45787

4. Richard Rubin and Kate Davidson, "Steven Mnuchin, a Newcomer, Tilts at Washington's Hardest Target: The Tax Code," *The Wall Street Journal*, September 25, 2017. https://www.wsj.com/articles/steven-mnuchin-a-newcomer-tilts-at -washingtons-hardest-target-the-tax-code-1506350555

5. Max Abelson and Zachary Mider, "Trump's Top Fundraiser Eyes the Deal of a Lifetime," Bloomberg News, August 31, 2016. https://www.bloomberg.com/news /articles/2016-08-31/steven-mnuchin-businessweek

6. Kevin Warsh, "Financial Intermediation and Complete Markets," speech at the European Economics and Financial Centre, London, June 5, 2007. https://www .federalreserve.gov/newsevents/speech/warsh20070605a.htm

7. Philip Rucker, Josh Dawsey, and Damian Paletta, "Trump criticizes Fed's policies as 'way off-base,'" *The Washington Post*, November 27, 2018, https://www.washing tonpost.com/politics/trump-slams-fed-chair-questions-climate-change-and-threatens -to-cancel-putin-meeting-in-wide-ranging-interview-with-the-post/2018/11/27/4362 fae8-f26c-11e8-aeea-b85fd44449f5_story.html

8. Peter Nicholas, Kate Davidson, and Michael C. Bender, "Inside Trump's Search for a Fed Leader," *The Wall Street Journal*, November 2, 2017. https://www.wsj .com/articles/inside-trumps-search-for-a-fed-leader-1509659537

9. Nick Timiraos and David Harrison, "Mr. Ordinary: Who Is Jerome Powell, Trump's Federal Reserve Pick?" *The Wall Street Journal*, November 2, 2017. https://www.wsj.com/articles/mr-under-the-radar-jerome-powell-trumps-federal -reserve-pick-signals-continuity-1509643306

10. Kai Ryssdal, "Fed Chair Jay Powell: We're 'independent of political consider- ations,'" *Marketplace*, July 12, 2018. https://www.marketplace.org/2018/07/12 /powell-transcript/

11. Jerome H. Powell, "Remarks at the Ceremonial Swearing-in," Washington, DC, February 13, 2018. https://www.federalreserve.gov/newsevents/speech/powell 20180213a.htm

12. Michael S. Derby, "Fed's Dudley Warns Trade Wars Aren't Winnable," *The Wall Street Journal*, April 18, 2018. https://www.wsj.com/articles/feds-dudley-warns -trade-wars-arent-winnable-1524088270

13. Akane Otani, Riva Gold, and Michael Wursthorn, "U.S. Stocks End Worst Week in Years," *The Wall Street Journal*, March 23, 2018. https://www.wsj.com/articles /stocks-slide-as-trump-kicks-off-trade-war-1521765378

14. "CNBC Transcript: President Donald Trump Sits Down with CNBC's Joe Kernen," July 20, 2018. https://www.cnbc.com/2018/07/20/cnbc-transcript-president -donald-trump-sits-down-with-cnbcs-joe-kern.html

Chapter 5

1. Jerome H. Powell, "Monetary Policy in a Changing Economy," Jackson Hole, Wyoming, August 24, 2018.

2. Nick Timiraos, "Fed Confronts a Dilemma Over the Hot Job Market," *The Wall Street Journal*, June 12, 2018.

3. Jason Cummins, "Fed needs to wake up and admit the economy is overheating," *Financial Times*, July 5, 2018.

4. Michael C. Bender, Rebecca Ballhaus, Peter Nicholas, and Alex Leary, "Trump Steps Up Attacks on Fed Chairman Jerome Powell," *The Wall Street Journal*, October 23, 2018. https://www.wsj.com/articles/trump-steps-up-attacks-on-fed -chairman-jerome-powell-1540338090

5. Peter Nicholas, Nick Timiraos, and Bob Davis, "Trump Faults Treasury Secretary Over Fed Pick," *The Wall Street Journal*, November 23, 2018. https://www.wsj.com /articles/trump-expresses-dissatisfaction-with-treasury-secretary-1543006250

6. Bob Davis, "Trump Expects to Move Ahead With Boost on China Tariffs," *The Wall Street Journal*, November 26, 2018. https://www.wsj.com/articles/trump-expects -to-move-ahead-with-boost-on-china-tariffs-1543266545

7. Author's interview.

8. Nick Timiraos, "President Trump Bashes the Fed. This Is How the Fed Chief Responds," *The Wall Street Journal*, November 30, 2018. https://www.wsj.com/articles /president-trump-bashes-the-fed-this-is-how-the-fed-chief-responds-1543566589

9. Ibid.

10. Bob Davis and Lingling Wei, *Superpower Showdown* (New York: HarperCollins, 2020), 309.

11. Matt Egan, "Why Jerome Powell's quiet show of defiance against Trump and Wall Street is so important," CNN.com, December 20, 2018. https://www.cnn .com/2018/12/20/business/powell-fed-trump-markets

Chapter 6

1. Peter Baker and Maggie Haberman, "For Trump, 'a War Every Day,' Waged Increasingly Alone," *The New York Times*, December 22, 2018. https://www.nytimes.com/2018/12/22/us/politics/trump-two-years.html

2. Nick Timiraos, "Trump's Advisers Seek to Assure Investors He Won't Fire Fed Chair," *The Wall Street Journal*, December 23, 2018. https://www.wsj.com/articles/trumps-advisers-seek-to-assure-investors-he-wont-fire-fed-chair-11545600685?mod=e2tw

3. Davis and Wei, 311.

4. Richard H. Clarida, "Monetary Policy Outlook for 2019," January 10, 2019. https://www.federalreserve.gov/newsevents/speech/clarida20190110a.htm

5. Peter Nicholas and Paul Kiernan, "A Trump-Powell Meeting: Chance of Rapprochement Fraught With Risks — for Both Sides," *The Wall Street Journal*, December 28, 2018. https://www.wsj.com/articles/a-trump-powell-meeting-chance-of-rapprochement-fraught-with-risksfor-both-sides-11546036082

6. Anne Flaherty, "Trump says of Fed Reserve chairman 'I've waited long enough,'" ABC News, June 14, 2019. https://abcnews.go.com/Politics/exclusive-trump-fed-reserve-chairman-ive-waited-long/story?id=63694021

7. Jeanna Smialek, "Trump Called Powell an 'Enemy.' 'Ugh' Was a Response Inside the Fed," *The New York Times*, January 30, 2020. https://www.nytimes.com/2020/01/30/business/economy/fed-trump-powell-ugh.html

8. Nick Timiraos, "How Fed Chairman Forged Rate-Cut Consensus," *The Wall Street Journal*, December 10, 2019. https://www.wsj.com/articles/how-fed-chairman-forged-rate-cut-consensus-11575973802

Chapter 7

1. Kate Davidson and Bob Davis, "How Mnuchin Became Washington's Indispensable Crisis Manager," *The Wall Street Journal*, March 31, 2020. https://www.wsj.com/articles/steven-mnuchin-is-trying-to-rescue-the-economy-from-the-coronavirus-11585654202

2. Matthew J. Belvedere, "Trump says he trusts China's Xi on coronavirus and the US has it 'totally under control,'" CNBC, January 22, 2020. https://www.cnbc.com/2020/01/22/trump-on-coronavirus-from-china-we-have-it-totally-under-control.html

3. Lael Brainard, Commencement Address at Claremont McKenna College, May 17, 2014, https://www.cmc.edu/news/read-the-commencement-address-by-dr-lael-brainard

4. Gili Lipman, "Fed Board Governor Dr. Lael Brainard '83 Drives the Economy Forward," *The Wesleyan Argus*, http://wesleyanargus.com/2017/04/10/fed-board-governor-dr-lael-brainard-83-drives-the-economy-forward/

5. Lawrence Summers, "Fed Choreography Was a Calamity: Summers," Bloomberg television interview. https://www.bloomberg.com/news/videos/2020-03-06/fed -choreography-was-a-calamity-summers-video?sref=1X5UIU0Y

6. Author's interview.

7. Colby Itkowitz, Ashley Parker, and Seung Min Kim, "Coronavirus continues its rapid spread, confounding efforts by global leaders," *The Washington Post*, March 7, 2020. https://www.washingtonpost.com/health/2020/03/07/coronavirus-contin ues-its-rapid-spread-confounding-efforts-by-global-leaders/

Chapter 8

1. Robert Costa, Josh Dawsey, Jeff Stein, and Ashley Parker, "Trump urged Mnuchin to pressure Fed's Powell on economic stimulus in explosive tirade about coronavirus," *The Washington Post*, March 11, 2020. https://www.washingtonpost.com /business/economy/trump-urged-mnuchin-to-pressure-feds-powell-on-economic -stimulus-in-explosive-tirade-about-coronavirus/2020/03/11/db7bfeea-63c9 -11ea-b3fc-7841686c5c57_story.html

2. Andrew Restuccia, Andrew Duehren, and Richard Rubin, "Lawmakers Rebuff Trump on Payroll-Tax Suspension for Outbreak," *The Wall Street Journal*, updated March 10, 2020. https://www.wsj.com/articles/white-house-intensifies-push-for -coronavirus-stimulus-measures-11583851800

3. Brookings Institution webinar, May 27, 2020. https://www.brookings.edu/wp -content/uploads/2020/05/es_20200527_financial_markets_transcript.pdf

4. Ayelen Banegas, Phillip J. Monin, and Lubomir Petrasek, "Sizing hedge funds' Treasury market activities and holdings," FEDS Notes, Board of Governors of the Federal Reserve System, October 6, 2021. https://www.federalreserve.gov /econres/notes/feds-notes/sizing-hedge-funds-treasury-market-activities-and -holdings-20211006.htm

5. Liz Hoffman, "Diary of a Crazy Week in the Markets," *The Wall Street Journal*, March 14, 2020. https://www.wsj.com/articles/diary-of-a-crazy-week-in-the-mark ets-11584143715

6. Lawrence Wright, "The Plague Year," *The New Yorker*, January 4, 2021.

7. Ibid.

Chapter 9

1. Author's interview.

2. Nick Timiraos and Julia-Ambra Verlaine, "Fed to Inject $1.5 Trillion in Bid to Prevent 'Unusual Disruptions' in Markets," *The Wall Street Journal*, March 12, 2020. https://www.wsj.com/articles/fed-to-inject-1-5-trillion-in-bid-to-prevent -unusual-disruptions-in-markets-11584033537

3. https://www.brookings.edu/wp-content/uploads/2020/05/es_20200527_financial _markets_transcript.pdf, 13.

Chapter 10

1. Author's interview.
2. Author's interview.
3. Author's interview.
4. Author's interview.
5. Jennifer Ablan, Ortenca Aliaj, and Miles Kruppa, "Ray Dalio caught wrongfooted with big losses at Bridgewater fund," *Financial Times*, March 14, 2020. https://www.ft.com/content/6addc002-6666-11ea-800d-da70cff6e4d3
6. Walter Bagehot, *Lombard Street: A Description of the Money Market* (Westport, CT: Hyperion, 1962), 25. https://fraser.stlouisfed.org/files/docs/meltzer/baglom62.pdf
7. Parinitha Sastry, "The Political Origins of Section 13(3) of the Federal Reserve Act," *FRBNY Economic Policy Review*, Issue 24-1, September 2018. 27 https://www.newyorkfed.org/medialibrary/media/research/epr/2018/epr_2018_political-origins_sastry.pdf
8. Matthew J. Belvedere, "El-Erian blasts Fed, saying it should have been 'laser-focused' on market failures and cut rates later," CNBC, March 16, 2020, https://www.cnbc.com/2020/03/16/el-erian-blasts-fed-says-it-should-have-cut-rates-after-other-moves.html
9. Sebastian Pellejero and Liz Hoffman, "Bond Market Cracks Open for Blue-Chip Companies — Then Slams Shut," *The Wall Street Journal*, March 18, 2020.
10. Author's interview.
11. Author's interview.
12. John Maynard Keynes, "From Keynes to Roosevelt: Our Recovery Plan Assayed," *The New York Times*, December 31, 1933, https://www.nytimes.com/1933/12/31/archives/from-keynes-to-roosevelt-our-recovery-plan-assayed-the-british.html
13. *PBS NewsHour* interview with Nancy Pelosi, March 25, 2020. https://www.pbs.org/newshour/show/were-ready-to-pass-senates-economic-relief-bill-in-the-house-says-pelosi#transcript
14. Ibid.

Chapter 11

1. Stacy Cowley and Anupreeta Das, "A Manhattan Bank Is Emptied of $100 Bills," *The New York Times*, March 16, 2020. https://www.nytimes.com/2020/03/14/business/coronavirus-cash-shortage-bank.html
2. Author's interview.
3. Author's interview.
4. Nick Timiraos, "The Fed Transformed: Jay Powell Leads Central Bank into Uncharted Waters," *The Wall Street Journal*, March 30, 2020. https://www.wsj.com

/articles/the-fed-transformed-jay-powell-leads-central-bank-into-uncharted
-waters-11585596210

5. Serena Ng and Nick Timiraos, "Covid Supercharges Federal Reserve as Backup Lender to the World," *The Wall Street Journal*, August 3, 2020. https://www.wsj .com/articles/fed-federal-reserve-jerome-powell-covid-coronavirus-dollar -lending-economy-foreign-currency-11596228151

6. Caitlin Ostroff and David Gauthier-Villars, "Pressure on Turkey's Economy Builds as Lira Nears Record Low," *The Wall Street Journal*, May 6, 2020. https:// www.wsj.com/articles/pressure-on-turkeys-economy-builds-as-lira-heads -to-record-low-11588769981

7. Nick Timiraos and Heather Gillers, "Fed Includes Municipal Debt in Money-Market Lending Backstop," *The Wall Street Journal*, March 20, 2020. https://www .wsj.com/articles/federal-reserve-to-increase-frequency-of-dollar-transactions -with-foreign-central-banks-11584712851

8. Michael Feroli and Jesse Edgerton, "The lamps are going out all across the economy," JPMorgan Chase & Co., March 18, 2020.

9. Warren Buffett, Berkshire Hathaway annual meeting, May 3, 2020. https://www .rev.com/blog/transcripts/warren-buffett-berkshire-hathaway-annual-meeting -transcript-2020

10. Craig Nicol and Jim Reid, "US Credit Strategy: Time for the Fed to step in?" Deutsche Bank Research, March 22, 2020.

Chapter 12

1. David Smith, "Trump throws tantrum over coronavirus question: 'You're a terrible reporter,'" *The Guardian*, March 21, 2020. https://www.theguardian.com/us -news/2020/mar/20/trump-coronavirus-question-attack-reporter-over-fears

2. Danielle Pletka, Marc Thiessen, and Glenn Hubbard, American Enterprise Institute podcast. https://www.aei.org/wp-content/uploads/2020/04/4.13.20-Glenn -Hubbard-transcript-PDF.pdf?x91208

3. Phil Mattingly, Clare Foran, and Ted Barrett, "Senate Republicans unveil $1 trillion economic stimulus package to address coronavirus fallout," CNN.com, March 20, 2020. https://lite.cnn.com/en/article/h_f4c2f69c836c6b6b79826f08 4411bd07

4. Author's interview.

5. Author's interview.

6. Jeff Stein, Josh Dawsey, and Robert Costa. "The dealmaker's dealmaker: Mnuchin steps in as Trump's negotiator, but president's doubts linger with economy in crisis," *The Washington Post*, March 28, 2020. https://www.washingtonpost.com /business/2020/03/27/trump-mnuchin-coronavirus-treasury/

7. Author's interview.

8. Carl Hulse and Emily Cochrane, "As Coronavirus Spread, Largest Stimulus in History United a Polarized Senate," *The New York Times*, March 26, 2020. www .nytimes.com/2020/03/26/us/coronavirus-senate-stimulus-package.html

9. https://www.speaker.gov/newsroom/32620-0

10. https://www.warren.senate.gov/newsroom/press-releases/warren-tweets-on -bailout-and-stimulus-negotiations

11. John Bresnahan and Marianne Levine, "Dems seize on 'slush fund' to oppose Republican rescue package," *Politico*, March 23, 2020. https://www.politico.com /news/2020/03/23/democrats-slush-fund-republican-rescue-package-143565

12. Erica Werner, Seung Min Kim, Rachael Bade, and Jeff Stein, "Senate falls far short of votes needed to advance coronavirus bill, as clash between Republicans and Democrats intensifies," *The Washington Post*, March 22, 2020, https://www .washingtonpost.com/us-policy/2020/03/22/vast-coronavirus-stimulus-bill -limbo-crunch-times-arrives-capitol-hill/

13. Ibid.

14. Author's interview.

15. Scott Horsley, "Fed Chair Said U.S. Economy Is On The Path To Recovery," NPR, March 25, 2021. https://www.npr.org/2021/03/25/981309889/fed-chair-said-u-s -economy-is-on-the-path-to-recovery

16. Serena Ng and Carrick Mollenkamp, "Hedge Funds Tapped Rescue Program," *The Wall Street Journal*, December 2, 2010. https://www.wsj.com/articles/SB1000 1424052748703865004575649233598560948

17. Steve Matthews, "U.S. Jobless Rate May Soar to 30%, Fed's Bullard Says," Bloomberg News, March 22, 2020. https://www.bloomberg.com/news/articles/2020-03 -22/fed-s-bullard-says-u-s-jobless-rate-may-soar-to-30-in-2q

18. Michael Feroli, "Powell rolls out Big Bertha," JPMorgan Chase & Co., March 23, 2020.

19. John Bresnahan, Marianne Levine, and Andrew Desiderio, "How the $2 trillion deal came together — and nearly fell apart," *Politico*, March 26, 2020. https:// www.politico.com/news/2020/03/26/inside-the-10-days-to-rescue-the -economy-149718

20. Siobhan Hughes, Natalie Andrews, and Lindsay Wise, "Trump Signs Record Stimulus Law — House-Approved Relief Package of $2 Trillion Offers Aid to Combat Damage of Pandemic," *The Wall Street Journal*, March 28, 2020. https:// www.wsj.com/articles/how-the-coronavirus-stimulus-deal-came-back-from -the-brink-11585338737

21. Narayana Kocherlakota, "The Fed Should Never Lend to Anyone Other Than Banks," *Bloomberg Opinion*, March 23, 2020. https://www.bloomberg.com /opinion/articles/2020-03-23/coronavirus-crisis-fed-should-never-lend-outside -banking-system

22. Stephen Cecchetti and Kermit Schoenholtz, "The Fed Goes to War: Part 2," *Money and Banking* blog. https://www.moneyandbanking.com/commentary/2020/3/25/the-fed-goes-to-war-part-2

23. Eric Morath, Jon Hilsenrath, and Sarah Chaney, "Record Rise in Unemployment Claims Halts Historic Run of Job Growth," *The Wall Street Journal*, March 26, 2020. https://www.wsj.com/articles/the-long-run-of-american-job-growth-has-ended-11585215000

Chapter 13

1. Author's interview.

2. Author's interview, March 24, 2020.

3. Author's interview.

4. Matt Wirz, "How Fed Intervention Saved Carnival," *The Wall Street Journal*, April 26, 2020. https://www.wsj.com/articles/how-fed-intervention-saved-carnival-11587920400

5. Ibid.

6. Author's interview.

7. Ben White, Victoria Guida, and Matthew Karnitsching, "Blank checks, taboos and bazookas: Inside the global battle to prevent another depression," *Politico*, April 13, 2020. https://www.politico.com/news/2020/04/13/inside-global-race-prevent-depression-182619

8. Author's interview.

9. Randal K. Quarles, "What Happened? What Have We Learned From It? Lessons from COVID-19 Stress on the Financial System," speech at the Institute of International Finance, via webcast, October 15, 2020. https://www.federalreserve.gov/newsevents/speech/files/quarles20201015a.pdf

10. Author's interview.

11. Aaron Klein and Camille Busette, "Improving the equity impact of the Fed's municipal lending facility," Brookings Institution, April 14, 2020. https://www.brookings.edu/research/a-chance-to-improve-the-equity-impact-of-the-feds-municipal-lending-facility/

12. Howard Marks, "Knowledge of the Future," memo to clients, April 14, 2020. https://www.oaktreecapital.com/docs/default-source/memos/knowledge-of-the-future.pdf

13. James Freeman, "'Waiting for Good Dough,'" *The Wall Street Journal*, April 21, 2020. https://www.wsj.com/articles/waiting-for-good-dough-11587491186

14. Author's interview.

15. Author's interview.

Chapter 14

1. https://twitter.com/ilhanmn/status/1255526030355451905?lang=en

2. https://twitter.com/zachdcarter/status/1251156024049856520?lang=en, accessible via Matthew Yglesias, "We should have done more bailouts," *Slow Boring* substack, May 18, 2021. https://www.slowboring.com/p/bailouts

3. Daan Struyven and Sid Bhushan, "Global Economics Comment: The US Jobs Comeback: Lessons from North of the Border," Goldman Sachs Economics Research, June 17, 2021.

4. Kate Davidson and Richard Rubin, "Steven Mnuchin Says U.S. Aims to Get Back Its Money From Fed Programs," *The Wall Street Journal*, April 29, 2020. https://www.wsj.com/articles/mnuchin-says-u-s-not-aiming-to-lose-money-on-fed-lending-facilities-11588178749

5. Nick Timiraos and Jon Hilsenrath, "The Federal Reserve Is Changing What It Means to Be a Central Bank," *The Wall Street Journal*, April 27, 2020. https://www.wsj.com/articles/fate-and-history-the-fed-tosses-the-rules-to-fight-coronavirus-downturn-11587999986

6. Author's interview.

7. Nick Timiraos, "Fed Had a Loan Plan for Midsize Firms Hurt by Covid. It Found Few Takers," *The Wall Street Journal*, January 4, 2021. https://www.wsj.com/articles/fed-had-a-loan-plan-for-midsize-firms-hurt-by-covid-it-found-few-takers-11609774458

8. Author's interview.

9. "Report on the Economic Well-Being of U.S. Households in 2019, Featuring Supplemental Data from April 2020," Board of Governors of the Federal Reserve System, May 2020, 53. https://www.federalreserve.gov/publications/files/2019-report-economic-well-being-us-households-202005.pdf

10. Virtual meeting at the Hoover Institution, April 21, 2021. https://www.hoover.org/events/policy-seminar-tyler-goodspeed-andrew-olmem-and-john-taylor

11. Author's interview.

12. Noah Smith, "Paul Krugman Is Pretty Upbeat About the Economy," *Bloomberg Opinion*, May 27, 2020. https://www.bloomberg.com/opinion/articles/2020-05-27/paul-krugman-is-pretty-upbeat-about-coronavirus-economic-recovery?sref=1X5UIU0Y

Chapter 15

1. Lisa Lambert, "White House's Kudlow floats cutting U.S. corporate tax rate in half," Reuters, May 15, 2020. https://www.reuters.com/article/us-health-coronavirus-usa-tax/white-houses-kudlow-floats-cutting-u-s-corporate-tax-rate-in-half-idUSKBN22R2FH

2. These figures would subsequently be revised. The official jobless rate peaked at 14.8 percent in April. The unemployment rate for Blacks reached 16.7 percent in April and held at that level in May. For Asians it peaked at 14.9 percent in May.

3. Lawrence H. Summers and Anna Stansbury, "Whither Central Banking?" *Project Syndicate*, August 23, 2019. https://www.project-syndicate.org/commentary/central -bankers-in-jackson-hole-should-admit-impotence-by-lawrence-h-summers-and -anna-stansbury-2-2019-08?barrier=accesspaylog

4. Author's interview, October 22, 2020.

5. Author's interview, September 28, 2020.

Chapter 16

1. Michael Feroli, Jesse Edgerton, and Dan Silver, "The 2021 US Economic Outlook: The needle and the damage undone," JPMorgan Chase & Co., November 20, 2020.

2. The early frontrunner for the job had been Lael Brainard. As a Fed governor, Brainard had at times been a few clicks to Yellen's left on monetary policy issues, most notably during the debate to lift interest rates from zero in 2015. During the Trump administration, she had been a lone voice on the Fed board arguing against a deregulatory impulse pushed by Randal Quarles and Powell. But Brainard's work in the Clinton and Obama administrations on free trade and currency issues had left labor unions skeptical of her candidacy, and the Biden team didn't consider her intensively for the job.

3. Jason Lange and Heather Timmons, "Biden says he has picked a Treasury secretary who will please all Democrats," Reuters, November 19, 2020. https://www .reuters.com/article/us-usa-election-dollar/biden-says-he-has-picked-a-treasury -secretary-who-will-please-all-democrats-idUSKBN27Z34L

4. Nick Timiraos, "Fed Had a Loan Plan for Midsize Firms Hurt by Covid. It Found Few Takers," *The Wall Street Journal*, January 4, 2021. https://www.wsj.com/articles /fed-had-a-loan-plan-for-midsize-firms-hurt-by-covid-it-found-few -takers-11609774458

5. Ibid.

6. Author's interview.

7. Heather Perlberg and Sonali Basak, "Trump Treasury Secretary Mnuchin Raises $2.5 Billion Fund," Bloomberg News, September 20, 2021, https://www.bloomberg .com/news/articles/2021-09-20/trump-treasury-secretary-steven-mnuchin -raises-2-5-billion-fund

8. Matthew S. Schwartz, "Up to 25,000 Troops Descend on Washington for Biden's Inauguration," National Public Radio, January 16, 2021. https://www.npr.org /sections/insurrection-at-the-capitol/2021/01/16/957642610/unprecedented -number-of-troops-descend-on-washington-d-c-for-bidens-inauguration

Chapter 17

1. Author's interview.

2. Janet L. Yellen, "Opening Statement of Dr. Janet Yellen before the Senate Finance Committee." https://www.finance.senate.gov/imo/media/doc/JLY%20opening%20 testimony%20%20(1).pdf

3. Ann Saphir, "Fed's Kaplan hopes to begin QE weaning this year," Reuters, January 11, 2021. https://www.reuters.com/article/us-usa-fed-kaplan/feds-kaplan-hopes -to-begin-qe-weaning-this-year-idUSKBN29G2TB

4. Howard Schneider, "Fed's Bostic says bond-buying 'recalibration' could happen in 2021," Reuters, January 4, 2021. https://www.reuters.com/article/us-usa-fed -bostic/feds-bostic-says-bond-buying-recalibration-could-happen-in-2021 -idUSKBN2992GI

5. Ann Saphir, "Fed's Kaplan: We are 'not anywhere close' to QE taper," Reuters, January 29, 2021. https://www.reuters.com/article/us-usa-fed-kaplan-qe/feds-kaplan -we-are-not-anywhere-close-to-qe-taper-idUSKBN29Y2ZA

6. Brian Cheung, "Atlanta Fed's Bostic: 'Not my expectation' to taper QE this year," *Yahoo Finance*, February 4, 2021. https://finance.yahoo.com/news/atlanta-feds -bostic-not-my-expectation-to-taper-qe-this-year-153018144.html

7. "Transcript: Fed Chief Powell Speaks to The Economic Club of New York," *The Wall Street Journal*, February 10, 2021, https://www.wsj.com/articles/transcript-fed -chief-powell-speaks-to-the-economic-club-of-new-york-11612992892

8. "IMF Seminar, Debate on the Global Economy," April 8, 2021, https://meetings .imf.org/en/2021/Spring/Schedule/2021/04/08/imf-seminar-debate-on-global -economy

9. Author's interview.

10. Author's interview https://www.wsj.com/articles/transcript-fed-chairman-jerome -powell-at-the-wsj-jobs-summit-11614889342

11. Author's interview.

12. Margot Patrick and Quentin Webb, "Archegos Hit Tops $10 Billion After UBS, Nomura Losses," *The Wall Street Journal*, April 27, 2021. https://www.wsj.com /articles/ubs-takes-surprise-774-million-archegos-hit-11619501547

13. Matt Phillips, "Recast as 'Stimmies,' Federal Relief Checks Drive a Stock-Buying Spree," *The New York Times*, March 21, 2021. https://www.nytimes.com/2021 /03/21/business/stimulus-check-stock-market.html

14. Author's interview.

15. Jordan Williams, "Larry Summers blasts $1.9T stimulus as 'least responsible' economic policy in 40 years," *The Hill*, March 20, 2021. https://thehill.com/policy/finance /544188-larry-summers-blasts-least-responsible-economic-policy-in-40-years

16. C. Peter McColough Series on International Economics with Lawrence Summers, Council on Foreign Relations, April 21, 2021. https://www.cfr.org/event/c-peter -mccolough-series-international-economics-lawrence-h-summers

17. Author's interview.

18. Paul Kiernan, "Fed's No. 2 Official Sees Time Approaching for Discussion on Cutting Asset Purchases," *The Wall Street Journal*, May 25, 2021. https://www.wsj .com/articles/feds-no-2-official-sees-time-approaching-for-discussion-on-cutting -asset-purchases-11621964259

19. Author's interview.
20. Powell press conference, June 16, 2021.
21. Author's interview.

Epilogue

1. Michael S. Derby, "Dallas Fed's Robert Kaplan Was Active Buyer and Seller of Stocks Last Year," *The Wall Street Journal*, September 7, 2021, https://www.wsj.com/articles/dallas-feds-robert-kaplan-was-active-buyer-and-seller-of-stocks-last-year-11631044094
2. Powell remarks to The Economic Club of Washington, DC, April 14, 2021. https://www.economicclub.org/sites/default/files/transcripts/powell_edited_transcript.pdf
3. Powell interview on *60 Minutes*, CBS News. https://www.cbsnews.com/news/jerome-powell-full-2021-60-minutes-interview-transcript/
4. Congressional Budget Office, "Federal Net Interest Costs: A Primer," December 2020, https://www.cbo.gov/system/files/2020-12/56780-Net-Interest-Primer.pdf
5. https://www.federalreserve.gov/releases/z1/dataviz/dfa/distribute/table/#range:2006.1,2021.1;quarter:126;series:Net%20worth;demographic:networth;population:1,3,5,7;units:levels
6. Raghuram G. Rajan, "Central Banks Are the Fall Guys," *Project Syndicate*, July 31, 2019. https://www.project-syndicate.org/commentary/central-bank-fall-guys-by-raghuram-rajan-2019-07
7. Author's interview.
8. Author's interview.
9. Author's interview.
10. Orla McCaffrey and Shane Shifflett, "During Covid-19, Most Americans Got Ahead—Especially the Rich," *The Wall Street Journal*, June 27, 2021. https://www.wsj.com/articles/during-covid-19-most-americans-got-richer-especially-the-rich-11624791602
11. Author's interview.
12. Transcript of Federal Reserve Board "Fed Listens" Event: How Is Covid-19 Affecting Your Community? May 21, 2020, 43. https://www.federalreserve.gov/mediacenter/files/fed-listens-transcript-20200521.pdf
13. Transcript, Fed Chairman Jerome Powell at the WSJ Jobs Summit. https://www.wsj.com/articles/transcript-fed-chairman-jerome-powell-at-the-wsj-jobs-summit-11614889342

INDEX